王昕 著

EFL（中国）语境下二语写作纠正性反馈机制研究

Effectiveness of Written Corrective Feedback on L2 Writing:
A Quantitative and Qualitative Perspective in an EFL Context

中国社会科学出版社

图书在版编目（CIP）数据

EFL（中国）语境下二语写作纠正性反馈机制研究 = Effectiveness of Written Corrective Feedback on L2 Writing：A Quantitative and Qualitative Perspective in an EFL Context：英文 / 王昕著 . —北京：中国社会科学出版社，2019.8
ISBN 978 - 7 - 5203 - 4543 - 9

Ⅰ. ①E⋯　Ⅱ. ①王⋯　Ⅲ. ①第二语言—写作—研究—英文
Ⅳ. ①H05

中国版本图书馆 CIP 数据核字（2019）第 110682 号

出 版 人	赵剑英
责任编辑	张　浱
责任校对	姜志菊
责任印制	李寡寡

出　　版	中国社会科学出版社
社　　址	北京鼓楼西大街甲 158 号
邮　　编	100720
网　　址	http://www.csspw.cn
发 行 部	010 - 84083685
门 市 部	010 - 84029450
经　　销	新华书店及其他书店

印　　刷	北京明恒达印务有限公司
装　　订	廊坊市广阳区广增装订厂
版　　次	2019 年 8 月第 1 版
印　　次	2019 年 8 月第 1 次印刷

开　　本	710 × 1000　1/16
印　　张	17.25
插　　页	2
字　　数	258 千字
定　　价	89.00 元

ABSTRACT

Corrective feedback (CF) often refers to negative evidence in second language acquisition (SLA) and sometimes is used interchangeably with error and grammar correction by researchers. Investigations have been undertaken to explore a variety of issues in SLA that are associated with CF in second language (L2) writing. Scholars debate whether CF contributes to improving L2 learners' grammatical accuracy in writing performance. On one hand, based on the impracticality of providing detailed CF for all L2 learners and detached grammar instruction in language classrooms, some researchers take a stance on the ineffectiveness of corrective feedback; on the other hand, many researchers promote the efficacy and significance of the role played by CF in the process of L2 writing.

Because controversies concerning CF are ongoing and inconclusive and the complexity of issues with CF tends to compound the difficulty of making claims about the efficacy of CF, the topic deserves further research. This research employs a quasi-experimental design and examines three major issues: (1) the extent to which CF facilitates or improves students' writing accuracy; (2) teachers' and students' expectations and preferences for CF; (3) the extent to which contextual and affective factors affect students' understanding of CF and their production of accurate L2 writing.

The research consists of 105 college level EFL learners and three teachers from three intact classes in an Eastern Chinese University. One class was assigned to the control group which did not receive any CF, but did receive comments on content and organization of their writing. The other two classes were then assigned to each of the two comparison groups which received different types of CF: indirect feedback or direct feedback. My study therefore is framed within a mixed-methods approach that incorporates both quantitative and qualitative research designs to address the research questions. Data collection for the quantitative approach includes student text/error analysis, treatments (i. e. , provision of corrective feedback) , examination of tests (i. e. , pretest, posttest and delayed posttest) , and questionnaires. Quantitative data were analyzed using SPSS including both descriptive (M and SD) and inferential statistics (i. e. , Correlation Coefficient and one-way ANOVA). Data collection for the qualitative approach includes interviews, surveys and classroom observations.

Within a research period of ten weeks, this study did not reveal statistically significant group differences between the two CF groups and the content-only (FC) group on individual error reduction or the total number of errors, but a time effect was observed within each group from the pretest to the delayed posttest. Thus, the stronger effect of CF was not significant enough to be observable on student writing accuracy, because the control (FC) group that did not receive CF also improved. Both students and teachers believed feedback was important and beneficial, but there is contradiction between what the teachers believed and their actual practices in the classroom. In addition, the study indicates that students' attitudes and the EFL learning context potentially suggest a clear and decisive relationship between students' perception of the difficulty in understanding and correcting the errors and their eventual improvement in writing accuracy. A number of implications and pedagogical recommendations for EFL teachers and CF research are also discussed.

Keywords: Adult EFL, Indirect CF, Direct CF, Targeted grammatical forms, Learner attitudes, SLA

TABLE OF CONTENTS

LIST OF TABLES

LIST OF FIGURES

Chapter 1: Introduction

Corrective feedback (CF) often refers to negative evidence in second language acquisition (SLA) and sometimes is used interchangeably with error correction/grammar correction by researchers. Russell and Spada (2006) defined corrective feedback as "any feedback provided to a learner, from any source, that contains evidence of learner errors of language form." (p. 134) Corrective feedback, in this case, does not refer to any feedback that is not related to grammatical forms.

One of the top responsibilities of language teachers is to provide feedback for student papers so that second language (L2) learners can see whether they are good writers or whether the pedagogical practices meet students' expectations of instruction. Corrective feedback provides critical information to inform students about their writing performance and transform students to critical and proficient L2 writers. Despite long debates since the 1970s, the most productive approach to providing corrective feedback in L2 writing has yet been precisely developed (Ferris, 2010), even though researchers and teachers have tried to "justify their faith in written corrective feedback with hard evidence" (Ellis et al. ,2008, p. 353).

According to Ferris (2010), because of the historical and theoretical trends, empirical research on corrective feedback in L2 writing was scarce before the mid-1990s. Influenced by Krashen's SLA theory (1981, 1982, &1985), corrective feedback was not valued then in writing instruction. After the 1990s, more research started addressing language issues in L2 writing, advocating the idea that error correction should be contextualized within the writing process, prioritized to focus on the most frequent and serious errors and should pay attention to individual learners' needs in writing.

Scholars debate whether corrective feedback contributes to improving L2 learners' grammatical accuracy in writing performance. Based on the impracticality of providing detailed corrective feedback for all L2 learners and detached grammar instruction in language classrooms (e. g. , some Intensive English Programs in the U. S. do not offer grammar instruction for intermediate and higher proficiency level ESL learners), some researchers take a stance on the ineffectiveness of corrective feedback (Robb, et al. , 1986; Kepner, 1991; Bruton, 2009; Truscott, 1996, 1999, 2004, 2007; Truscott & Hsu, 2008). Kepner (1991) found no significant effects of feedback on language forms in L2 college students' writing, and concluded that corrective feedback is ineffective for developing learners' grammatical accuracy in writing. Truscott (1996) denied the relationship between the usefulness of error feedback and L2 learning and claimed that error correction is ineffective and harmful in improving students' L2 learning. He even made a strong argument that error correction " should be abandoned" (p. 328). In particular, Truscott (1996) doubted the value of error correction from both the theoretical and practical aspects. His research drew immediate attention, provoked immediate debates, increased interests on the topic, and led to heated discussion in the research field of L2 writing.

On the other side, some researchers found corrective feedback to be effective for written errors. A consensus has since appeared among many researchers who promote the efficacy and significance of the role played by corrective feedback in the process of L2 writing. The researchers examine how students who receive appropriate corrective feedback show better performance in the accuracy and quality of writing. Researchers who advocate grammar correction also emphasize strategy training in order to develop L2 learners' ability of being autonomous editors of their own writing(Bitchener & Knoch, 2009, 2010; Ferris, 2010; Ferris, Guenete & Lyster, 2013; Liu, Sinba, & Senna, 2013; Van Beunnigen, De Jong, & Kuiken, 2012; Vyatkina, 2011). Russell and Spada (2006) in a meta-analysis provided support for the effectiveness of corrective feedback in general for L2 grammar learning. The meta-analysis showed a medium to large effect size for the majority of the primary studies that investigated the effects of corrective feedback on written performance and confirmed a positive effect for corrective feedback on L2 acquisition. Kang and Han (2015) took a meta-analytic approach and synthesized 21 empirical primary studies. The findings of the meta-analysis also revealed a beneficial role corrective feedback plays in leading to greater grammatical accuracy in L2 writing.

As shown by the research that demonstrates the effectiveness of corrective feedback, the extent to which type of corrective feedback may play a better role in improving L2 learners' accuracy of writing becomes an interesting issue to consider. Typically, studies have primarily categorized corrective feedback into explicit vs. implicit, direct vs. indirect, focused vs. unfocused, and metalinguistic feedback. Implicit feedback refers to no evident indication that an error has been committed, whereas explicit does focus on error correction. Carroll and Swain (1993) also defined explicit feedback as "any feedback that overtly states that a learner's output was not part of the language-to-be-learned" (p. 361). Direct error correction refers to an explicit correction of linguistic features, and teachers provide a correct form for students. By contrast, indirect correction is defined as the way that teachers simply locate the errors in students' writing, which draws students' attention to them and requires students' self-correction. Focused feedback is an approach teachers use to selectively treat student errors by targeting only a limited range of error types (e. g. , English articles and subject-verb agreement) , while unfocused feedback should be more comprehensive involving correcting all student errors in L2 writing (Van Beuningen, 2010). Metalinguistic feedback requires teachers to provide students with some form of explicit comments about the nature of the errors by using error codes or abbreviated labels as well as grammatical explanations (Ellis, 2009).

In fact, metalinguistic correctionor metalinguistic feedback is a type of corrective feedback that is less common than direct and indirect feedback (Russell and Spada, 2006). As Ellis (2009) suggested, this may be due to its limited application to the majority of student writers, such as low and intermediate L2 learners, as well as the practicality issue for teachers because it is much more time consuming and requires sufficient metalinguistic knowledge from teachers. He further noted that metalinguistic feedback unfortunately may also demotivate and discourage students because of its overwhelming focus on linguistic explanations. Ellis (2009) argued that although with limited evidence, it cannot be denied that metalinguistic feedback is valuable to equip advanced level students with specified grammatical knowledge and to help them achieve a greater level of accuracy in the long run.

As arguments for and against corrective feedback are investigated in SLA literature, a growing body of empirical research (Ferris, 2011; Ferris, et al. , 2013; Jernigan & Mihai, 2008; Lee, 2005; Lee, 2008; McMartin-Miller, 2014) explores another crucial issue: students' and teachers' perceptions and preferences towards corrective feedback in L2 writing. Previous research suggests that, for both ESL and EFL learners, beliefs about error correction as an effective instructional technique differ substantially from the belief and practices of their teachers. For example, students prefer to have all their errors corrected, while teachers only address the errors when communication is affected in writing (Jernigan & Mihai, 2008). Therefore, attention needs to be paid to how corrective feedback is perceived by L2 learners and teachers.

Controversies concerning corrective feedback are ongoing and inconclusive. Because no studies to date have examined the topic adequately or systematically enough (e. g. , due to methodological issue) , research on corrective feedback in L2 writing still requires further investigation. Though a positive outcome for error correction in L2 writing may be found, few studies conducted so far have focused on whether corrective feedback improves L2 students' writing accuracy over a long period of time. Scholars have yet to address whether corrective feedback is effective in helping learners to eliminate errors in new pieces of writing. In addition, though abundant literature examines how teachers should balance different types of corrective feedback, learners' perspectives are also an ignored area in investigations of the effectiveness of CF (Ferris & Roberts, 2001 ; Mustafa, 2012). Students' perspectives can produce influential outcomes for pedagogical practices or decision-making for educators in language teaching and learning. In addition, error patterns in different genres and types of student writing need consideration and consistent error patterns among L2 learners call for more studies.

Other variables that have been identified in the CF literature have not been systematically investigated as well in a sufficient quantity of studies to be able to synthesize the overall results. For example, few studies examined the impact of individual learner characteristics in relation to CF including motivation, attitudes and beliefs. Previous studies also lack clarity about whether participants are skilled writers growing up in an EFL (English as Foreign Language) or ESL (English as Second Language) context. Thus, further investigations on error correction need to take into consideration L2 learners' individuality with their cultural and educational backgrounds. Another frequently mentioned issue in previous research is that few studies are empirically conducted on a comprehensive identification of all the error types in learners' production of writing. Recent research also suggests that specific grammatical forms need to be distinguished from one another so as to effectively evaluate the role of different types of corrective feedback. Therefore, the above-mentioned possibilities are the major factors that motivate this investigation. The complexity of issues with corrective feedback tends to compound the difficulty of making claims about the efficacy of CF and thus the topic deserves further research.

1.1   Context Analysis

1.1.1   EFL Context in China.

Today, English is extensively used in many provinces of China. By 2016, China had the largest English speaking population in the world. Concurrently, English instruction in China has becomes more intensively studied. Various teaching approaches and pedagogies have been investigated at different levels of schools. In 2002, the Chinese Ministry of Education announced that English would become a required course starting from the third grade(Liu & Braine, 2005). Since then, English has become an important part of the curriculum, which covers listening, speaking, reading, writing and grammar; Chinese English learners start practicing and studying English skills intensively in middle school, and English even has a decisive role for students' admission to universities and functions as a crucial criterion for their entrance to workplace.

In China, formal instruction and grammatical accuracy are emphasized in English teaching and learning, and the traditional teaching approach still prevails. Most of the time, L2 writing in English has primarily been seen as a matter of filling in blanks, following pattern drills and producing linguistically controlled writing due to the test-oriented feature of English instruction. This pattern of learning leads students to a low English speaking and writing ability but helps students obtain high scores in reading and listening. Research indicates that there is a gap between Chinese literacy instruction and EFL language instruction due to the reality of communicative purpose(Wang,2011).

At the university level, all undergraduates are required to take English courses. English instruction in many areas of China mostly focuses on grammar instruction and translation of Chinese sentences into English expressions. Other skills, such as writing and speaking, have been ignored to some extent. Despite the fact that English writing instruction has become increasingly important and highly demanded, Chinese students' English writing proficiency is inadequate to some extent in terms of the accuracy, fluency, and organization of their L2 writing.

1.1.2 Context of the Study.

This study is situated in an EFL learning context. Unlike most of the current studies that have focused more on advanced English learners in an ESL context, the population of the research is college level EFL learners in an Eastern Chinese University. 105 full-time students who were enrolled in the freshman course were recruited. Their ages ranged from eighteen to twenty. The participants were already randomly assigned into three classes when they entered college after they took the Chinese College Entrance Examination(i. e. ,"Gao Kao"). The three classes were then assigned to one control group which received feedback on content and organization of writing and two comparison groups which received different types of corrective feedback: indirect CF and direct CF. All the participants were English majors, had a common L1 (i. e. Mandarin Chinese) background, and had studied English for the same number of years, but with varied previous English learning experiences. All students had formal instruction on grammar and writing in college and they were expected to spend time studying grammar and practicing writing outside of the classroom. Students had a midterm and final exam each semester, in which writing tasks are heavily weighted in evaluating students' competence and performance of English. Therefore, the research tasks provided practice with feedback for the final assessment.

Formal grammar instruction in this university generally centers on accuracy of form and learning of rules, along with mechanical exercises. Grammar is still being taught in a traditional way in a non-integrative manner (e. g. , not integrated with skill practice). Both teachers and L2 learners see rule learning as important and teachers feel written grammar practice is very useful.

Teachers for the three classes are in general encouraged to follow a holistic grading system and rubric to provide feedback for students' writing. For example, content and organization are placed ahead of grammar in terms of student assessment; written policy also warns instructors against the tendency to edit the whole papers for students, which may overwhelm students, but instead teachers are asked to only correct repeated errors.

As an Intensive English Program (IEP) instructor before, I received complaints from L2 learners that a lack of grammar instruction, insufficient focus on grammar errors in students' writing, and students' inadequate self-editing skills inhibited L2 learners' full learning experiences. Also, a noticeable lack of confidence in L2 learners' self-identification of their writing ability was detected. The problem observed, based on my personal experience as a language teacher, triggered my study to further look into this issue and to propose appropriate instructional techniques for the specific EFL learning context.

Given the complexity and slow process of grammar learning, L2 learners inevitably make grammatical errors in their production of language. Considering many L2 learners' strong desire for corrective feedback (Ashwell, 2000; Ferris, 2012; Lee, 2004, 2008) , the study addressed the following three issues:

- Effectiveness of corrective feedback. To be specific, whether accuracy in the use of certain grammatical structures improves as a result of the provision of corrective feedback in their L2 writing and which type of corrective feedback (i. e. , indirect CF and direct CF) better helps facilitate students' L2 writing.

- Students' beliefs and reactions and teachers' expectations and preferences for different feedback on the improvement of students' writing. For example, which component among grammar, content and organization do students value the most in their understanding of effective feedback? How do students evaluate their own potential for improving their writing ability? What expectations do students have of grammar corrections in their writing? How do students' perceptions and preferences vary between different groups?

- Contextual (e. g. , prior learning experience, EFL vs. ESL) and affective (e. g. , attitudes, motivations, and beliefs) factors associated with corrective feedback in L2 development.

1.2   Outline of the Study

The structure of the study is as follows: In Chapter 2, I review the past work of both descriptive and experimental research associated with corrective feedback in L2 writing in an effort to discover controversies about the effectiveness of corrective feedback. Topics discussed in Chapter 2 also include form-focused instruction, implicit vs. explicit knowledge, learner and teacher perceptions of CF as well as the potential factors that may influence the effectiveness of corrective feedback. In chapter 3, I present both quantitative and qualitative research designs that were framed within a mixed-methods approach, which I applied in order to address each of the three research questions in the study. In Chapter 4, I report the quantitative findings for Research Question 1 and the results of the statistical analysis regarding the extent to which CF improves students' writing accuracy. In Chapter 5, I explore the mixed-methods results for Research Question 2 considering students' preferences and expectations for CF based on their responses to the two questionnaires. In Chapter 6, I report the qualitative findings for Research Question 3, which are the contextual and individual factors in relation to student production of writing accuracy and uptake of CF based on a combination of interviews and classroom observations. In Chapter 7, I review the results and further discuss each research question in connection to each other and other studies in the literature. In Chapter 8, I summarize the major results for the three research questions, provide suggestions for pedagogical practices in L2 classrooms, state the strengths and limitations of the current study, and also propose further directions for future research.

Chapter 2: Literature Review

Investigations have been undertaken to explore a variety of issues in second language acquisition (SLA) that are associated with corrective feedback (CF) in second language (L2) writing. The following sections discuss these issues, including the contributions of form-focused instruction, the need to develop both implicit and explicit L2 knowledge, the role of learning grammar in L2, controversies surrounding the effectiveness of CF, learner and teacher expectations, preferences, and perceptions of CF as well as the importance of certain relevant factors that may influence the effectiveness and efficiency of CF. Through a thorough analysis of both descriptive and experimental research into CF, the importance of this pedagogical practice will be demonstrated. This review will also help teachers and learners build connections between the potential influencing variables (e. g. , type of CF and learner variables) in ultimate language acquisition and how to achieve congruence between teachers and learners for successful language learning.

2.1　Form-focused Instruction (FFI) in SLA

A recent debate has been discussed regarding how language input should be presented to L2 leaners in classrooms. There is also widespread acceptance that L2 acquisition requires learners' attention to form. Many studies present a scope of research on form-focused instruction (FFI) and how it has changed over years (Nassaji, 1999; 2016). Form-focused instruction or grammar instruction in a broad sense refers to any instructional techniques or strategies that attempt to draw learner attention to specific grammatical structures(Ellis,2001,2005; Nassaji,1999). Such strategies are reflected in different forms, which are distinct from one another in a variety of ways. For instance, they can occur implicitly and explicitly, reactively(e. g. ,CF in response to student errors) or proactively in a predetermined manner, deductively or inductively, integratively or separately(Nasaji & Fotos, 2010). Spada (1997) defined FFI as " any pedagogical effort which is used to draw the learners' attention to form either implicitly or explicitly ⋯ within meaning-based approaches to L2 instruction [and] in which a focus on language is provided in either spontaneous or predetermined ways. " (p. 73)

2. 1. 1 **Naturalistic Exposure vs. Formal Instruction.**

Over the past forty years, research on the role of form-focused instruction has gone through many changes. Much research concentrated on whether form-focused instruction makes any difference in the development of learner language. This question has been motivated by the debate in the field of SLA in terms of the role of naturalistic exposure versus formal instruction.

To start the discussion on researchers' different views ofform-focused instruction in L2 learning, it is worthwhile to review Krashen's five hypotheses in SLA, that is, the Acquisition-Learning hypothesis, the Monitor hypothesis, the Natural Order hypothesis, the Input hypothesis, and the Affective Filter hypothesis(Krashen, 1981, 1982). Krashen's Acquisition and Learning hypothesis makes a distinction between acquisition and learning. Acquisition is related to implicit knowledge and occurs when learners engage in natural and meaningful communication, whereas learning is related to explicit knowledge and occurs when learners focus on forms as result of classroom instruction and activities, such as provision of corrective feedback. In the Monitor Hypothesis, Krashen does not completely deny a monitoring role for learning and points out that learners' monitor enables them to draw on their explicit knowledge if they have sufficient linguistic knowledge. In his Natural Order Hypothesis, Krashen states that a predictable order exists for learners' acquisition of linguistic knowledge of the target language. This order cannot be changed by the order that linguistic forms are taught in class. In his Input Hypothesis, Kranshen takes a very strong position on the importance of input. He asserts that the only causative variable in SLA is comprehensible input, and exposure to comprehensible input alone is sufficient for L2 acquisition. Krashen also points to studies showing the length of residence in a foreign country is related to language proficiency and the positive relationships between the amount of reading and proficiency.

Thus, from Krashen's viewpoint, form-focused instruction (FFI) has little beneficial effect on language acquisition. Some researchers followed Krashen's position and argued that the acquisition processes of L1 and L2 are similar to each other, and L2 learners need a naturalistic exposure for successful L2 acquisition rather than learning through formal instruction (Prabhu, 1987; Schwartz, 1993; Zobl, 1995).

However, a number of researchers have reassessed the role of form-focused instruction (FFI) and made an argument for its beneficial use in L2 pedagogy. These researchers claim that FFI can be potentially effective if it is provided and used appropriately. Here are the reasons for the argument. First, from a theoretical perspective, it is problematic to state that language can be learned without conscious attention to form (Schimidt, 1990, 1993, 1995). Schmidt's Noticing Hypothesis (1990, 2001) pointed out that there is no learning without conscious attention to form. Noticing or drawing learners' attention to the target language forms is essential for effective L2 learning. Second, much research shows that it is inadequate to primarily or solely focus on meaning and communication in learning without paying attention to grammatical forms (Harley & Swain, 1984; Swain, 1985; Lapkin, Hart & Swain, 1991). For example, empirical research shows that L2 learners in immersion programs and content-based classrooms may develop a high level of comprehension skills or fluency, but fail to develop a high level of grammatical accuracy in their L2. In addition, a number of studies demonstrated evidence that form-focused instruction is beneficial in helping L2 learners not only achieve a high level of accuracy in language use but also leads to the ultimate acquisition of language (Long, 1983; Ellis, 1995; Lightbown & Spada, 1990; Larson-Freeman & Lon, 1991; Ellis, 1994; Spada, 1997; Norris & Ortega, 2000, 2001; Ellis, 2001).

2.1.2 Focus on Forms(FonFs) vs. Focus on Form(FonF).

Research has shifted its focus on whether form-focused instruction (FFI) is effective to what type of instruction is more beneficial. Long (1991) made a distinction between Focus on Forms(FonFs) and Focus on Form(FonF) instruction. According to Long (1991), FonFs employs a traditional structural syllabus to language teaching, in which language is not presented to learners in a contextualized way. This approach presents a sequence of discrete pre-selected grammar structures. FonF is defined as an approach to instruction that involves drawing learners' attention to grammatical forms as they arise from communication and in the context of meaning-focused instruction. In certain conditions, FonF also reacts to linguistic problems that occur incidentally during communicative tasks. Both draw learners' attention to the linguistic features of language while FonF prefers to focus on content and meaningful communication and interactions in language learning by focusing learners' attention on understanding the message being conveyed through the L2.

Ellis(2002) also pointed out the two types of form-focused instruction: Focus on Forms(FonFs) and Focus on Form(FonF). In response to Long (1991), Ellis(2002) defined FonFs as the instruction that emphasizes the structures and accuracy of language, where the activities are directed intensively at a single grammatical form. This approach involves teaching grammar in separate lessons. On the other side, FonF implies no separate lessons on language forms. It stresses the importance of meaning in language learning and pays attention to teaching forms integrated into a curriculum consisting of communicative activities.

A number of theoretical studies have examinedthe differences between FonFs and FonF. The debate so far reveals considerable theoretical disagreement in terms of which type of form-focused instruction (FFI) is more effective in developing implicit knowledge. Some researchers strongly argue that focus on forms is more effective because it helps the automatisation of explicit knowledge during grammar learning (Dekeyser, 1998). This approach supports the value of explicit language teaching which proceduralizes language structures. However, other researchers (Long, 1988, 1991; Doughty, 2001) argue that Focus on Form is better to promote interlanguage development because acquisition of implicit knowledge occurs due to learners' attention to linguistic forms as well as learner engagement in understanding and producing meaningful information. However, there is significant agreement between the two viewpoints, which is that instruction needs to help students connect grammatical forms and meaning in communication.

Other researchers expanded the concept of FonF to include both incidental and preplanned FonF and argued that FonF can take place on a broader scale depending on how and when it is implemented (Spada, 1997; Doughty & Williams, 1998; Lightbown, 1998; Nassaji, 1999; Ellis, 2001; Nassaji & Foto, 2010). Ellis (2002) claimed that FonF can be pre-planned, where attention is drawn to the predetermined grammatical features and is intensive. FonF can also be incidental, where attention to form in communicative activities is not predetermined but occurs according to learners' linguistic needs in the activities. By using this approach, teachers cover a wide range of grammatical structures with an existing syllabus.

Spada et al. (2014) examined the effects of two other types of form-focused instruction (FFI) on L2 learning and the development of L2 grammatical knowledge: integrated FFI and isolated FFI. Integrated FFI is embedded within communicative practice and isolated FFI is separated from communicative practice. In Spada et al. (2014), two groups of adult ESL learners received the two types of FFI on the English passive voice. Results showed that learners in both groups made significant gains on the two language measures, which suggests that explicit attention to form within meaning-based instruction contributes positively to the development of L2 grammatical knowledge.

Furthermore, another issue noted in Nassaji (2016) is that the theoretical perspectives underlying instructional studies have started shifting from a purely cognitive perspective to those that incorporated more social, cultural and sociocultural perspectives. Many researchers examined the various forms of FFI in different contexts and with different learners as well as different factors that affect their use and effectiveness.

Table 2.1 shows a timeline with some examples of the studies on FFI based on the chronological order of their evolution over time. All the studies can be classified into the following nine categories as suggested in Nassaji(2016).

1. Theoretical and background issues

2. Definition of constructs

3. FFI vs. no instruction

4. Types of instruction

   a. Explicit vs. implicit

   b. Isolated vs. integrated

   c. Deductive vs. inductive

   d. Interactional/corrective feedback

   e. Consciousness raising tasks

   f. Incidental FonF

5. Factors affecting the use/effectiveness of instructional strategies

    g. Learners characteristics

    h. Feedback characteristics

    i. Types of tasks

    j. Linguistic target

    k. Linguistic/developmental level

6. Learners' and teachers' attitudes and perception

7. Context of instruction/interaction

    l. Second language

    m. Foreign language

8. Context of research

    n. Classroom

    o. Laboratory

    p. Computer-assisted

9. Narrative reviews/meta-analysis of research

Table 2. 1

Example of Key Studies on Form-Focused Instruction(FFI)

Studies	Theme
Long, M. (1983) Does second language instruction make a difference? A review of the research. *TESOL Quarterly*, 17, 359-382. Long found that instruction has positive effects on L2 learning compared to no instruction.	I
Sanz, C. & Morgan K. (2004). Positive evidence versus explicit rule presentation and explicit negative feedback: A computer assisted study. *Language learning*, 54, 35-78. Sanz and Morgan examined the effects on computer-delivered explicit information on learning Spanish.	G(b) H(c)
Mackey, A. (2006). Feedback, noticing, and second language development: An empirical study of L2 classroom interaction. *Applied Linguistics*, 27, 405-430. Mackey in the study found a positive relationship between feedback, noticing and the acquisition of L2 forms.	F
Spada, N. &Lightbown, p. (2008). Form-focused instruction: Isolated or integrated? *TESOL Quarterly*, 42, 181-207. Spada and Lightbown discussed two types of FFI: isolated and integrated. Both the two types of FFI were effective but in different ways.	B E(b)

(Contd.)

Studies	Theme
Nassaji, H. & Simard, D. (2010). Current developments in form-focused interaction and second language development. *Canadian Modern Language Review*, 66, 773-977. Nassaji and Smiard examined a number of studies that contribute to focused interaction and feedback on L2 development.	D
Spada, N. (2011). Beyond form-focused instruction: Reflection on past, present and future research. *Language Teaching*, 44, 225-236. Spada pointed out that questions regarding form-focused instruction have still remained because of different linguistics forms, timing of instruction and individual learner characteristics.	A
Tomita, Y. , & Spada, N. (2013). Form-focused instruction and learner investment in L2 communication. *The Modern Language Journal*, 97, 591-610. Tomita and Spada examined Japanese learners' investment in L2 communication. Results showed that FFI encouraged learners to invest in L2 communication by helping them create learner identity.	C

In the literature on instructed SLA, there is a consensus that a combination of form and meaning focused instruction is effective for L2 learning, and there is increasing evidence to support explicit attention to form through instruction and corrective feedback, particularly in content- and meaning-based L2 classrooms (Norris & Ortega, 2000; Spada, 2011). Attention has also been paid to the timing in the instructional sequence to draw learners' attention to form. Influenced by Spada (1997), FFI is described as occurring in L2 classrooms where the primary focus is on meaning and where attention to form is included. Thus, the central differences between the two types of instruction—FonFs vs. FonF— is when attention to form is provided. Doughty and William (1998) also discussed the issue of timing when making pedagogical decisions in FFI. In addition, Spada and Lightbown (2008) outlined a conceptual framework for distinguishing the isolated FFI and integrated FFI that differ in timing of attention to form. Isolated FFI separates form from content/communicative-based instruction, while integrated FFI combines attention to form within communicative/content-based teaching.

Moreover, existing SLA research on FFI (Ferris, 2004 and Doughty, 1998) strongly suggests that adult L2 learners in particular need teachers to explicitly point out the errors and make them salient to them for the avoidance of fossilization and continued development of their linguistic competence.

2.1.3 Explicit vs. Implicit Knowledge and Learning.

Another issue discussed by SLA researchers considers whether grammar should be taught as explicit or implicit knowledge (i. e. , explicit vs. implicit learning). Learners may not have difficulties articulating the rules of grammar, but they may have problems using it accurately and properly in communication, or vice versa.

Explicit knowledge refers to the linguistic knowledge learners have learned or been taught of the language. It relates to consciousness and is accessed through controlled processing when learners experience some linguistic difficulty in using L2 (Ellis, 2006). According to Ellis (2006), explicit knowledge has two types: explicit knowledge as analyzed knowledge and as metalinguistic explanation. Analyzed knowledge is a conscious awareness of how language structures work. Metalinguistic explanation is the knowledge of grammatical metalanguage and the ability to understand explanations of rules. This is related to metalinguistic awareness, which is important to the development of L2 competence. Jessner (2006) adopted the term *metalinguistic awareness* in his study to refer to " what learners know about language through reflection on and manipulation of language. " (p. 43) There exists certain consensus regarding the function of metalinguistic awareness in SLA because it regulates learners' conscious attention and plans, and monitors learners' linguistic production. Explicit learning therefore helps learners to develop their metalinguistic awareness, be able to process it, and internalize the grammatical forms for comprehension (Jessner, 2006).

Whether there is any value in teaching explicit knowledge of grammar is one of the most controversial issues in L2 acquisition. Two questions necessitate consideration in order to make sense of the position: first, is explicit knowledge valuable in itself; second, is explicit knowledge valuable in facilitating the development of implicit knowledge. The first question concerns the extent to which learners are able to use explicit knowledge in actual performance. One position from Krashen(2003)is that the ability is limited. Krashen (2003) argued that learners can only use explicit knowledge when they monitor themselves, which requires them to focus on form rather than on meaning and have sufficient time to access the knowledge. Another position argues that explicit knowledge can be used by learners to formulate messages, self-monitor, and access explicit memories for these purposes(Ellis,2005).

To answer the second question, according to Krashen (2003) , explicit knowledge cannot be converted into implicit knowledge because they are entirely distinct. Krashen's point of view leads to a zero grammar approach. Contrary to Krashen, there is increasing evidence showing that explicit attention to grammar can contribute to spontaneous production (Sheen, 2005; Spada & Tomita, 2010). DeKeyser (1997) insisted that explicit knowledge can become implicit through practice, provided that learners are developmentally ready to acquire the grammar. Ellis (2005) also claimed that explicit knowledge can convert into implicit knowledge if learners are ready to acquire the target language features or if they attend to the structures from input and notice the gap between the input and their output as well as if they seek opportunities to practice their communicative skills. N. Ellis(2005) argued as well that while most language acquisition takes place implicitly as learners use the language, explicit knowledge does have a role in affecting implicit knowledge by recruiting learners ' consciousness, thereby enhancing their ability to recognize patterns while they are negotiating meaning.

In addition, Norris & Ortega (2000) found a positive effect of explicit teaching. Swain &Lapkin (1998) also found benefits when students made opportunities for themselves to discuss grammar explicitly in "language related episodes", where students talk together about the language they are using and discuss which correct form they should produce. As DeKeyser and Preto Botano (2014) stated, whatever the source is, ultimately what is important is how much explicit knowledge learners have to proceduralize and automatize.

However, Lightbown (2008) pointed out an issue that even though learners are developmentally ready to acquire a given structure and they have received targeted explicit instruction on that structure, the learners may not immediately use the structure productively because the explicit instruction may be disconnected with language use. It is also possibly because the fact that grammar learning is a gradual process and it involves learners' interlanguages processing through transitional stages (Ellis, 2008).

In contrast to explicit knowledge, implicit knowledge is unconscious and can be immediately accessible for use in fluent communication. Many SLA researchers agree that language competence in the L2 is primarily a matter of implicit knowledge (Krashen, 1981; N. Ellis, 1998). One may ask if there is a best way to teach grammar for implicit knowledge. Two conflicting theoretical positions prevail regarding this issue. According to skill-building theory (DeKeyser, 1998), implicit knowledge derives from proceduralization through practice of explicit knowledge. In contrast, Krashen (1982) and N. Ellis (1998)'s emergentist theories believe implicit knowledge develops naturally from meaning-focused communication. In addition, Ellis (2005, 2006) considers two instructional options to answer the pedagogical question: input-based and output-based instruction. Input-based instruction attempts to draw learners' attention to the structures of the target language in the following ways: providing examples of the target structure in the input materials, highlighting the structure, and directing students' attention to form-meaning mappings. Output-based instruction is reflected in both skill-building theory as mentioned earlier and in the sociocultural theory of L2 learning, which refer to the fact that learners learn from social interaction in which learners attempt to produce new grammatical structures.

Regardless of the different theoretical positions, there is agreement between Krashen and Ellis that input is important to develop a high level of implicit knowledge in order to become a competent L2 communicator. Learners need opportunities to practice in communicative activities to develop implicit knowledge. Moreover, instruction needs to be directed at developing implicit knowledge of L2 while not neglecting explicit knowledge. There exists a possibility that implicit knowledge arises out of explicit knowledge, when the explicit knowledge is proceduralized through practice.

Overall, a number of studies (Andringa & Curcic, 2015; Carroll & Swain, 1993; Ellis, 2002, 2006; Sanz & Short, 2004) compare the effectiveness of explicit and implicit learning, but still with mixed findings, which lead to an ongoing debate on the two instruction approaches for the future.

2.1.4　The Role of Grammar Instruction in Pedagogy.

Grammar teaching has inspired a considerable amount of research. A number of issues are controversial in terms of how to teach L2 grammar in the field of SLA. Larsen-Freeman(2015) raised several questions regarding grammar instruction. For example, should students be given grammar rules? Should the rules remain explicit or implicit? She presented various ways of teaching grammar, such as providing learners with explicit rules, inductive versus deductive learning, input based instruction and focused tasks, and also identified two research positions on grammar instruction, which are the non-interface positon and form-focused instruction.

In the early research on SLA , grammar teaching was considered to have little impact on the natural language acquisition process. Krashen (1981 ,1982) argued that grammar plays no role in acquisition. Learners would automatically acquire language as long as they receive comprehensible input and are sufficiently motivated. Therefore , based on Krashen's hypotheses , what learners need is the abundant comprehensible input for sufficient language development. Evidence in support of this position was derived from naturalistic L2 acquisition theory in SLA research which showed there was a natural order of acquisition for learners for certain grammatical features , and learners only need to follow the natural and developmental stages to master grammatical structures. Conscious grammar instruction would not contribute to subconscious language acquisition and would not lead to learners' grammatical competence. Thus , Krashen maintained a non-interface position that no connection exists between what is taught to learners explicitly and the implicit knowledge necessary for fluent communication.

Although Krashen's ideas were widespread and popular among teachers , the ideas were criticized by researchers because Krashen failed to consider the importance of receiving feedback for learners on their performance (White , 1987). For students enrolled in L2 Immersion Programs , research showed that grammatical errors persisted after years of the approach Krashen recommended (Harlwy & Swain , 1984). Against these arguments , Krashen defended his non-interface position and stated that learning rules and drills are only of marginal value for learners.

However , in many classroom situations , the reality is that despite teachers' use of communicative language teaching and comprehensive input for students , much class time is devoted to providing grammatical explanations and rules (Gatbonton & Segalowitz , 2005). The question raised here is why teachers still have not abandoned explicit grammar instruction as they have been advised to. One reason is the power of students and teachers' attitudes and beliefs which were no doubt informed by their own learning experiences (Borg, 1999). For example, Schulz's (2001) research surveyed attitudes about grammar teaching among students and teachers who speak different languages. The findings suggested that grammar instruction is perceived as effective and necessary for students, although students may not enjoy working with it.

Moreover, from Larsen-Freeman's points of view, non-interface position is ineffective because of the strong and long-standing views on the importance of grammar teaching by teachers and by those who set the educational policy. She suggested there should not be change based on findings from SLA research because researchers often seek to define what is minimally necessary to explain language acquisition. What is minimally needed may not necessarily be what is optimal for classroom instruction or for all language learners, especially for those whose only contact with the target language is limited to what they receive in the classroom.

Therefore, many researchers do not adopt Krashen's ideas on excluding grammar teaching from classroom instruction. Long (1991), who favors FonF, argued that teaching grammar should not be prohibited and should be taught in a way that does not interfere with natural acquisition. In particular, Long advocated the use of explicit explanations of the grammatical forms as they arise from communication and called for learners' attention to grammatical features through corrective feedback. While Long's focus is primarily reactive, that is, learners' attention is directed to the grammatical forms once they have committed an error (Spada, 1997), some other researchers believe grammar instruction includes a pre-emptive treatment of grammatical features, which is often initiated by students and which can be integrated into meaningful language use(Ellis, Basturkmen & Loewen, 2001). Both approaches indicate that grammar instruction and helping students notice errors are important in pedagogy. This is especially important for structures that are vulnerable to fossilization, which may be subject to cross-linguistic influence (Han & Odlin, 2006).

There is also evidence showing that grammar instruction contributes to both acquired and learned knowledge. Some researchers found that instructed learners progressed more rapidly and achieved higher level of grammatical competence than naturalistic learners. Some others argued the case that in order for grammar instruction to work effectively, it needs to take into account learners' development of interlanguage. There are many controversies regarding how interlanguage develops and how grammar instruction facilitates that development.

Traditional syllabi emphasized teaching form over meaning. Current syllabi pay more attention to the functions of grammatical forms and the meanings that different grammatical forms convey in communication. If grammar fails to describe the connection between grammatical forms and meaning, then acquisition of the L2 will be inadequate. Thus, establishing connections between form and meaning is critical for language acquisition.

However, it is controversial to choose which grammatical structures to teach. One position is from Krashen (2003) , who argued that grammar teaching should be limited to a few simple rules that can be used to monitor learners' output from the acquired system. Most learners are not capable of mastering complex rules because the rules go beyond their ability to notice and correct through monitoring. Other researchers concluded that grammar holds a central place in language teaching and learning, and needs to be taught in a way that was comparable with the naturalistic order of acquisition.

Given the controversies, Ellis (2002) proposed the theory of instructed language learning addressing the role of grammar instruction in L2 acquisition. According to Ellis (2002) , there is a considerable amount of research that demonstrates the effectiveness of teaching grammar, and there should not be just one preferred approach to teaching grammar. Acquisition of grammar is a complex process which should be assisted by different approaches. The following are some of the ideas addressed by Ellis (2002), which provide a basis for argument and reflection in SLA: First, the traditional approach to grammar teaching based on explicit explanations and drills is unlikely to lead to acquisition of implicit knowledge that is needed for fluent and accurate communication. Grammar should not only emphasize form, but also the meaning and uses of different grammatical features. Second, teachers should focus on teaching the grammatical forms that are most problematic to learners rather than teaching the entirety of grammar. Third, grammar is better taught to learners who have already acquired a certain ability to use the language. It can also be taught through corrective feedback (CF). Fourth, explicit learning assists implicit learning. Teaching explicit knowledge can be incorporated into both the FonFs and FonF approaches.

Ellis (2002) particularly addressed that the need for instruction to ensure that learners predominantly focus on meaning. Two types of meaning are involved: the semantic meaning relating to specific lexical and grammatical structures, and the pragmatic meaning that arises in communicative tasks. It is important for learners to focus on both types of meaning, but the pragmatic meaning is more crucial to language learning because it views L2 as a tool for communication. Only when learners are engaged in decoding and encoding messages in the context of communication, is acquisition more likely to occur, and pragmatic meaning helps learners activate linguistic knowledge and develop their L2 fluency.

In addition, instruction needs to ensure learners' focus on forms (FonFs) based on SLA theories, which is necessary for acquisition to take place. A number of approaches can be used in instruction to focus on forms (Larsen-Freeman, 2015). For example, grammar lessons can be designed to teach specific grammatical forms by using an inductive approach, which encourages learners' noticing of forms, or a deductive approach that seeks to develop an awareness of grammatical rules. Grammar instruction can also use focused tasks to require learners to comprehend and process specific grammatical structure in the input or to produce the structures in output.

2.2　Positive Evidence vs. Negative Evidence in SLA

Second language learners can be exposed to two types of input: positive evidence and negative evidence. Positive evidence refers to input which provides learners with the acceptable or correct information of their L2(Shintani et al. ,2014). It can come from native speaker discourse, in a modified language which simplifies or elaborates the input to facilitate learner comprehension, or the extensive input learners access either inside and outside the classroom, such as movies, extensive reading materials, music, etc. Many successful L2 learners seek opportunities to experience the language outside the classroom. Receiving positive evidence is an effective way to achieve a high level of L2 proficiency. In contrast, negative evidence provides learners with information regarding what is unacceptable in their L2, such as corrective feedback(Shintani et al. ,2014). Negative evidence can be used before errors occur or afterwards to indicate or correct non-targetlike use of the language in learner output.

In SLA literature, the term negative evidence is used interchangeably with corrective feedback (CF) to indicate any non-target like use of language. A great deal of research has been done on the topic of corrective feedback in SLA, and there has been disagreement about the role of errors in language learning. In early years, errors in writing were not tolerated. Later, some linguists argued that errors in SLA were acceptable because it is part of the developmental process in language learning, which is similar to the L1 learning process (Doughty &Williams, 1998; R. Ellis, 2007, Long, 1996, 2007; Lyster, Lightbown &Spada, 1999; Russel & Spada, 2006).

The idea of "we learn from mistakes" has long been a source of debate in the field of SLA. Krashen (1982) argued against corrective feedback as it aims at rectifying explicit rather than implicit knowledge, which makes little or no contribution to true linguistic development. Long (1996), as one of the principle challengers of Krashen' position, agreed that meaningful input is essential to L2 acquisition but claimed that having only comprehensive input is insufficient. Long asserted that even if negative evidence is not absolutely necessary for SLA to occur, it may play a facilitative role in the process(Long,2007).

Many other SLA researchers have advocated the use of negative evidence as well to promote learning, noticing of errors, and internalization of correct forms(Doughty & Williams,1998; R. Ellis,2007,Long,1996, 2007; Lyster, Lightbown & Spada, 1999; Russel & Spada, 2006). For example, Russel and Spada(2006)'s meta-analysis of corrective feedback between 1982-2004 found a large effect size of 1. 04 of primary studies, indicating a beneficial effect CF has on L2 development, although not all corrective feedback types are equally effective, for some are more effective than others. Schmidt(1990) contended that learner attention to linguistic forms is necessary for their internalization. N. Ellis (2001) echoed this position in his assessment of the importance of noticing forms in L2 learning.

Overall, those researchers and L2 specialists agree that CF plays a role in SLA, even though the role is still in dispute. The accuracy issue in writing undervalues the linguistic gaps that many L2 learners bring into advanced learning situations. L2 learners' knowledge and experience is not the same as that of native speakers. Therefore, L2 learners need additional pedagogical intervention to help with their writing.

2.3   Corrective Feedback in L2 Writing

Questionsand issues about the role of corrective feedback (CF) in L2 writing are involved in heated debates , generating a great deal of theoretical and empirical research. Does corrective feedback facilitate the overall performance of L2 writing? If the answer is affirmative , what type of corrective feedback is more effective? Researchers have investigated the facilitative role of corrective feedback in L2 writing; however , the claims have not been decisively concluded. In order to better understand these questions and move forward the research in the area of corrective feedback , it is important to examine previously conducted research on the impact of corrective feedback in L2 development , especially the effectiveness of corrective feedback for L2 learners in an EFL learning context , particularly those students which not only are based on classroom observation but also on teachers' and learners' perceptions by taking into account teacher , learner , and context variables on corrective feedback. Although each empirical study examines different research questions , consistencies and similarities appear in the questions. Basically , four categories of issues are identified in the previously conducted research : (1) language teachers' perceptions of corrective feedback in relation to the contextual factors ; (2) learners' perceptions on teachers' feedback and to what extent teachers' corrective feedback is related to language learners' motivation and attitudes ; (3) the effect of teachers' written feedback on the revision process in learners' academic performance and their application of and reactions to teacher feedback ; (4) the effects of individual preferences and attitudes toward technology in relation to their choice of feedback and L2 academic performance.

Discussion arising in the SLA literature reveals a great deal of empirical support from researchers , teachers , and learners who believe either a positive or negative relationship exists between corrective feedback and L2 learning and development. On one hand, some researchers show a strong stance on the ineffectiveness of corrective feedback (Bruton, 2009; Truscott, 1996, 1999; Robb, 1986); on the other hand, a growing consensus appears among the many researchers who promote the efficacy of corrective feedback in L2 writing. L2 teachers and learners also hold a positive attitude towards and concern about the significance of the role played by corrective feedback in the process of L2 development (Baleghizadeh & Gordani, 2012; Evan, Hartschorn, & Krause; 2011; Guenete & Lyster, 2013; Vyatkina, 2011). The researchers examine how students who receive appropriate corrective feedback show a better performance in the accuracy and quality of writing (Bitchener & Knoch, 2009, 2010; Ferris, 2010; Ferris, Liu, Sinba, & Senna, 2013; Van Beunnigen, De Jong, & Kuiken, 2012). Among the extensive research that explores the effectiveness of corrective feedback, the extent to which type of corrective feedback can play a better role in improving L2 learners' accuracy of writing also becomes an interesting issue to consider.

In the following sections, both theoretical and empirical studies on corrective feedback in L2 writing will be discussed. In particular, four main issues will be explored in detail: first, does corrective feedback play a positive role in helping L2 writers? To be more precise, do L2 learners who receive corrective feedback produce more accurate texts than those who receive no corrective feedback? Secondly, what type of corrective feedback leads to more accurate writing by L2 students (e. g. , direct CF and indirect CF)? Third, what are students' and teachers' expectations and preferences for the corrective feedback on L2 writing? Fourth, how are contextual, affective and other individual factors associated with corrective feedback (CF) in L2 development? All the discussions will be explored by looking at researchers' positions and teachers' and learners' perceptions.

2.3.1   Positions on Corrective Feedback in L2 Learning

2. 3. 1. 1   **Arguments against Corrective Feedback.** A considerable number of investigations center on the subjects of corrective feedback in L2 and pose controversies among L2 researchers and language teachers. Based on previous studies, some researchers take a position regarding this issue and argue that corrective feedback does not facilitate L2 learners' language performance. One of the well-known position papers was published by Truscott(1996), which inspired increased interest in the topic of corrective feedback on the part of researchers. Truscott (1996) denied the relationship between the usefulness of error feedback and L2 learning and took a strong position that grammar correction has no place in L2 writing and should be abandoned.

To briefly describe the reasons stated by Truscott (1996), first, few research takes serious attempts to justify the effectiveness of corrective feedback on an empirical basis. Much existing research shows that grammar correction is ineffective and none shows it is helpful in any interesting sense. Second, for both theoretical and practical purposes, grammar correction is expected to be ineffective. Many researchers do not critically examine the nature of correction process and language learning, do not consider the impracticality of correction, and ignore some theoretical problems involved in correction. Third, grammar correction may have harmful effects, such as its effects on students' attitudes, wasting time and consuming energy in classroom practice.

In terms of the ineffectiveness of grammar correction, Truscott(1996) claimed that grammar correction does not work and it does not have any effect in terms of students' proficiencies varying from beginning to advanced levels. Truscott provided some examples of evidence against grammar correction from research, including from Hendrickson (1976), Cohen and Robbins (1978). Hendrickson (1976) claimed that correcting all the errors was not better than correcting only the errors that caused communicative problems, and both the two methods had little or no significant effects on students writing ability. Cohen and Robbin (1978) looked at the effect of corrective feedback on advanced ESL learners' writing and reached the same conclusion with Hendrickson that corrections did not have significant effects on students' improvement of errors in writing. Some other studies also showed that no significant differences between the first draft and the revised composition in students' improvement of writing ability either in lasting a semester or a quarter. Therefore, corrective feedback had no benefits for students' writing.

Truscott(1996) also pointed out some potential limitations of research that examined the effectiveness of grammar correction because different researchers had different interpretations and other factors may have also influenced the results of the research. For example, there may be a delayed effect of correction that did not show in the research, and research resultsmay also be affected by different methods of assessment and instruction. Many researchers did not provide much detailed information, but in this regard, different instructions used in classroom may suggest substantial variation in L2 research. For instance, some teachers devote most of the class time to correction practice in L2 writing; some other teachers put more emphasis in extensive writing practice with a focus on selective grammar instruction. In addition, researchers in some studies did not require students to do anything with the corrections before students rewrote. Some other researchers, however, set aside class time for students to correct the errors and then rewrite.

Therefore, it is not realistic to examine the benefits of correction because a number of variables should be considered, such as educational experiences, age, gender, attitudes, and anxiety. It may also depend on teacher characteristics, the learning environment, as well as the interaction among all the potential factors and other unknown and uncontrolled factors. In this case, research cannot identify accurately and properly the benefits of correction and is highly unlikely to be able to do so in the future. Truscott's arguments on the limitations of research reach the same conclusion with the previous argument he made, which is grammar correction does not work.

In addition, Truscott (1996) made the argument that even some research shows the effectiveness ofgrammar correction, none of it is able to answer the question: does grammar correction make students better writers? Some studies did have interesting and valuable findings. For example, the group of students who received corrections produced better final drafts than the group without receiving any comments on their writing. However, the results still did not answer the question: does grammar correction make students better writers in the future because of receiving grammar corrections? None of the studies ever suggested an answer to the issue, thus, there is no relationship between correction and learning (Truscott, 1996). Students will repeat the errors, even after being corrected many times. Therefore, in Truscott's point of view, none of the studies sufficiently supports grammar correction as an effective classroom practice, while a number of studies have found corrections are not effective.

Moreover, Truscott (1996) considered from both theoretical and practical aspects to explain why grammar correction cannot work. From the theoretical perspective (i. e. , orders of acquisition, interlanguage, and the role of L2 intuition vs. metalinguistic knowledge) , Truscott pointed out two specific theoretical problems of grammar correction. First, grammar correction only deals with the superficial part of grammar and ignores the underlying process of language development. Truscott argued that many teachers intuitively assume that students can understand and remember the corrections and are able to use them properly in their future writing. However, becoming proficient in English is a complex and long process. Acquisition of grammar is a gradual process rather than relying on transfer of knowledge or a sudden discovery based on teaches' intuitive viewpoint of learning. It involves inherent and consistent order or sequence of the acquisition of certain grammatical structures. Therefore, teachable moments and developmental sequences need to be taken into account. Providing correction can encounter problems due to our ignorance of the sequences of language acquisition. Truscott claimed that it is possible that research on developmental sequences can be applied to classroom practice, but this goal has not been and will not be achieved.

Another theoretical problem is described as pseudolearning. It means that learners can have acquired good knowledge of the target language but are not able to use it. Grammar correction is a practice that produces pseudolearning. It is a superficial form of learning. Much research shows that the ability to correct errors is different from the ability to state the rules of grammar correction. Sometimes, students are not willing to make corrections they receive. Students may fully understand the corrections but still make errors in their writings.

Therefore, in view of the theoretical problem, the acquisition of certain grammatical structures follows the developmental sequence rather than an intuitive acquisition process. Instead of simply distributing error correction to students, teachers cannot expect error correction to work efficiently unless they ensure the teachable moments when students have the readiness to receive the information. L2 learners need to go through a fairly regular sequence regardless of their L1. Some learners may progress at slower or faster rates based on a variety of factors, such as age, affective issues, and prior education experiences. Based on Truscott's arguments, error correction can be beneficial only if teachers take into account students' developmental conditions and individuality in order to take advantage of the teachable moments.

Truscott(1996) also doubted the value of grammar correction based on a practical consideration. First, teachers may fail to notice the errors, especially for teachers who are not native speakers of the target language.

Even if teachers realize and correct the errors, they may not have a good understanding of the correct use of grammar due to lack of knowledge and lack of time. Although they can understand it well, they may not be able to provide good explanations. While teachers are capable of providing good explanations, they may not have time and patience as they are dealing with a large number of students' writing assignments. The quality of the corrections becomes a problem in this case. Also, teachers are not consistent and systematic in their corrections, especially when they are dealing with many students and with many different errors. This inconsistency makes it more difficult for students to understand and remember the errors. Another problem is that even if teachers can give good explanations and students can deal with the errors, they both may not be motivated to do so, especially if they need to deal with many of them. Students do not pay attention to corrections and are not motivated to think about the correction in future writing. Many students do not seriously deal with corrections because they see it as a form of punishment.

One may suggest that teachers selectively provide corrections instead of comprehensive corrections so as to reduce their work and to avoid overwhelming students. However, Truscott believed that this is not going to work because selective correction needs to be consistent with learners' developmental stages if it is to be effective. In this case, teachers have to obtain a high level of knowledge about developmental stages and need to take care of each individual student's grammatical errors. This, however, adds an extra burden to teachers. Also, it takes time for teachers to decide which errors need to be corrected. Teachers have to find all the relevant errors for selective correction, identify them and avoid being overly inclusive.

To conclude, from the practical angle, a point in support of the uselessness of corrective feedback is that it is only a superficial phenomenon. The idea is that error correction promotes a reduction of errors that students are prompted to immediately correct and carefully treat in their performance. However, evidence that proves students will avoid making the same errors on subsequent language tasks is scarce. The literature does not support claims that corrective feedback ensures an ultimate application of that feedback in L2 development in the long run.

In addition, researchers and scholars (Truscott, 1996, 1999) stated that grammar correction has harmful effects on learners themselves. Learning is most successful when it is less stressful and enjoyable. Students find corrections discouraging because they do not like to be corrected repeatedly all over their writing. Many students who do not receive corrections tend to have a more positive attitude toward writing. Research also shows that because of the positive attitudes uncorrected students develop toward writing, they tend to write more and show a superior grasp of grammar, such as sentence boundaries. On the other side, the corrected students tend to simplify their writing in order to avoid being corrected. They do not learn as much as uncorrected students because of the negative attitude toward learning.

Another reason researchers believes correction is harmful is because of its time-consuming nature. Students who take corrections seriously have to spend more time thinking about and correcting their errors. The time they spend should be spent on other, more productive learning activities. The time problem for teachers is even greater because correcting many students' writing absorbs enormous amount of teachers' time, which can be spent more efficiently on other things. Focusing on grammar correction distracts students and teachers' attention from other, more important, "high level" aspects of writing, such as organization and content of writing. Error-focused feedback led students to pay too much attention to grammatical features and unfortunately neglected the fluency in their writing. A number of L2 teachers mentioned that because language is mostly used for communication, grammatical errors should not be prioritized if students make good points in their writing. Another argument added by Truscott (1996) was that even though teachers are responsible for helping students learn and students express their willingness to be corrected because they think corrections are helpful, this does not mean teachers should provide correction to them.

Overall, Truscott and researchers in L2 writing (Bruton , 2009 , Robb , 1986 , Truscott , 1996) extensively argued grammar correction is not helpful and even harmful. They presented research on grammar correction and provided evidence for ineffectiveness of grammar, and finally suggested that teachers should not provide corrections for students.

2. 3. 1. 2　**Arguments for Corrective Feedback.** Regarding the importance of corrective feedback in L2 learning, a growing number of L2 researchers (Lee , 2004 ; Bitchner , 2008 ; Bitchnener and Knoch , 2008 , 2010) argue in favor of the positive contribution corrective feedback makes to L2 learning, especially for a consistent learning process. Extensive research makes it clear that corrective feedback should be a part of the instruction in language classroom because of its facilitative role in second language acquisition (SLA).

Ferris is the most prominent advocate of grammar correction. Ferris (1999) evaluated Truscott's viewpoints on the ineffectiveness of grammar corrections. She claimed Truscott's arguments on grammar correction are premature and overly strong. Ferris believed that error correction is a great concern in L2 writing and a controversial issue for researchers and classroom teachers. Her own teaching experience and extensive empirical research tells that many students benefit from corrective feedback, and have even made great improvements in their accuracy of writing. According to Ferris (1999) , corrective feedback at least results in short term learning outcomes and possibly an indicator of long term improvements as well. Ferris then provided the reasons that addressed the need to continue the practice of grammar correction. First, students themselves are concerned about accuracy and expect to receive feedback from teachers. Many grading rubrics of writing explicitly outline that poor use of grammar prevents students from achieving high scores in writing proficiency examinations. Thus, the absence of grammar feedback can frustrate students, and thus negatively affect students' motivation and confidence in their writing. Second, some instructors in college are not tolerant of typical ESL errors, because they feel the errors would affect the overall evaluations of students' papers. Third, appropriate corrective feedback can enhance learners' metalinguistic awareness, which is crucial for students to be capable to self-edit their own writing(Ferris, 1999, 2004, 2010).

With regard to the significance of corrective feedback, other researchers also point out that L2 learners who receive error correction produce more accurate texts than those who do not. From the long-term perspective, with repeated improvements in accuracy, corrective feedback leads to the development of L2 learners' overall language proficiency overtime. Especially for adult L2 learners, explicit error feedback greatly decreases the likelihood of fossilization during their L2 learning (Kang&Han, 2015; Polio, 2012, Shintani, Ellis, & Susuki, 2014). Fossilization is a phenomenon that occurs during second language acquisition, in which L2 learners tend to formulate their own rules in language production. The rules are influenced either by their first language (L1) structure or their correct or incorrect perception of L2 structure. If the rules turn into a permanent feature, this phenomenon is called fossilization, which hinders students' L2 acquisition and learning. Thus, without corrective feedback, L2 learners have difficulty realizing why and how the errors happened and to further develop an advanced skill of language.

Myles(2002) claimed in her study that the emphasis on the writing process, including invention and multiple drafts, is only appropriate and effective for L2 learners if they are both able to get sufficient feedback from teachers with regard to their errors in writing, and are proficient enough in their L2 to implement self-correction strategies. At this point, feedback is crucial in L2 learners' writing instruction and learning processes. Without adequate concentration on errors, students will hardly become sufficient self-editors and improvement in writing will barely occur.

Bitchener(2008) conducted an empirical study as well exploring the efficacy of corrective feedback. He found students who received corrective feedback outperformed those who did not receive any feedback in the immediate post-test, and the outcome due to corrective feedback was still maintained in the delayed post-test two-month later without any additional feedback and classroom instruction. The other contribution of this study is that it successfully evidenced corrective feedback fosters the degree of accuracy in a new piece of writing rather than a subsequent writing of the same task.

2. 3. 1. 3 **Types of Corrective Feedback.** Among the extensive research that explores the effectiveness of corrective feedback, the question of which type of corrective feedback prompts more improvements in L2 learners' language performance has been an interesting issue to consider. A rich literature has investigated the effects of different types of corrective feedback on L2 learning (Chandler, 2003 ; Sheen, Wirght, & Moldawa, 2009 ; Van Beuningen, De Jong, & Kuiken, 2008). Some evidence shows that explicit and direct corrective feedback is more effective in eliciting learners' immediate revisions and subsequent correct use, while some theoretical arguments support implicit and indirect corrective feedback because this is more related to focus on meaning. However, few conclusions tell us which one is more effective for L2 acquisition.

It is necessary to take a close look at specific problems that are posed by researchers regarding the effect of different types of corrective feedback in language learning. For example:

 · What is a better way of giving students feedback for improvement on their accuracy?

- How explicit should teacher feedback be?
- Which corrective feedback do L2 learners prefer?

Many researchers support the use of indirect CF because it is claimed to encourage students' analytic reflection to guide their own learning, engagement in the problem-solving process, and processing of the feedback they receive (Chandler, 2003; Ferris & Robert, 2001; Shintani & Ellis, 2013). Thus, indirect feedback brings benefits to a long-term improvement in students' L2 learning. In one of the few longitudinal classroom-based studies investigating teachers' CF strategies and student progress over time, it was found that while direct correction led to a higher level of correction in short-term revision, greater gains were found in long-term written accuracy as a result of indirect feedback. For direct feedback, however, teachers may inappropriately interpret students' intention and provide the wrong corrections for students. Chandler (2003) conducted an empirical study by comparing an experimental and control group so as to examine the usefulness of indirect feedback for L2 writers. Results emphasized the value of indirect feedback, which contributed to reducing long-run errors. Participants in this study also showed their preference for the indirect error correction because it engaged them in self-discovery learning, which would eventually assist them in advancing their writing proficiency.

Nevertheless, other researchers (Bitchener and Knoch, 2008, 2010) questioned the effectiveness of indirect feedback and are in favor of the direct correction of errors because direct approach reduces the confusion if students do not understand what the error means. Direct feedback requires minimal cognitive processing, helps students deal with more difficult and complicated errors, and obtain an immediate improvement in their L2. Thus, direct feedback is particularly appropriate for beginning language learners (Lee, 2003). However, in light of indirect feedback, only identifying errors may cause students' confusion and difficulties in comprehending and decoding the errors.

Regarding the fundamental question of how explicit the error correction should be, recent research (Bitchener and Knoch, 2010; Ferris and Roberts, 2001) with a focus on the adult L2 learners strongly suggested that the more explicit the error marks are, the better language competence adult L2 learners are able to develop. Writing major error patterns in feedback along with marking sample errors in the text is one of the most successful techniques of leading students to make considerable revisions. Bitchener and Knoch(2010) carried out an experimental study that investigated the effects of different types of error correction provided for advanced L2 learners, who had already developed a high level of language accuracy. Participants were college students in the U. S. and varied from different L1 backgrounds(i. e. , mostly from East and South Asia). They were divided into three groups: those who received metalinguistic explanation, indirect error correction, and metalinguistic feedback plus form-focused instruction. The targeted linguistic features measured in their study were two articles: *a* and *the*. A pre-test, a post-test, and a delayed post-test were conducted during a 10-week period of time. Results confirmed that all students who received error correction on their pre-test texts revealed improved accuracy immediately. However, only the students who received metalinguistic explanation and form-focused instruction were able to retain their writing accuracy over the 10-week period. Based on the results of this study, corrective feedback needs to be adopted by L2 teachers even though some feedback types cannot retain a longitudinal effect on the accuracy of L2 writing. The outcomes also suggest that a clear and simple metalinguistic explanation functions more effectively if targeting on a long-term improvement of accuracy in L2.

In terms of the controversies prevalent in the investigation of different types of feedback, Ferris (2010) clarified one possible condition that can determine the use of specific type of corrective feedback. In a L2 composition class, indirect feedback may be more appropriate and effective because indirect feedback encourages students to learn how to revise and edit their L2 writing. By contrast, if in a language learning class, direct feedback is preferred over other forms of corrections because direct feedback is easier to guide students to recognize and resolve the errors.

Ferris (20004, 2010) also argued that corrective feedback that is insufficiently provided is not helpful to students, but effective error correction which is selective, prioritized, and clear can at least help some students in their L2 writing. In this case, teachers need more preparation and practice as they need a solid grounding of linguistic theory and how to teach grammar to L2 learners. Teachers also need more practice in error analysis and providing feedback for their students. To make error corrections effective for students, it is also important for teachers to selectively choose the errors and help students develop their awareness and knowledge of their most frequent and serious grammar problems. The strategy of prioritizing increases the chance of being more accurate in teachers' feedback. Effective corrective feedback also needs to take into account students' L1 and L2 background, language proficiency, motivation, attitudes, etc. Teachers need to listen to students' needs regarding how to provide feedback to their writing. Providing feedback and strategy training enables students to take seriously the need to improve their editing skills and raise their awareness of the importance of accuracy in L2 writing.

2.3.2 Perceptions of Corrective Feedback in L2 Learning

Linguistics errors are pervasive in L2 writing, and may cause different degrees of irritation or even communication breakdown to teachers or other readers. Thus, student errors in writing becomes a major concern for students and providing corrective feedback for student writing has been an essential practice for teachers. Much discussion arising in second language acquisition (SLA) reveals a great deal of empirical support from researchers, teachers, and learners who believe positive relationship exists between corrective feedback and L2 learning and development. Students need corrective feedback and it is an effective pedagogical practice in L2 writing. A growing body of research has also explored learner characteristics including the affective aspects (e. g. , motivation and attitudes) , age, proficiency level, learning style, instructional context, and cultural backgrounds, which may influence learners' reactions and the efficacy of corrective feedback(Hyland,2003; Kormo,2012; Lee,2005). A negative outcome of feedback is called affective damage, which can lead to negative feelings and emotions, such as low self-esteem, poor motivation and attitude, and language anxiety. Affective damage can inhibit or discourage learning, damage learners' feelings and attitudes, and negatively influence the effectiveness of corrective feedback (Agudo, 2013). Therefore, the potential affective damage corrective feedback causes for learners needs to be seriously taken into consideration when interacting with students. The following exploratory studies examined the particular beliefs of students and teachers regarding the role of corrective feedback and students' reactions to teachers' feedback in language learning.

2. 3. 2. 1   **Negative Perceptions.** Some research in SLA has suggested that students who have not received error correction hold more positive attitudes towards writing because students may be frustrated when errors are marked repeatedly, though they accept the fact that making errors is part of the learning process(Truscott,1996; Truscott and Hsu,2008). At this point, students are inclined to avoid using complex sentence structures or advanced vocabularies with the purpose of avoiding corrections. There exists a great possibility that students who have received numerous corrections do not perform as well as those with only few amendments because their pessimistic feelings toward learning develop over time.

Individuals may argue that if teachers correct a few important errors continuously, it would be easy for students to take care of the corrections and improve for the future. However, this is not applicable for teachers because they have to look at a large number of students' writings, which requires patience and consumes time. Besides, under certain conditions in which students will repeat the errors that they made over a long time, teachers would consider students sluggish and inattentive. Both the situations can leave room for teachers to possibly overlook students' errors and simply conclude that error correction is ineffective (Bruton, 2009; Lee, 2003; Truscott & Hsu, 2008).

Furthermore, as discussed in Lee (2003), because of insufficient linguistic knowledge, some unconfident teachers express their concerns in providing appropriate error corrections for students. Even though language teachers are able to easily recognize students' grammatical errors, some teachers cannot fully and successfully explain them, which causes teachers' irritation and anxiety in dealing with the problems. Accordingly, this lack of confidence may result in the inconsistency of teachers' error correction practices with their beliefs and insufficient preparation to help students with their self-editing skills in language production.

2.3.2.2 **Positive Perceptions.** The negative viewpoints mentioned above have ignored students' individuality and affective factors (e. g. , their strong desire and necessity) for corrective feedback. The following studies show the researchers, teachers and students who believe that corrective feedback is necessary in any language classroom. In particular, it is helpful in enhancing L2 learning in adults.

In evaluating ESL students' attitudes toward corrective feedback in a college-level English writing class, Leki's (1991) research indicated that ESL students were concerned with their written errors and believed that high quality writing should be error-free. They expected teachers to have all their errors corrected in their writing. Schulz's (2001) study also investigated students' and teachers' perceptions regarding the role of corrective feedback in adult L2 learning regarding the effectiveness of corrective feedback in American and non-American learning contexts. Results revealed that students in Colombia and the U. S. would like to be corrected and felt teachers should correct their errors in speaking and writing. Teachers in both cultures showed little disagreement as well, and agreed that students' errors in the target language should be corrected.

As Ferris(2004) stated, studies concentrating on L2 learners' attitudes and opinions about error feedback are very consistent in demonstrating that L2 student writers show a general preference and strong expectation for error correction. They regard error feedback from their teachers as an essential contributor to the success of their language production. Since L2 learners not only care about but also frequently struggle with linguistic accuracy, L2 learners believe in the importance and benefit of teachers pointing out the errors for the purpose of eliminating the possibility of making grammatical errors during their L2 development. Conversely, the lack of feedback from teachers can be harmful due to students' strong belief about this issue. As Ferris(1999) claimed about L2 writing:

"··· the absence of any form of grammar feedback could frustrate students to the point that it might interfere with their motivation and confidence in the writing class, particularly when grading rubrics and writing proficiency examination results tell them that their language errors could prevent them from achieving their educational and professional goals." (p. 8)

Ferris (1999) also argued that students highly value teachers' comments on grammar, as feedback triggers them to make effective revisions, which further affects their writingperformance. Similarly, Hyland (2003) conducted another study that examined students' perception of the effect of error feedback on their L2 writing product and revision strategies. Subjects who engaged in Hyland's research varied in different levels of

English proficiency and backgrounds. The researcher pointed out that an affirmative relationship exists between error feedback and the quality of students' writing. Students' engagement with form-focused feedback motivated them to develop their self-revision skills in writing and eventually helped them make good progress in the problems that are addressed in the feedback. Though error feedback may not have an immediate effect, students hold a firm belief that continual feedback from teachers would ultimately benefit them. Without feedback, students would be more likely to fail to notice the errors.

Research also reveals that since accuracy is one of the fundamental criteria for the assessment of academic performance, some language teachers, especially at the college level, are less or even not at all tolerant of "typical" ESL errors compared to the "typical" errors committed by native speakers, and therefore demand linguistically error-free academic performance from L2 writers (Ferris, 1999). Hence, it seems that a stigma exists in academia in terms of students' inaccurate language performance. For example, teachers feel linguistic errors can adversely affect their overall evaluation of students' papers.

2.3.3 Factors in Relation to Corrective Feedback

Students' attitudes, beliefs, and expectations about corrective feedback can be informed by a number of potential contextual, affective, and individual factors. It is important to not only address the importance of corrective feedback in improving L2 learners' writing, but also to point out those factors that affect students' understanding and preferences of corrective feedback. Understanding whether the factors have the potential to facilitate or impede L2 development in writing can help us understand why some learners develop L2 knowledge more easily and quickly than others and why some learners fail to benefit from corrective feedback. Based on the following studies, this issue is examined from diverse perspectives in terms of student prior learning experiences, proficiency level, educational and cultural background, attitudes, and motivation. For example, variations in students' understanding of corrective feedback might be due to the way an L2 is taught or assessed in different language learning environments. Teachers' individual factors also come into play, including their experiences and personalities. For example, some teachers may have benefitted from corrective feedback in their own language learning process. Teachers' pedagogical approaches might be a factor that influences student reactions to teacher feedback. Also, teachers' personalities could be another factor that explains the high and low proficiency students' different attitudes to error feedback.

2.3.3.1 **Prior Learning Experience.** With regard to written feedback, learners' beliefs about what feedback works best for them can be informed by their prior learning experiences, such as the teaching and learning context they are exposed to. Two studies have explored factors that have an impact on the effectiveness of CF for L2 development.

In Bitchener and Knoch (2008), 144 learners were assigned to different groups. The first groups were EFL learners from Asia who were used to receiving written CF and formal English instruction in their L2 classrooms. However, the other group were migrants from diverse cultural backgrounds, who had received little formal English instruction including written CF before they arrived in New Zealand. The target linguistic form in the study was English articles. It was assumed that the group with EFL learners would be more likely to respond to CF with greater accuracy compared to the group with migrants. However, the result was surprisingly that no difference existed in the performance of the two groups. The researchers suggested that there may have been an overlap in the learning background of the two groups. Participants in group two may have had more exposure to form-focused instruction and written accuracy than they had indicated in their background bio-statement that they filled out at the beginning of the research.

Rummel (2014) not only investigated the potential of prior learning experiences to influence L2 learning, but also particularly focused on student beliefs about CF that may help improving their L2 writing. Participants in Rummel (2014) were EFL learners from Kuwait and Laos, who received CF on their use of present perfect and past simple tense. Results showed that learner beliefs about the type of CF they attend to are helpful for improving their L2 knowledge. Although this does not seem to have an effect on the learners from Kuwait, it is reflected in the accuracy performance of learners from Laos, who were able to improve their written accuracy after they received the type of CF they favored (i. e. , indirect feedback). Rummel (2014) also suggested that learners' prior learning experience may have an influence on learner uptake of CF because all the learners from Laos who preferred indirect feedback had previous experiences of receiving this types of feedback.

2.3.3.2 **Proficiency Level.** High and low proficiency students have different preferences toward teachers' feedback. Lee's (2008) study examined students' reactions to teachers' feedback in Hong Kong secondary classrooms and discussed the contextual factors that may have influenced students' responses. Results showed that regardless of proficiency level, students in general want more feedback from teachers. However, high proficiency students react to teacher feedback more positively than their low proficiency counterparts, and teacher feedback caused more frustration among low proficiency than high proficiency students.

Agudo's (2013) study also looked at secondary school ESL learners' perceptions of the affective effect that corrective feedback may produce for them. This study revealed that learners emotionally responded to teachers' corrective feedback in different ways. Most secondary ESL students acknowledged the needs and usefulness of corrective feedback in classrooms situations, and expected teachers to correct their errors regularly, but they may feel upset if they did not understand what was being corrected and why their teachers were correcting them, especially when teachers' feedback was not consistent or it was ambiguous. Also, some students found corrective feedback inhibiting, discouraging and embarrassing to varying degrees.

2.3.3.3 **Cultural Factor.** Culture is the "learned patterns of perception, values, and behaviors, shared by a group of people, which is also dynamic" (Nelson, 2006, p. 51). Cultural backgrounds can have an influence on students' behaviors regarding peer review in groups. Language learners from certain cultures may prefer not to impose social strain or embarrassment in the classroom. For example, it has been reported that Chinese students expressed their desire for a positive group climate (Nelson, 2006). This affects their attitudes towards peer feedback and results in them not criticizing their peers' written work in order to avoid arguments and promote harmony in group interactions. Nelson's (2006) article suggests that students with a common language and cultural expectations tend to have more successful peer response interaction than students with varied cultural backgrounds. The language used in peer interaction is also a factor. For example, students participating in peer review in their L1 are more confident in providing effective feedback for their peers.

Schulz(2001) also examined cross-cultural similarities and differences reflected in students' and teachers' perceptions of feedback in two different learning contexts: Colombia and the U. S. results revealed that there were no significant discrepancies between learners in Colombia and in the U. S. toward corrective feedback. However, there were striking discrepancy rates between U. S. learners and teachers in their perceptions of the role of error correction. For example, 4% of the students versus 22% of the teachers thought that students disliked being corrected in class; 90% of the students versus 30% of the teachers agreed that students should be corrected when they make errors in speaking and writing. The discrepancies between Columbian students and teachers resembled the U. S. pattern.

Lee's (2008) study examined Chinese students' reactions to teachers' feedback in Hong Kong secondary classrooms and discussed the contextual factors that may have influenced students' responses. Results showed that regardless of proficiency level, students in general wanted more feedback from teachers, which focuses not only on language but also on other issues such as organization and content. Based on their educational experiences, Chinese students tend to demand greater effort on the part of teachers, that is, more written comments and more explicit error feedback by providing correct answers or categorizing error types. Such a reaction could be a direct role ofa teacher-centered approach to feedback, which does not provide opportunities for student-centered activities, such as peer/self-evaluation. Therefore, students become increasingly passive and reliant on the teacher.

2.4   Next Step for Classroom Practice

2.4.1   Challenges.

Current empirical and classroom studies seem to yield few conclusive answers for language teachers and learners in terms of the effectiveness of corrective feedback in improving L2 grammatical accuracy. In addition, due to the inconsistencies in research design(Ferris, 2004; Truscott, 2007), L2 teachers choose to not rely on the concrete research findings. Instead, they tend to design corrective feedback that relies on their experiences, intuition, and students' expectations (Ferris, 2011; Hyland & Hyland, 2006). Assuming that corrective feedback is helpful in theory, a question is posed in terms of *how should teachers provide feedback that fits the teaching context* so that corrective feedback is helpful in assessing and improving students' written accuracy.

Chapter 3: Methodology

This research employs a quasi-experimental design with a pretest, posttest, and delayed posttest treatment, using three intact EFL classes as explained in the following section, and examines three major issues: effectiveness of two types of corrective feedback (i. e. , indirect CF and direct CF) , students' and teachers' perceptions of the effectiveness of corrective feedback in improving their L2 writing, and individual factors associated with corrective feedback in L2 writing. My study therefore is framed within a mixed-methods approach that incorporates both quantitative and qualitative research designs to address the research questions for my study. The mixed-methods approach in the research will fulfill its goals by using triangulated methods including qualitative and quantitative data, which will be capable of informing one another throughout the research process and provide valuable information to answer the research questions and to reveal different interpretations. This ensures the reliability and validity of the research through the researcher's prolonged engagement and triangulation.

3.1　Research Questions

1. Does accuracy in the use of certain grammatical structures improve as a result of the provision of corrective feedback (CF) in L2 writing? What type of CF will better help facilitate students' L2 writing accuracy

(e. g. indirect CF and direct CF) ?

2. What are students' and teachers' preferences and expectations for the feedback on students' writing? (E. g. , which component among grammar, content and organizations, do students value the most in their understanding of effective feedback? How do students evaluate their own potential for improvement of their writing ability? What expectations do students have of grammar corrections in their writing?)

3. What are the contextual (e. g. , EFL vs. ESL) and affective (e. g. , attitudes and beliefs) factors associated with EFL learners' understanding the effectiveness of corrective feedback in L2 writing?

3. 2   Participants

The population of the research consists of college level EFL learners and teachers in an Eastern Chinese University. 105 full-time students who were enrolled in freshman course were recruited. Their ages ranged from 18 to 20. The participants were already randomly assigned into three classes when they entered college after they took the Chinese College Entrance Examination (also called "Gao Kao"). One class was assigned to the control group which did not receive any corrective feedback, but did receive comments on content and organization of their writing from the researcher. The other two classes were then assigned to each of the two comparison groups which received different types of corrective feedback: indirect feedback or direct feedback. All the participants were English majors with the same English proficiency based on the grades they received on the Chinese College Entrance Examination. They had a common L1 (i. e. , Chinese) background and years of previous English learning experiences. All students receive formal instruction on grammar and writing in college and they are expected to spend time studying grammar and practicing writing outside of the classroom. Students have a midterm and final exam per semester, in which writing tasks take a great portion for the whole evaluation of students' competence and performance of English. Therefore, the research tasks, which were conducted within two months, provided practice with feedback for the assessment. Each group was expected to be representative of the larger population of EFL learners in China in order to be used for error analysis in L2 writing. Three teachers who taught grammar and writing, intensive reading and extensive reading courses also participated in the study for the interview. All the teachers spoke Mandarin Chinese and had at least five years of English language teaching experience.

Learner characteristics and task variables are presented below in Table 3.1 and Table 3.2.

Table 3.1

Learner Characteristics

Learner variables	
Age of contributors	Young adults(18-20 years old)
Learning context	EFL
Status of contributors	College students, English Major
Nationality	Chinese
Proficiency level	High/advanced

Table 3.2

Task Variables of Pretest, Posttest and Delayed-posttest

Pretest(Week 1)	Argumentative essays
	Cover a wide variety of topics
	300 words in length on average expected
	60-90 minutes
Posttest(Week 5)	Argumentative essays
	Cover a wide variety of topics
	300-400 words in length on average expected
	60-90 minutes(including planning and writing)

(Contd.)

Learner variables	
Delayed-posttest(Week 9)	Argumentative essays Cover a wide variety of topics 400 words in length on average expected 60-90 minutes(including planning and writing)

3.3   Dependent and Independent Variables

In this study, the dependent variable is accuracy of L2 writing. The level of accuracy is related to the frequency of grammatical errors that learners made in their L2 writing and includes both lexical and sentence-level accuracy. Independent variables in the study include two types of corrective feedback received by L2 learners: indirect feedback and direct feedback, as well as the contextual, affective, and other individual factors associated with L2 learners, such as their educational experiences, cultural and linguistic backgrounds, attitudes towards grammar learning and error correction, beliefs, expectations of corrective feedback, and learning styles. These factors can also become the confounding factors in the research because they may affect EFL learners' understanding of the effectiveness of corrective feedback in their writing.

3.4   Data Collection and Analysis

The mixed-methods research design is discussed in the following sections to address the three research questions. The data collection procedure provides a quantitative and numeric description as well as an interpretative understanding of trends, and yields both objective, generalizable data and the subjective interpretations of the study. Data

collection for the quantitative approach includes student text/error analysis,
treatment (provision of corrective feedback), examination of tests, and
questionnaires. Data collection for the qualitative approach includes
interview, surveys and classroom observation.

3.5   Research Question #1

3.5.1   Data Collection.

105 essays were examined for all types of grammatical errors that were
committed by the EFL learners, such as subject-verb agreement, article,
tense, verb, preposition, parts of speech, etc. The researcher then selected
the top seven most common types of grammatical errors EFL learners made
to define the treatment of CF on them. 105 participants from three classes
were divided into one control group and two comparison groups. Therefore,
each group had 35 students. The data consisted of the writing texts from
college EFL learners in China. All the subjects majored in English. They
had finished from 6-8 years formal English instruction at school and were
taking English courses, including English writing, reading, listening and
grammar in college. Three types of research instruments: a pretest, a
posttest, and a delayed posttest were used. All the three testing procedures
were scheduled during the class time.

Overa research period of two months, the researcher collected three
different writing texts from each student, which were under timed
conditions: a diagnostic essay in Week 1 (i. e. , the pretest), a midterm
examination in Week 5 (i. e. , the posttest) and a final examination essay in
Week 9 (i. e. , the delayed posttest). All the three essay tasks were
argumentative writing. The three timed writing tasks were graded and
required as part of the course curriculum for students in order to assure
students' full participation in the study.

The researcher then collected and responded to the texts produced during the timed-writing assessments because they were written to the same type of prompt as well as under the same condition so that the researcher can compare the results across different groups of students. Most importantly, students had an awareness that these writing tasks were critical to their overall course evaluation. In this case, the researcher could assume that the students would be highly motivated to engage in the revision section and interviews to reflect upon the high-stakes assessment tasks. Fortunately, all the participants completed the three writing tasks at 100% in addition to the revision section and interviews. The following explains the three treatments in details.

The pretest (i. e. , the argumentative writing task) was delivered by the researcher in Week 1. Students were asked to write an argumentative text of 300 words in a time allotted of 60-90 minutes. The prompt for the pretest was:

Pretest prompt:

Positive effect vs. Negative effect of technology: Does technology affect our lives? How? *Please provide at least three reasons for your argument.*

Students were asked to write freely and to express their positive and negative viewpoints of the topic. Each written text from EFL students was treated as an observation; that is, a total of 105 observations were analyzed. The construct was the linguistic accuracy of L2 writing, and the operationalized variables were the seven primary error types that were chosen by the researcher to be targeted by measuring the error rates in student writing. The distribution of each type of grammatical error was distinguished, categorized and analyzed by calculating the frequency (i. e. , simply counting the number of errors made by students in one writing text).

To more sufficiently and effectively collect the data, it was important to follow certain principles to examine the accuracy of students' writing. First, a manual examination was applied to examine the accuracy. One college teacher and the researcher cooperated during data collection in order to accurately identity all types of the grammatical errors committed by student participants. Second, scoring criteria were developed to evaluate the accuracy (numbers of grammatical errors) of student L2 writing. Individual error rates were calculated for the control and the two comparison groups in terms of their accurate use of the top seven target grammatical features. An overall accuracy score for the target grammatical forms was also calculated depending on the total error numbers for each error type. (see Appendix A. for grading criteria)

The relative difficulty of different grammatical features potentially affects whether or not the errors are correctable/treatable through corrective feedback. Ferris (1999) defines treatable errors as errors that occur "in a patterned [and] rule governed ways" and untreatable errors as those that "no handbook or set of rules students can consult" (p. 6), such as irregular verb tense. Ferris and Robert (2001) then examined the larger subcategories of "treatable" and "untreatable" errors by targeting five major categories of grammatical errors, that is, verbs, noun endings, articles, word choice, and sentence structure. Bitchener et al. (2005) also targeted verb tense, English article and prepositions for investigation of the effect of corrective feedback. Building on Sheen's (2007) study of the effects of written CF on the acquisition of English articles, Sheen, Wright and Moldawa (2009) examined the written correction at errors in the following linguistic structures, which were articles, copula 'be', regular past tense, irregular past tense, and prepositions. Therefore, drawing on previously conducted research (e. g. , Ferris, 1999; Ferris & Robert, 2001; Bitchener et al. 2005; Sheen, 2007; Sheen et al. , 2009), it is important for the researcher to identify the most common grammatical errors for the focus of the different feedback groups for the current study.

During the examination of student errors in terms of accuracy, the syntactic structures and certain factors that the criteria would consider are shown in Table 3. 3.

Table 3. 3

Syntactic Structures for Grammar Accuracy

Grammar Accuracy
Subject-verb agreement: S-V-O structure
Verb tense and aspect(present, past, progressive, present perfect)
Plural vs. Singular
Verbs(modal verb, main verb, copula verb)
Articles(definite vs. indefinite)
Prepositions
Pronouns(possessive, reflexive, demonstrative, relative pronoun)
Possessive
Existential *there*
Comparatives
Parts of speech
Word order(mistakes may occur in more complex structures when the subject gets separated from the verb)

After identifying and categorizingall types of errors and selecting the most common ones from the first writing task, Group One, a fulltime class of 35 students, received indirect corrective feedback; indirect feedback occurred when the researcher indicated that an error existed by circling or underlining the errors in student text but did not provide direct correction. This left the errors for students to correct them. For example (from students' pretest writing) :

(1) *The invention of computers dramatically increases work efficiency and help compete many difficult tasks that were impossible in the past.* (indicates a wrong word form)

(2) *Thanks to* ✓ *development of science and technology , the society has enjoyed continuous prosperity and more convenience.* (✓ means a missing word)

Group Two received zero error correction but feedback on the content, coherence and organization of their writing. Examples of feedback for Group Two in pretest writing are shown below:

(3) *You did a good job presenting your ideas on one side of the argument. I enjoyed reading your writing, which was very interesting. You were good at using transition words. This made your writing go smoothly.*

(4) *Good job with the discussion about the positive effect oftechnology. Your ideas flew very well and very straightforward. I hope to see your progress on the next writing.*

Group Three received direct CF, which took the form of full and explicit error correction above the underlined errors. For example (from students' pretest writing):

(5) *The invention of computers dramatically increases work efficiency*
        helps
and help compete many difficult tasks that were impossible in the past.

       the

(6) *Thanks to* ✓ *development of science and technology , the society has enjoyed continuous prosperity and more convenience.*

The researcher then returned the feedback to students three days after students competed their first writing task. The student participants were given four weeks outside of class to revise their writing, and make any changes or corrections in response to the errors.

The posttest was conducted one month after students received feedback from the researcher for their first writing task (i. e. , pretest) , and a delayed posttest was administrated at the last week , that is , four weeks after students received feedback from the researcher for their second writing task (i. e. , posttest). In the posttest and delayed posttest , students were asked to write the second and third argumentative essay respectively , which was a similar type compared to the first writing task in the pretest but had a different prompt. Here were the prompts:

Posttest prompt:

Competition vs. Cooperation: Which is good for college students? *Please provide at least three reasons for your argument.*

Delayed posttest prompt:

Do colleges put too much stock in standardized test scores? *Please provide at least three reasons for your argument.*

The posttest and delayed posttest provided students with an opportunity to use the top seven targeted linguistics forms as identified by the researcher. Participants were measured again on the quantitative variable: accuracy of their performance. Students' writing tasks were marked by both the classroom teacher and the researcher to guarantee the interrater reliability for error identification and categorization. When the researcher and teachers disagreed with each other regarding the identification and categorization of particular errors, they discussed them and reached a consensus. Between each two writing tasks, no additional explicit instruction on the targeted linguistic errors were given by the researcher. Certain instructions on grammar may have been given by the classroom teachers because the content could be part of the curriculum for students. Additional input or practice that occurred outside of class time were not controlled for.

3.5.2 **Data Analysis.**

Preliminary analysis of the data involved identification and classification of different errors committed by the EFL learners from the control and experimental groups, such as subject-verb agreement, plurals, English articles, verbs, tense, prepositions and parts of speech. Quantitative data were elicited from the pretest, the posttest, and the delayed posttest to discover whether the two different types of corrective feedback positively affect students' L2 writing outcome, and to compare the longitudinal effects caused by the two types of corrective feedback and the feedback on content, which were measured on the quantitative variable: accuracy performance in student L2 writing. Descriptive statistics, such as the mean score(M) and standard deviation (SD), for each type of errors in writing were computed. Accuracy regarding the rate of occurrence of each type of errors in each text was calculated using the raw count and percentage of correct use of each targeted linguistic form. For example, the number of correct uses of a linguistic form from the total number of occurrences gives an accuracy performance score. In addition, in order to compare across texts of different lengths, the distribution of different types of errors in each student text was distinguished and analyzed by the normed frequencies (Biber, et al. 1999), which were reported as the rate of occurrences per 1000 words in this study.

Moreover, Paired Sampled T-Test was conducted to examine the time effect of different types of feedback on improving students' writing accuracy within the three groups. In order to examine interactions between factors and the effects of individual factors, a one-way ANOVA was chosen as an appropriate statistical procedure for each dependent variable, and to determine if there were statistically significant differences among the three groups. Additionally, if a test revealed statistical significance, post hoc tests were conducted to evaluate differences among specific means. It is expected that the findings will provide a practical perspective on how L2 teachers can better develop correction strategies applicable for EFL learners in their language learning.

3.6   Research Question #2 & #3

3.6.1   Questionnaires.

Questionnaires were used to answer Research Question #2 and #3. Here are some specific examples of questions that appeared in questionnaires: how do students feel about their English language use in writing? What are students' perceptions of the corrective feedback on their L2 writing? To be specific, what expectations do students have of grammar correction in their writing? Do students understand the type of corrective feedback they received? And whether or not student feel discouraged about the error correction.

3.6.1.1   **Data Collection.** Questionnaires included multiple choice items and open-ended questions to inform both the quantitative and qualitative portion of the research. All student participants in the three classes were asked to complete questionnaires about their writing and language learning backgrounds (e. g. , information of students' formal English instruction and schooling in China) before they started the first writing task(the pretest). For example, how do you feel about your English language use, especially grammar, in writing? Regarding this question, they chose from three statements— bad(meaning: I know little about grammar and my English grammar is a big problem in my writing) , good(English grammar is not a serious problem for me, but sometimes it interferes with my writing) , very good(I feel confident using it, and I use it correctly most of the time) (see Table 3.4).

Then, students from all three classes were required to fill out another questionnaire after the delayed posttest, which compared the different types of teacher feedback at the end of the research. Students were asked about the questions that were specifically related to the effectiveness of corrective feedback. The questions asked were, for example, "in your opinion, what is the best way for your English teacher to give feedback about your grammatical errors in your writing? What is the easiest way for you to correct your errors? Which type of corrective feedback do you think you can learn the most from?" Before they filled out the questionnaire, students were informed from the researcher of the meaning of accuracy. The level of accuracy is related to the frequency of grammatical errors that learners make in their L2 writing and includes both lexical and sentence-level accuracy. Having a good understanding of the concept of accuracy helped students complete the questionnaire more efficiently and effectively. (see Table 3.4 and 3.5)

Table 3.4

Questions in Questionnaire 1

---

1. In English classes you have taken before, have you ever learned any English grammar rules?
   Yes, a lot   Yes, but few   No
   If yes, what? _____
   If no, why? _____
2. Have you ever received feedback from teachers?
   Yes, a lot   Yes, but few   No
   If yes, what? _____
   If no, why? _____
3. Do you think teacher feedback is helpful?
   Yes, very helpful   Yes, but not much   No
4. Do you worry about making mistakes in writing or your language class?
   Yes, a lot   Yes, but few   No
5. How do you feel about your English language use, especially grammar, in writing?
   Very good   Good   Bad
6. How do you feel when the teacher immediately correct your error in your writing or in language classroom? (e. g. , angry, embarrassed, sorry, happy, satisfied, bothered, indifference, nervous, and overwhelmed)

---

7. What feedback do you expect teachers to provide for your writing?

---

8. Anything else you want to share with the researcher?

Table 3. 5

Questions in Questionnaire 2

---

1. What is the best way for your English teacher to give feedback on your writing?

   Feedback on grammar feedback on content feedback on organization none of these If others, what is it? _____

2. What is the best way for your English teacher to give feedback about your grammatical errors in your writing?

   Direct correction   underline or circle   description and explanation   none of these

   If others, what is it? _____

3. What is the easiest way for you to correct your errors?

   Direct correction underline or circledescription and explanation none of these

   If others, what is it? _____

4. Which type of corrective feedback do you think you can learn the most from?

   Direct correction underline or circledescription and explanation none of these

   If others, what is it? _____

5. Whytype of corrective feedback do you like most?

   Direct correction underline or circle description and explanation none of these

   If others, what is it? _____

6. Do you like the current type of corrective feedback you received from the researcher?

   Very much   mostly   a little   not at all

7. Do you understand the type of corrective feedback you received from the researcher?

   Very much   mostly   a little   not at all

8. Do you feel discouraged about the correction?

   Very much   mostly   a little   not at all

9. Do you think you will apply the correction to your future writing?

   Very much   mostly   a little   not at all

10. What did you think or what did you do after you received your writing with feedback from the researcher?

    I was eagerly to see the errors I made and wanted to correct the errors immediately because I really wanted to improve my English writing.

    I was thinking about the reasons why I made the errors, but I did not know how to correct them and revise my writing.

    I just left it on my desk and did not want to look at or revise it.

    I believed that I wish I had not written anything.

11. Any other comments?

   _____

---

3. 6. 1. 2 **Data Analysis.** Quantitative data from questionnaires were analyzed using SPSS including both descriptive (*M* and *SD*) and inferential statistics (i. e. , *Correlation Coefficient*) to analyze the multiple-choice items and to discover whether the three different types of feedback positively affect ESL learners' L2 writing outcome and their perceptions. For example, the Mean and Standard Deviation for each item in the questionnaires were calculated, which told us how much variability is in students' responses; the correlation coefficient was reported to see if there was any relationship existing between students' attitudes and their accuracy performance. A one-way ANOVA was conducted as well to reveal if there was any significant difference in students' responses across the three groups. In addition, like case studies, questionnaires were also used to draw flexible responses and detailed input from students in terms of their responses to corrective feedback. This helped the researcher infer the possible factors contributing to students' errors in writing and their perceptions of corrective feedback. The research design would also help teachers develop effective pedagogy and practices for language learners. Individual responses were collected and analyzed in terms of the open-ended questions in the questionnaires.

3. 6. 2 **Interview.**

Interviews were also used to address Research Questions #2 and #3 for qualitative data collection. The advantage of using interviews for data collection is that it encourages participants to freely talk about their thoughts, and allows the researcher to elicit in-depth inquiries based on the initial responses from participants. It provides explanation of the generalized data from the quantitative analysis, and allows for a detailed exploration with a few individuals who can provide a complete picture of the researched issue (Creswell ,2007).

Thus, in this research, interviews tended to draw detailed input from EFL learners and teachers in terms of their responses to corrective feedback to complement the results received from the quantitative approach. This also helped the researcher speculate about possible factors contributing to students' errors in writing and their perceptions of corrective feedback so asto help teachers develop effective pedagogies and practices for language learners.

3.6.2.1   **Data Collection.** After the delayed posttest, 10 students from each group and three teachers participated in the interviews, through which further questions and explanations were explored. The interview questions covered various issues that were worthy of exploration of individual learners, such as their English learning background, their feelings about corrective feedback and self-editing strategies, as well as their responses to the research project and suggestions to their teachers in terms of the way of corrective feedback was provided. The guideline of the interview questions was created to facilitate the interviews, as listed in Table 3.6.

Table 3.6

Interview Questions in English（see Chinese version in Appendix C）

For students:

1. Which component of writing do you most expect to receive feedback from teachers, grammar, content, or organizations?
2. Do you like the type of feedback you received from the teachers and the researcher?
3. Are you confident of your own writing and self-editing ability?
4. What expectations do you have of grammar corrections in your writing from teachers?
5. What difficulties did you encounter during your revision process?
6. What other contextual and individual factors (e. g. , attitude, belief, and motivation) do you think may influence your writing ability to benefit from corrective feedback?
7. Do you have anything else that you want to share with the researcher?

(Contd.)

For teachers :

1. Which component do you think among grammar, content and organizations, students value the most in their understanding of effective corrective feedback?

2. Do you regularly help students practice their writing and self-editing ability?

3. What expectations do you think students would have of grammar corrections in their writing from teachers?

4. What contextual and individual factors do you think may influence your students' writing ability to benefit from corrective feedback? Any factors from teachers?

5. Do you have anything else that you want to share with the researcher?

During the interviews, the researcher, students, and teachers were only allowed to talk about the interview questions in Chinese (see Appendix D for the Chinese version of interview questions). The researcher controlled any other input that could potentially affect the research results by discouraging these questions. For example, additional questions about corrective feedback on specific targeted linguistic forms and instructions on grammar were consciously avoided.

Before the interview, the researcher was prepared to bring the list of marked errors students made and corrections for each text. Other materials were also required, such as student questionnaires, the first writing text per student with error making and revisions, and the essay prompt used to generate student writing. These materials were available for discussion during the interview. Participants were interviewed at different points so that the researcher was able to have a sense of how students perceived their writing process, particularly as to accuracy as time went along. Interviews ranged from 20-30 minutes long and were audio-recorded. The researcher also took notes during the interview. Three classroom teachers were also interviewed to get their insights about how the class had been taught and their impressions about the effectiveness of corrective feedback.

3.6.2.2   **Data Analysis.** After the interviews, the researcher listened to the audio-recorded scripts and transcribed them into English. Both word-to-word and colloquial translations with abbreviations were used based on the importance of the information, which showed the meanings and structures of the sentences in an effort to present the intended meaning of the utterances rather than the literal meaning.

After two months of research, the researcher collected the data and created data files for each student that included their writing texts, questionnaires, retrospective interviews, and thedata files for each teacher who regularly teaches the classes. The researcher organized students' information as follows: background information, self-identified strengths and weaknesses, opinions about corrective feedback, and insights about language knowledge and revision process. Then, the researcher compared the findings across different participants.

3.6.3   Classroom Observation.

In order to better examine the potential effect that teacher instruction may have on the revision process and writing products of EFL learners in an academic context, detailed notes of classroom observation were also collected to reinforce the data obtained from interviews and surveys, and to provide information about the EFL classrooms where the teachers' and students' interactions occur. Also, classroom observation enabled the researcher to have more comprehensive understanding of the three research questions. According to McMillan (2012), classroom observation needs to be objective and standardized. It yields "first hand data without the contamination that may arise from tests, inventories, or other self-report instruments" (p. 163). Classroom observation also allows for the description of naturally occurring behaviors and lets the researcher to take into account contextual factors, which are important for the interpretation and use of the research results.

I was the "complete researcher" during classroom observation (McMillan ,2012 ,p. 289). "Complete researcher"in the study means that I was solely an observer ,who was detached from the participants and did not participate in group discussions or any other classroom activities. During classroom observation ,I determined the content and sequence of what were written down or recorded ,and identified the teacher behaviors and practices as well as student performance in the EFL classroom. I also paid attention to certain specific behaviors and contextual factors ,which may lead to inferences for the research questions. Although other factors ,such as curriculum and classroom planning were important ,it was students' daily experiences in the classroom with teachers and peers that may have the greatest influence on how much students are able to learn from their writing and grammar classes.

I visited each classroom in Week 6 and the observation sessions lasted 90 minutes for each group in their grammar and writing class. I kept an in-depth and comprehensive recording of what was going on in the classroom. As discussed in McMillan (2012), there are two types of filed notes : descriptive and reflective. McMillan (2012) defines *descriptive* as using pictures ,words, maps, etc. which captures as many details as possible of what is observed in classrooms. Researcher's interpretations are avoided in descriptive field notes. For *reflective* field notes, the researchers' speculations, feelings, and interpretations are involved. For my study, reflective notes that included thoughts about emerging behaviors and issues in classrooms were collected.

Before I entered the classroom for observation ,I talked to the instructor so that I had a clear understanding of all the background work the students had done. I also anticipated the problems that might be encountered in classrooms so as to avoid being completely unprepared.

During classroom observation ,written notes were the primary means of recording observation data ,and it was important for the written notes to be accurate and extensive (see Table 3. 7). I sat down at the back of the classroom to briefly note down activities, items written on the white board, etc. while observing and then expanded the notes with more detailed descriptions after I left the classroom. I also used my laptop after observing to write up even more complete and expanded notes on a daily basis. The computerized text then was inspected and organized for later data interpretation and analysis. Then, I interpreted and analyzed the notes to address the research questions and problems.

Table 3. 7

Outline for Classroom Observation

	Classroom 1	Classroom 2	Classroom 3
Setting · Classroom			
Events/Lesson Sequence · Grammar · Writing			
Interactions · Teacher · Students			
T Assessment/ Feedback			
Ss' Reaction			

Classroom observation concentrated on teacher instruction and student learning activities in the grammar and writing class. In particular, I looked at the following issues in terms of teacher and student practice in two classes: first, what did the teacher do to establish and communicate learning goals, track student progress, and present the sequence of instruction? Second, what did the teacher do to help students effectively interact with new learning materials and knowledge? Third, what did the teacher do to help students practice and deepen their understanding of new knowledge? Fourth, what did the teacher do to engage students? A productive classroom provides clearly defined learning activities for students, and in an effective classroom, the teacher is able to look for opportunities to engage students in active participation, and effectively facilitate student learning with well-timed questions and comments that expand students' involvement. Also, it is important for teachers to provide an appropriate level of instructional support, such as feedback, focusing on the performance and the process of learning. It is possible that teacher feedback provides students with specific information about their work in order to help students reach a deeper understanding of concepts than they could get on their own. Classrooms may also engage in ongoing, back-and-forth exchanges between the teacher and students on a regular basis. Teachers facilitate language development when they encourage, respond to, and expand on student talk.

Moreover, I paid attention to the following factors during the classroom observations. First, I looked at the classroom climate as well as social and emotional support from the teacher and classmates. It was assumed that students who were more motivated and connected to teachers and peers demonstrated positive development in their academic learning. In classrooms with a positive climate, teachers and students are enthusiastic about learning and respectful of one another. Teachers and students have positive relationships with each other and clearly enjoy being together and spending time in the classroom. Second, I paid attention to teacher sensitivity. Teachers are sensitive when they consistently respond to students and are effective in addressing students' questions, concerns, and needs. There is an expectation that the teacher is able to anticipate areas of student learning difficulty and provide appropriate levels of support for all students in the classroom. Another point concerns student perspectives. Teachers who value student perspectives provide opportunities for students to make decisions and take active roles in classrooms. It was expected that teachers made content useful and relevant to students, made sure that student ideas and opinions were valued, and encouraged meaningful interactions with peers.

Chapter 4: Quantitative Results: Pretest, Posttest and Delayed Posttest

The research mainly investigated three issues: (1) the extent to which corrective feedback (CF) facilitates or improves students' writing accuracy; (2) teachers' and students' preferences and expectations for CF; (3) the extent to which contextual and affective factors affect students' understanding of effective CF and their production of accurate L2 writing. The following Chapter 4, Chapter 5, and Chapter 6 present the results for each research question including: (1) comprehensive within-group analysis of the effectiveness of CF including both descriptive and inferential statistics for each group (Chapter 4); (2) individual data analysis examining individual learners' development of writing accuracy overtime after the provision of CF (Chapter 4); (3) a comparison and contrast of the effectiveness of CF across groups (Chapter 4); (4) the extent to which each of the top seven (i. e. , most frequently occurring) errors are more prone to be affected by CF (Chapter 4); (5) students' attitudes towards CF by the examination of the questionnaires and the extent to which responses are associated with their production of writing accuracy (Chapter 5); (6) exploration of the contextual and individual factors in relation to the effectiveness of CF on their writing accuracy from the interviews and classroom observation (Chapter 6). All the findings will be returned to in the discussion in Chapter 7. The three research questions are listed below.

*RQ*1: Does accuracy in the use of certain grammatical structures improve as a result of the provision of CF in student L2 writing? Which type of corrective feedback (i. e. , indirect CF and direct CF) better helps facilitate students' L2 writing accuracy?

*RQ*2: What are students' and teachers' preferences and expectations for the feedback on students' writing? (E. g. , which component among grammar, content and organizations, do students value the most in their understanding of effective feedback? How do students evaluate their own potential for improvement of their writing ability? What expectations do students have of grammar corrections in their writing?)

*RQ*3: What are the contextual (e. g. , EFL vs. ESL) and affective (e. g. , attitudes and beliefs) factors associated with EFL learners' understanding the effectiveness of corrective feedback in L2 writing?

4. 1   RQ1: Overall Effectiveness of CF and the Type of CF in Relation to Students' Improvement in L2 Writing Accuracy

4. 1. 1   Descriptive Statistics for Indirect Corrective Feedback (Indirect CF) Group.

After reading and assessing students' essays, the researcher found that students preferred to use simple sentence structures and academic vocabulary to develop their ideas in their writing. There was a total of 196 grammatical errors found in student essays from the Indirect CF Group in the pretest, 91 errors in the posttest, and 65 errors in the delayed posttest. Table 4. 1 offers the total number of different error patterns students of the Indirect CF group made on the three tests. As can be seen, 13 error patterns were found in the pretest, 12 error types occurred in the posttest, and 9 error types in the delayed posttest, which mainly include subject-agreement, plural, tense, article, verbs, prepositions, parts of speech, etc.

Many of them also have subcategories. For examples, errors on verb have the subcategories of wrong use after modals, missing main or copular verbs, redundant use of main verb, wrong main verb, and wrong use of passive voice; article errors include redundant use, incorrect use, and insufficient use. (Refer to Appendix E for examples of student errors in the pretest, the posttest and the delayed posttest)

As expected, the total number of errors and error types gradually decreased from the pretest to the posttest and from the posttest to the delayed posttest in Indirect CF student essays. Figure 4. 1 shows a tendency of consistent decrease of errors across the three tests. Table 4. 1 shows the seven most frequent error types were subject-verb agreement, plural, verb, article, tense, preposition, and parts of speech, which represented 25%, 22. 73%, 12. 5%, 10. 51%, 9. 66%, 5. 97% and 5. 68%, respectively. Pronoun (1. 99%), possessive (1. 99%), comparatives (1. 42%), existential there (1. 14%), the use of 'to' (0. 85%) and 'that' (0. 57%) were the six least frequent errors. Based on the frequency of errors, the seven primary error types will be further statistically analyzed in the following sections, including subject-agreement, plural, tense, article, verbs, prepositions, and parts of speech.

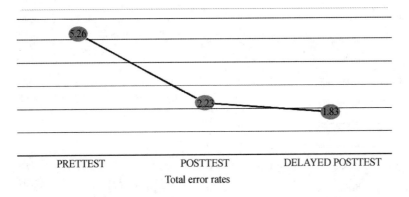

| PRETTEST | POSTTEST | DELAYED POSTTEST |

Total error rates

Figure 4. 1 **Mean of the error rates in the three tests in Indirect**

CF Group

Table 4.1

Raw Number and Percentage of Different Error Types for Indirect CF Group
$(n = 35^a)$

Error[b]	Sub-categories	Pre[c]	Post[c]	Delay[c]	Total[d] Pre(%)	Total[d] Post(%)	Total[d] Delay(%)	Total[d] (%)
Sva		49	15	24	49 (25.00)	15 (16.48)	24 (36.92)	88 (25.00)
Plural		38	20	22	38 (19.39)	20 (21.98)	22 (33.85)	80 (22.73)
Verbs	Wrong use after modals	9	6	2	16 (8.16)	20 (21.98)	8 (12.31)	44 (12.50)
	Missing main/ copula verb	5	6	4				
	Redundant main verb	2	2	2				
	Wrong main verb	0	1	0				
	Passive voice	0	5	2				
Article	Wrong	2	2	2	27 (13.78)	7 (7.69)	3 (4.62)	37 (10.51)
	Missing	4	0	1				
	Redundant	21	5	0				
Tense		27	3	4	27 (13.78)	3 (3.30)	4 (6.15)	34 (9.66)
Prep.	Wrong	6	8	0	9 (4.59)	12 (13.19)	0	21 (5.97)
	Missing	3	2	0				
	Redundant	0	2	0				
Pos.	Wrong adj.	7	0	1	18 (9.18)	1 (1.10)	1 (1.54)	20 (5.68)
	Wrong adv.	6	0	0				
	Wrong verb	3	0	0				
	Wrong noun	2	1	0				
Pro.	Missing	1	1	0	4 (2.04)	3 (3.30)	0	7 (1.99)
	Redundant	2	1	0				
	Missing subject	1	1	0				

(Contd.)

Error[b]	Sub-categories	Pre[c]	Post[c]	Delay[c]	Total[d] Pre(%)	Total[d] Post(%)	Total[d] Delay(%)	Total[d] (%)
Poss.	Wrong	1	4	0	1 (0.51)	6 (6.59)	0	7 (1.99)
	Missing	0	2	0				
Com.	Wrong	3	2	0	3 (1.53)	2 (2.18)	0	5 (1.42)
'there'	Wrong	2	1	1	2 (1.02)	1 (1.10)	1 (1.54)	4 (1.14)
'to'	Missing	1	1	1	1 (0.51)	1 (1.10)	1 (1.54)	3 (0.85)
'that'	Redundant	1	0	1	1 (0.51)	0	1 (1.54)	2 (0.57)
Total					196	91	65	352 (100.00)

Note. [a]: all 35 students from Indirect CF group participated in the research from the beginning to the end, and no one quitted in the middle.

[b]: sva—subject-verb agreement; prep. —preposition; pos. —parts of speech; pro. —p pronoun; poss. —possessive; com—comparatives; 'there'—existential there; 'to'—'to' in infinitive clause; 'that'—'that' in clauses

[c]: Pre = pretest(conducted in Week 1); Post = posttest(conducted in Week5); Delay = delayed posttest(conducted in Week 9).

[d]: Total Pre = the total number of the specific type of error made by the 35 students in the pretest; Total Post = the total number of the specific type of error made by the 35 students in the posttest; Total Delay = the total number of the specific type of error in the posttest made by the 35 students in the delayed posttest. Total = the total number of the specific type of error made by the 35 students in the three tests; (%) = percentage of the errors (raw count of the specific type of error / the total number of all errors)

As Table 4. 1 shows, in the pretest, subject-verb agreement (25%), plural (19. 39%), tense (13. 78%) and article (13. 78%) were the four most frequent error patterns in student texts. Errors with parts of speech(9. 18%), verb(8. 16%), and preposition(4. 59%) appeared at comparatively higher frequencies than the other error types. Even though the production of grammatical errors was not extremely high, it showed a wide range of error patterns produced, including pronoun, possessive, existential there, the use of 'to' infinitives and 'that' in clauses, etc.

Concerning the number of errors students produced in the posttest, the frequency gives an impression of a great change for certain grammatical features but staying stable for other error types. For example, the number of errors on subject-verb agreement dropped from 49 (25%) in the pretest to 15 (16. 48%) in the posttest. Errors regarding plural dropped from 38 (19.3%) to 20(21.98%). Article errors reduced from 27(13.78%) to 7 (7.69%), tense errors decreased from 27 (13.78%) to 3 (3.3%), and parts of speech errors dropped from 18 (9.18%) to 1 (1.1%). This indicates that that students attempted to make use of the CF to correct the errors produced in their writing. Other types, such as pronoun, existential there, comparatives, the use of 'to' infinitives, and 'that' in clauses, the number of errors either remained the same or dropped only one error. In contrast, it was interesting to note that errors of verb, preposition and possessive increased, even though not much, from the pretest to the posttest. Errors on verbs rose from 16 (8.16%) to 20 (21.98%); prepositional errors increased from 9 (4.59%) to 12 (13.19%); and possessive errors grew from 1 (0.51%) to 6 (6.59%). The increase of errors does not exactly mean that these errors were more attempted by students. It does not necessarily mean that students did not make effort to digest the indirect CF, either. It is probable that students forgot to pay attention to or had difficulty processing the CF.

In the delayed posttest, the raw count of errors on subject-verb agreement rose compared to the posttest from 15 (16.48%) to 24 (36.92%). Quite a low number of errors on article, verb, existential there, and parts of speech appeared while errors on preposition, pronoun, possessive and comparatives disappeared in the delayed posttest. This was not surprising because it was expected that indirect CF could play a certain role, either positive or negative, in reducing students' production of errors in writing.

With regard to the data from the pretest to the delayed posttest, the raw count of certain errors dropped substantially but the percentage of the errors rose accordingly. For example, errors on subject-verb agreement, plural, verbs dropped from 49 (25%) to 24 (36. 92%) , 38 (19. 39%) to 22 (33. 85%) ,16 (8. 16%) to 8 (12. 31%) , respectively. As can be seen, their percentage of errors rose by almost 12% , 15% and 4%. For the errors on article (13. 78% to 4. 62%) , tense (13. 78% to 6. 15%) , preposition(4. 59% to 0) , parts of speech (9. 18% to 1. 54%) , pronoun (2. 04% to 0) , possessive(0. 51% to 0) and comparatives(1. 53% to 0) , both their raw count and percentage dropped from the pretest to the delayed posttest. The rest of the error patterns remained at the same or a similar raw count or percentage from the pretest to the delayed posttest. It might be concluded that after receiving indirect CF students were capable of using corrective feedback to help themselves with self-editing in their writing, and some of them successfully corrected errors and avoided the reoccurrence of errors in the new piece of writing.

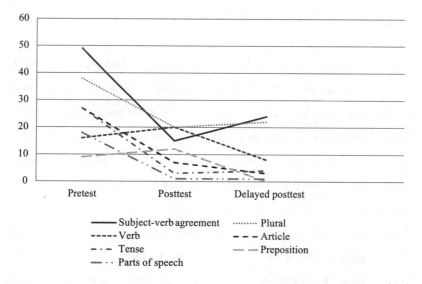

Figure 4. 2 **Developmental trend in relation to raw count of the top seven error types for Indirect CF group in the three tests**

Table 4. 2

Means and Standard Deviations of Seven Primary Error Types by Indirect CF Group in the Three Tests   ($n = 35$)

Test	Sva[a]		Plural		Verb		Article		Tense		Prep. [b]		Pos[c]	
	M	SD	M	SD	M	SD	M	SD	M	SD	M	SD	M	SD
1	1.40	1.59	1.09	1.07	.46	.92	.77	1.09	.77	1.09	.26	.51	.51	.95
2	.43	.74	.57	.85	.57	.82	.20	.41	.09	.28	.34	.64	.03	.17
3	.69	1.08	.63	1.24	.29	.62	.09	.28	.11	.40	.00	.00	.03	.17

Note. [a]: Sva = subject-verb agreement. [b]: Prep. = preposition. [c]: Pos. = parts of speech.

Figure 4. 2 presents the raw error count of the seven most frequent errors in the pretest, posttest and delayed posttest. Table 4. 2 displays the means and standard deviations of the seven most frequent error patterns made by students in the Indirect CF group on the three tests. As seen, the developmental trend of the seven error types across the three tests was generated and clearly represented in Figure 4. 2. The x-axis represents the three tests, and the y-axis represents the frequency of errors in each test. The seven most frequent error types produced by the Indirect CF students demonstrated four shapes of developmental trends. There was no linear decrease or increase pattern as displayed in Figure 4. 2, indicating the Indirect CF group did not exhibit an ideal developmental pattern expected, which was reasonable in the L2 learning process. However, as seen, article was the error type that constantly decreased from the pretest to the delayed posttest, which had a similar developmental pattern with the linear decrease. For verbs and prepositions, error rates slightly increased from the pretest to the posttest, indicating a growth of errors over a four-week period of time. Then, a clear drop of the number of errors occurred from the posttest to the delayed posttest, which was even below the errors in the pretest. Although this was not a perfect or the best developmental pattern, it was still desirable in L2 learning. In contrast, for subject-verb agreement, plural, tense and parts of speech, the total number of errors remarkably decreased from the pretest to the posttest, indicating a constant reduction of errors over a four-week period of time. However, the difference was that subject-verb agreement was then followed by a slight increase in the delayed posttest but still below the errors in pretest; plural, tense and parts of speech were followed by a parallel development in the delayed posttest. In summary, all the developmental patterns in the Indirect CF group showed a decline in the number of errors from the pretest to the delayed posttest.

In order to control the effect of writing length on students' error rates, normed frequencies were calculated (i. e. , number of errors/ total number of words * 1,000). Figure 4. 3 shows the developmental tendency in terms of the total number of each of the seven primary error types in the three tests based on their normed frequencies. As seen, article was the only error pattern that showed a continuous decrease across the three tests. Although errors rates on the other six error patterns (i. e. , subject-verb agreement, plural, tense, verb, parts of speech, and preposition) to certain extent picked up either in the posttest or delayed posttest, it still can be said that they conformed to the trend for the whole occurrence of errors. In other words, the overall developmental pattern for each of the seven primary errors showed a concordance with the previous analysis, indicating an eventual reduction of errors from the pretest to the delayed posttest in the Indirect CF group.

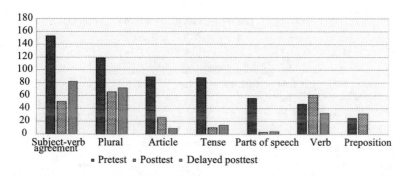

Figure 4. 3 **Normed frequencies of the top seven error types for Indirect CF in the three tests**

Table 4.3,4.4 and 4.5 present the Indirect CF students' aggregate performance with regard to frequency of different error types that occurred in the three tests. Most students made fewer errors along with the treatment from the pretest to the delayed posttest. For example,62.86% of students made errors on subject-verb agreement in the pretest. Then,it dropped to 31.43% in the posttest,which was a 30% decrease,and remained stable in the delayed posttest. There were 65.71% of students who made plural errors in the pretest. It then dropped to 37.14% (almost 30% decrease) in the posttest and still kept stable in the delayed posttest. In addition,a total of 34% decrease was shown from the pretest (42.86%), the posttest (20%) to the delayed posttest (8.57%) for the article errors; 48.57% of students made tense errors and dramatically dropped to 8.57% in the posttest and delayed posttest; and 31.43% of students made errors on parts of speech and had a noticeable drop to 2.86% in the posttest and delayed posttest. This was a promising phenomenon, indicating more frequent attempts by students in their application of indirect CF in their writing.

Table 4.3

Indirect CF Students' Aggregate Performance in Accuracy in the Pretest($n = 35$)

Number of Error	Sva(%)[a]	Plural(%)	Verb(%)	Article(%)	Tense(%)	Prep. (%)	Pos. (%)
0	13 (37.1)	12 (34.3)	25 (71.4)	20 (57.1)	18 (51.4)	27 (77.1)	24 (68.6)
1	10(28.6)	13 (37.1)	7 (20.0)	7 (20.0)	11 (31.4)	7 (20.0)	7 (20.0)
2	5 (14.3)	6 (17.1)	1 (2.9)	5 (14.3)	4 (11.4)	1 (2.9)	2 (5.7)
3	2 (5.7)	3 (8.6)	1 (2.9)	2 (5.7)	1 (2.9)	0	1 (2.9)
4	2 (5.7)	1 (2.9)	1 (2.9)	1 (2.9)	0	0	1 (2.9)
5	3 (8.6)	0	0	0	1 (2.9)	0	0
Total	35	35	35	35	35	35	35

Note. [a]:(%) = number of students/ 35

Table 4.4

Indirect CF Students' Aggregate Performance in Accuracy in the Posttest

$(n = 35)$

Number of Error	Sva(%)[a]	Plural(%)	Verb(%)	Article(%)	Tense(%)	Prep. (%)	Pos. (%)
0	24 (68.6)	22 (62.9)	21 (60.0)	28 (80.0)	32 (91.4)	26 (74.3)	34 (97.1)
1	8 (22.9)	7 (20.0)	9 (25.7)	7 (20.0)	3 (8.6)	6 (17.1)	1 (2.9)
2	2 (5.7)	5 (14.3)	4 (11.4)	0	0	3 (8.6)	0
3	1 (2.9)	1 (2.9)	1 (2.9)	0	0	0	0
Total	35	35	35	35	35	35	35

Note. [a] : (%) = number of students/ 35

Table 4.5

Indirect CF Students' Aggregate Performance in Accuracy in the Delayed-posttest

$(n = 35)$

Number of Error	Sva(%)[a]	Plural(%)	Verb(%)	Article(%)	Tense(%)	Prep. (%)	Pos. (%)
0	22 (62.9)	25 (71.4)	28 (80.0)	32 (91.4)	32 (91.4)	35 (100.0)	34
1	6 (17.1)	4 (11.4)	4 (11.4)	3 (8.6)	2 (5.7)	0	1 (2.9)
2	4 (11.4)	3 (8.6)	3 (8.6)	0	1 (2.9)	0	0
3	2 (5.7)	1 (2.9)	0	0	0	0	0
4	1 (2.9)	1 (2.9)	0	0	0	0	0
5	0	1	0	0	0	0	0
Total	35	35	35	35	35	35	35

Note. [a] : (%) = number of students/ 35

Nevertheless, it was interesting that exceptions happened on the verbs and prepositions. 28.57% of students made verb errors in the pretest while it unexpectedly rose to 40% in the posttest but eventually dropped to 20% inthe delayed posttest. For prepositions, 22.86% of students made errors in the pretest, then a slight increase from the pretest to posttest (25.71%), and finally achieved 100% accuracy in the delayed posttest. The initial increased and final decrease in percentage of students could indicate more students paid attention to or attempted to correct their errors but failed or had difficulty processing error correction at the beginning, but eventually many had improved accuracy of their writing after they received further treatment of the indirect CF.

4. 1. 2   Descriptive Statistics for Feedback on Content (FC) Group.

A total of 69 grammatical errors occurred in the FC Group student essays in the pretest, 62 errors occurred in the posttest, and 34 errors in the delayed posttest. Table 4.6 below shows the total number of different error patterns in the FC group students made in the three tests. As shown in Table 4. 6, 9 error patterns were found in the pretest, 10 error types occurred in the posttest, and 5 error types in the delayed posttest. Based on error frequency, the primary seven error types for the FC group include subject-agreement, plural, tense, article, verbs, prepositional, and part of speech errors.

The total number of errors and error types in the FC Group student essays slightly decreased from the pretest to posttest and from the posttest to delayed posttest as well. Figure 4. 4 below shows a tendency for a continuous decrease of errors across the three tests. Table 4. 6 illustrates detailed statistics regarding all the types of produced errors. The seven most frequent error types, including plural, subject-verb agreement, verb, article, tense, parts of speech and preposition, represented 32.73%, 27.88%, 10.30%, 6.67%, 6.67%, 6.06% and 5.45%, respectively.

This clearly shows that errors on plural and subject-verb agreement account for the greatest portion (60. 61%) among the seven most frequent error types. In contrast, comparatives (2. 42%), pronoun (0. 61%), possessive (0. 61%), existential there (0. 61%) were the four least frequent errors. Compared to the Indirect CF group, errors on 'to' in infinitive clause and the use of 'that' did not occur for the FC group students in the three tests.

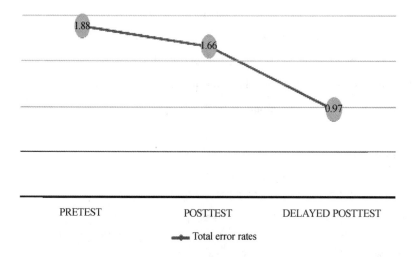

Figure 4. 4 **Mean of the error rates in the three tests in FC Group**

Figure 4. 5 above is a visual representation of the raw error count of the seven most frequent error types in the three tests for the FC group. As displayed, the seven most frequent error types produced by the FC group students demonstrates four different shapes of developmental trends. In comparison to the Indirect CF group, a linear decrease pattern was observed in students' production of plurals. An initial decrease of errors was observed from the pretest to the posttest, followed by a continued drop from the posttest to the delayed posttest. This means that plural error was the only error type that consistently decreased from the pretest to the delayed posttest in the FC group. For verb errors, article errors, prepositional errors, and parts of speech errors, error rates slightly increased from the pretest to the posttest, followed by a decline in the number of errors in the delayed posttest, which was also less than the errors in the pretest. The number of errors on subject-verb agreement had an initial decrease from the pretest to the posttest, then followed by a slight increase in the delayed posttest. However, there were more errors in the delayed posttest than in the pretest. Errors on tense also initially dropped from the pretest to the posttest, but were followed by a parallel development in the delayed posttest. Except for subject-verb agreement errors, the FC group showed a desirable development trend of L2 learning because of the constant decrease in the total number of errors across the three tests. There was no linear increase pattern observed for this group as well.

Table 4.6

Raw Number of Different Error Types for FC Group (n = 35[a])

Error[b]	Sub-categories	Pre[c]	Post[c]	Delay[c]	Total[d] Pre(%)	Total Post(%)	Total Delay(%)	Total (/%)
Plural		27	18	9	27 (39.13)	18 (29.03)	9 (26.47)	54 (32.73)
Sva.		16	13	17	16 (23.19)	13 (20.97)	17 (50%)	46 (27.88)
Verbs	Wrong use after modals	0	1	1	6 (8.67)	8 (12.90)	3 (8.82)	17 (10.30)
	Missing main/ copula verb	0	0	1				
	Redundant use of main verb	5	6	1				
	Wrong use of main verb	0	0	0				
	Passive voice	1	1	0				

(Contd.)

Error[b]	Sub-categories	Pre[c]	Post[c]	Delay[c]	Total[d] Pre(%)	Total Post(%)	Total Delay(%)	Total (/%)
Article	Wrong	1	0	0	4 (5.80)	5 (8.06)	2 (5.88)	11 (6.67)
	Missing	0	0	0				
	Redundant	3	5	2				
Tense		5	3	3	5 (7.25)	3 (4.84)	3 (8.82)	11 (6.67)
Pos.	Wrong adj.	1	3	0			0	
	Wrong adv.	1	0	0	4 (5.80)	6 (9.68)		10 (6.06)
	Wrong verb	1	1	0				
	Wrong noun	1	2	0				
Prep.	Wrong	2	2	0	4 (5.80)	5 (8.06)	0	9 (5.45)
	Missing	2	2	0				
	Redundant	0	1	0				
Com.		2	2	0	2 (2.90)	2 (3.24)	0	4 (2.42)
Pro.	Missing	0	0	0	0	1 (1.61)	0	1 (0.61)
	Redundant	0	0	0				
	Missing subject	0	1	0				
Poss.	Wrong use	0	0	0	0	1 (1.61)	0	1 (0.61)
	Missing	0	0	0				
'there'		1	0	0	1 (1.45)	0	0	1 (0.61)
'to'		0	0	0	0	0	0	0
'that'		0	0	0	0	0	0	0
Total					69	62	34	165 (100.00)

Note. [a]: all 35 students from Feedback on Content group participated in the research from the beginning to the end, and no one quitted in the middle.

[b]: sva—subject-verb agreement; prep. —preposition; pos. —parts of speech; pro. —p pronoun; poss. —possessive; com—comparatives; 'there'—existential there; 'to' — 'to' in infinitive clause; 'that' — 'that' in clauses

[c]: Pre = pretest(conducted in Week 1); Post = posttest(conducted in Week 5); Delay = delayed posttest(conducted in Week 9).

[d]: Total Pre = the total number of the specific type of error made by the 35 students in the

pretest; Total Post = the total number of the specific type of error made by the 35 students in the posttest; Total Delay = the total number of the specific type of error in the posttest made by the 35 students in the delayed posttest. Total = the total number of the specific type of error made by the 35 students in the three tests; (%) = percentage of the errors(raw count of the specific type of error / the total number of all errors)

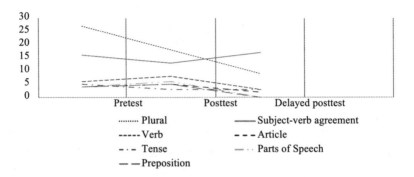

Figure 4. 5 **Raw count of the top seven error types for FC group in the three tests**

Regardingeach error pattern produced in the pretest, as Table 4. 6 shows, plural (39. 13%), subject-verb agreement (23. 19%), verb (8. 67%) and tense(7. 25%)were the four most frequent error patterns in student texts, which is slightly different from the Indirect CF group. Article, verb, prepositional, and part of speech errors appeared at comparatively higher frequencies than the rest of the error types, which is 5. 80% for all three error patterns. Compared to the Indirect CF group, the production of grammatical errors in the FC group was comparatively lower, and the range of error patterns produced was not as wide as the Indirect CF group. As an example of the group difference, missing 'to' in infinitive clauses and redundant use of 'that' did not occur in FC group students' writing in any of the three tests.

In light of the number of errors students produced in the posttest, the frequency did not have as great a change as the Indirect CF group did, and most of the grammatical features stayed quite stable from the pretest to the posttest and from the posttest to the delayed posttest. However, a noticeable decrease was still seen for certain types of errors from the pretest to the posttest. For example, errors on plural dropped from 27 (39. 13%) to 18 (29.03%). The number of errors on subject-verb agreement fell from 16 (23. 19%) in the pretest to 13 (20. 97%) in the posttest. Errors on tense decreased from 5 (7. 25%) in the pretest to 3 (4. 84%) in the posttest. It was interesting to note that both the raw number and percentage of errors on verb, article, parts of speech, prepositional and comparative errors slightly increased from the pretest to the posttest (i. e. , verbs from 8. 67% to 12.9% ; article from 5. 8% to 8. 06% ; parts of speech from 5. 8% to 9. 68% ; preposition from 5. 8% to 8. 06% ; comparatives from 2. 9% to 3. 24%).

In the delayed posttest, the raw count of errorson subject-verb agreement increased compared to the posttest from 13 (20. 97%) to 17 (50%). Errors on plural (26. 47%) , verb (8. 82%) , article (5. 88) , and tense (8. 82%) occurred less frequently while errors on preposition, parts of speech, and comparatives disappeared in the delayed posttest. With regard to the data from the pretest to the delayed posttest, only plural had a considerable drop from 27 (39. 17%) to 9 (26. 47%) , which was about a 13% change from the pretest to the delayed posttest. Subject-verb agreement slightly increased from 16 (23. 19%) in the pretest to 17 (50%) in the delayed posttest. Other errors, such as verb, article, and tense did not change much from delayed posttest to pretest.

Therefore, based on the previous analysis, a general trend of the development of accuracy for the FC group was observed, demonstrating a great improvement on plural errors and a slight improvement on other error types from the pretest to the delayed posttest, such as verb, tense, article, prepositional, and part of speech errors. Nevertheless, the positive trend did not extend to the delayed posttest for subject-verb agreement, on which students showed a higher percentage and number of errors in the delayed posttest. It may be concluded that even though the FC group students received feedback on content and without any focus on grammar, students were still attending to certain error patterns regarding their writing accuracy. In other words, feedback works to a certain extent to improve students' writing no matter which type it is.

Table 4.7

Means and Standard Deviations of Seven Most Frequent Error Typesby FC Group in the Three Tests (n = 35)

Test	Sva[a]		Plural		Verb		Article		Tense		Prep. [b]		Pos[c]	
	M	SD	M	SD	M	SD	M	SD	M	SD	M	SD	M	SD
1	.46	.66	.77	1.11	.17	.45	.11	.32	.14	.36	.11	.40	.11	.40
2	.37	.65	.51	.66	.26	.44	.14	.60	.09	.28	.14	.43	.17	.71
3	.49	.92	.26	.61	.09	.37	.06	.24	.09	.37	.00	.00	.00	.00

Note. a. Sva is the acronym of subject-verb agreement. b. Prep. is the acronym of preposition.

c. Pos is the acronym of parts of speech.

Table 4.7 above presents the means and standard deviations of the seven most frequent error patterns made by the FC group students in the three tests. As indicated in Table 4.7, the trend of four out of seven error types was an increase from the pretest to the posttest, and then a decline from the posttest to the delayed posttest (i. e. , verb, article, preposition and parts of speech). Errors on subject-verb agreement showed a positive trend from the pretest to the posttest but did not extend to the delayed posttest. Errors on plural and tense decreased from the pretest to the delayed posttest, indicating students' continually improved accuracy on the two error patterns.

Just as with the Indirect CF group, normed frequencies were also calculated (i. e. , number of errors/ total number of words * 1,000) in order to control for the effect of writing length on students' writing accuracy for the FC group. Figure 4.6 shows the developmental tendency in terms of the total number of each the seven primary error types in the three tests based on their normed frequencies. As seen, plural was the only error pattern that continuously declined across the three tests. The number of tense errors dropped as well at the beginning, followed with a parallel development in the delayed posttest. Subject-verb agreement seems like an exception, as there was no change in the overall developmental trend. For verb, article, preposition and parts of speech, they initially rose in the posttest and eventually fell in the delayed posttest, and errors on preposition and parts of speech finally disappeared in the delayed posttest.

According to the results from the normed frequencies, it can be concluded that error occurrences by the FC group in general showed an overall decline across the three tests. The developmental pattern for each of the seven primary errors also showed an eventual reduction of errors from the pretest to the delayed posttest except for subject-verb agreement.

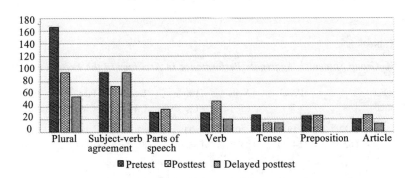

Figure 4. 6 **Normed Frequencies of the top seven error types for FC group in the three tests**

Table 4. 8, Table 4. 9 and Table 4. 10 present the FC group students' aggregate performances with regard to the different errors that occurred in the three tests. Students tended to make fewer errors after the treatment from the pretest to the delayed posttest. For example, there were 37. 1% of students who made errors on subject-verb agreement in the pretest. Then, it dropped to 25.7% in the delayed posttest. There were 45.7% of students who made plural errors in the pretest, then it dropped to 17.1% (an almost 29% decrease) in the delayed posttest. A slight decrease was shown from the pretest(11.4%) to the posttest(5.7%) for the errors on article usage, and remained stable in the delayed posttest(5.7%). 14.3% of students made errors on tense, which dropped to 8.6% in the posttest and 5.7% in the delayed posttest. 8.6 % of students made errors in parts of speech in both the pretest and the posttest and there was a noticeable drop to 0 in the delayed posttest.

Exceptions happened on the errors with verbs and prepositions. 14.3% of students made verb errors in the pretest. Then, it unexpectedly raised to 25.7% in the posttest but eventually dropped to 5.7% in delayed posttest. 8.6% of students made errors on prepositions in the pretest, followed by a slight increase from the pretest to the posttest(11.4%), and finally achieved 100% accuracy in the delayed posttest.

Table 4.8

FC Group Students' Aggregate Performance in Accuracy in the Pretest(n = 35)

Number of errors	Sva(%)[a]	Plural (%)	Verb (%)	Article (%)	Tense (%)	Prep. (%)	Pos. (%)
0	22 (62.9)	19 (54.3)	30 (85.7)	31 (88.6)	30 (85.7)	32 (91.4)	32 (91.4)
1	10 (28.6)	11 (31.4)	4 (11.4)	4 (11.4)	5 (14.3)	2 (5.7)	2 (5.7)
2	3 (8.6)	0	1 (2.9)	0	0	1 (2.9)	1 (2.9)
3	0	4 (11.4)	0	0	0	0	0
4	0	1 (2.9)	0	0	0	0	0
Total	35	35	35	35	35	35	35

Note. [a] :(%) = number of students/ 35

Table 4.9

FC Group Students' Aggregate Performance in Accuracy in the Posttest(*n* = 35)

Number of errors	Sva (%)ᵃ	Plural (%)	Verb (%)	Article (%)	Tense (%)	Prep. (%)	Pos. (%)
0	25 (71.4)	20 (57.1)	26 (74.3)	33 (94.3)	32 (91.4)	31 (88.6)	32 (91.4)
1	7 (20.0)	12 (34.3)	9 (25.7)	0	3 (8.6)	3 (8.6)	2 (5.7)
2	3 (8.6)	3 (8.6)	0	1 (2.9)	0	1 (2.9)	0
3	0	0	0	1 (2.9)	0	0	1 (2.9)
Total	35	35	35	35	35	35	35

Note. ᵃ: (%) = number of students/ 35

Table 4.10

Feedback on Content Group Students' Aggregate Performance in Accuracy in the Delayed-posttest(*n* = 35)

# of errors	Sva (%)ᵃ	Plural (%)	Verb (%)	Article (%)	Tense (%)	Prep. (%)	Pos. (%)
0	26 (74.3)	29 (82.9)	33 (94.3)	33 (94.3)	33 (94.3)	35 (100.0)	35 (100.0)
1	3 (8.6)	3 (8.6)	1 (2.9)	2 (5.7)	1 (2.9)	0	0
2	4 (11.4)	3 (8.6)	1 (2.9)	0	1 (2.9)	0	0
3	2 (5.7)	0	0	0	0	0	0
Total	35	35	35	35	35	35	35

Note. ᵃ: (%) = number of students/ 35

In conclusion, the increased percentageof error-free writing may indicate that more students paid attention to their writing with teacher feedback or attempted to self-edit their writing. In addition, as seen from the tables abbove, the FC group students in general showed comparatively lower percentages in their accurate use of subject-verb agreement and plurals, and higher percentages in their use of article, tense, verb, preposition and parts of speech.

4. 1. 3　Descriptive Statistics for Direct Corrective Feedback (Direct CF) Group.

Similar to the Indirect CF group, students in the Direct CF group also revealed a tendency to use simple sentence structures and specialized and infrequent vocabulary to develop their ideas in their writing. There was a total of 219 grammatical errors found in student essays from the pretest, 71 errors from the posttest, and 71 errors from the delayed posttest. Table 4. 11 presents the total number of different error patterns students from the Direct CF group made on the three tests: 11 error patterns were found in the pretest, 10 error patterns occurred in the posttest, and 9 error patterns were found in the delayed posttest.

Table 4. 11

Raw Number of Different Error Types for Direct CF Group (n = 35[a])

Error[b]	Sub-categories	Pre[c]	Post[c]	Delay[c]	Total[d] Pre(%)	Total Post(%)	Total Delay(%)	Total (%)
Sva.		59	14	33	59 (26.94)	14 (19.72)	33 (46.48)	106 (29.36)
Plural		47	15	18	47 (21.46)	15 (21.13)	18 (25.35)	80 (22.16)
Verbs	Wrong useafter modals	8	11	1	23 (10.50)	18 (25.35)	7 (9.86)	48 (13.30)
	Missing main/copula verb	8	5	4				
	Redundantmain verb	4	2	2				
	Wrong main verb	2	0	0				
	Passive voice	1	0	0				

(Contd.)

Error[b]	Sub-categories	Pre[c]	Post[c]	Delay[c]	Total[d] Pre(%)	Total Post(%)	Total Delay(%)	Total (%)
Article	Redundant	15	3	0	22 (10.05)	4 (5.63)	2 (2.82)	28 (7.76)
Pos.	Missing	2	0	0	21 (9.59)	3 (4.23)	2 (2.82)	26 (7.20)
	Wrong adj.	6	0	0				
	Wrong	5	1	2				
	Wrong adv.	3	0	2				
	Wrong verb	1	1	0				
	Wrong noun	11	2	0				
Tense		13	8	4	13 (5.94)	8 (11.27)	4 (5.63)	25 (6.93)
Prep.	Wrong	8	2	2	18 (8.22)	3 (4.23)	3 (4.23)	24 (6.65)
	Missing	5	1	1				
	Redundant	5	0	0				
Pro.	Missing	1	0	0	7 (3.20)	4 (5.63)	1 (1.41)	12 (3.32)
	Redundant	2	1	0				
	Wrong	1	1	0				
	Missing subject	3	2	1				
Com.		5	0	0	5 (2.28)	0	0	5 (1.39)
'to'		3	2	0	3 (1.37)	2 (2.82)	0	5 (1.39)
'that'		1	0	1	1 (0.46)	0	1 (1.41)	2 (0.55)
Poss.		0	0	0	0	0	0	0
there		0	0	0	0	0	0	0
Total					219	71	71	361 (100.00)

Note. [a] : all 35 students from Group 1 participated in the research from the beginning to the
end, and no one quitted in the middle.

[b] : sva—subject-verb agreement; prep.—preposition; pos.—parts of speech; pro.—
pronoun; poss.—possessive; com—comparatives; 'there'—existential there;
'to'—'to' in infinitive clause; 'that'—'that' in clauses

[c] : Pre = pretest (conducted in Week 1); Post = posttest (conducted in Week 5); Delay =
delayed posttest (conducted in Week 9).

[d] : Total Pre = the total number of the specific type of error made by the 35 students in the
pretest; Total Post = the total number of the specific type of error made by the 35
students in the posttest; Total Delay = the total number of the specific type of error in
the posttest made by the 35 students in the delayed posttest. Total = the total number
of the specific type of error made by the 35 students in the three tests; (%) =
percentage of the errors (raw count of the specific type of error / the total number of all
errors)

In the Direct CF student essays, the total number of errors and error
types showed a continued decrease from the pretest to the posttest and from
the posttest to the delayed posttest. This tendency is visually reflected in
Figure 4. 7 below based on the mean of error rates. Table 4. 11 above
shows the seven most frequent error types were subject-verb agreement,
plural, verb, article, tense, preposition, and parts of speech, which
represented 29. 36% , 22. 16% , 13. 3% , 7. 76% , 7. 20% , 6. 93% and
6. 65% , respectively. As similar to the Indirect CF group, pronoun
(3. 32%) , comparatives (1. 39%) , lack 'to' in infinitive clause (1. 39%)
and the use of 'that' (0. 55%) were the four least frequent errors.

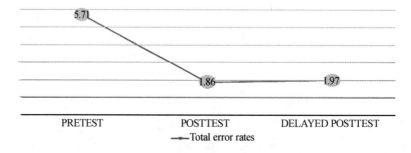

Figure 4. 7 **Mean of the error rates in the three tests in Direct CF group**

Regarding error patterns in the pretest , as Table 4. 11 displays , subject-verb agreement (26. 94%) , plural (121. 46%) , verb (10. 50%) and article (10. 05%) were the four most frequent error patterns in student texts in the pretest. Parts of speech (9. 59%) , preposition (8. 22%) , and tense (5. 94%) appeared at comparatively higher frequencies than the other error types. There were no errors on possessives and existential *there*. The rate of production of grammatical errors by the Direct CF group was noticeably higher than the Indirect CF and FC group , and showed a broad range of error patterns.

In terms of the number of errors students produced in the posttest , the frequency had a great change for certain grammatical features but kept steady for other error types. For example , the number of errors on subject-verb agreement dropped from 59 (26. 94%) in the pretest to 14 (19. 72%) in the posttest. Errors with plurals dropped from 47 (21. 46%) to 15 (21. 13%). Errors with articles reduced from 22 (10. 05%) to 4 (5. 63%) ; errors with parts of speech dropped from 21 (9. 59%) to 3 (4. 23%) ; and prepositional errors declined from 18 (8. 22%) to 3 (4. 23%). For verb , tense , pronoun , and ' to ' infinitives , the raw counts of these errors decreased while their percentages slightly increased. For example , verb errors dropped from 23 to18 but the percentage of total errors rose from 10. 50% to 25. 35%. Tense errors dropped from 13 to 8 with an increase in the percentage from 5. 94% to 11. 27% in the posttest. Comparative errors (2. 28%) in the pretest and ' that ' errors (. 46%) in clauses did not occur in the posttest.

In the delayed posttest , the raw count of errors on subject-verb agreement raised compared to the posttest from 14 (19. 72%) to 33 (46. 48%) , but was still lower than the number in the pretest. Plural errors also slightly raised from 15 (21. 13%) to 18 (25. 35%) , which was still less that the pretest. Errors on verb (9. 86%) , article (2. 82%) , parts of speech (2. 82%) , tense (5. 63%) , prepositions (4. 23%) , and pronouns

(1. 41%) occurred less frequently and errors on ' to ' infinitives disappeared in the delayed posttest.

With regard to the error change from the pretest to the delayed posttest, the raw counts of certain errors dropped impressionistically but the percentage of the errors raised accordingly. For example, errors on subject-verb agreement and plural dropped from 59(26. 94%) to 33(46. 48%) ,47 (21. 46%) to 18 (25. 35%) , respectively. For the errors on verb (from 10. 50% to 9. 86%) , article(from 10. 05% to 2. 82%) , tense(5. 94% to 5. 63%) , preposition (8. 22% to 4. 23%) , parts of speech (9. 59% to 2. 82%) , pronoun(3. 20% to 1. 41%) and comparatives (2. 28% to 0) , both their raw count and percentage dropped from the pretest to the delayed posttest. This indicates a trend towards increased accuracy.

The general trend of the development of accuracy for the Direct CF group, as indicated by the raw error counts demonstrates a certain degree of improvement on all error types from the pretest to the posttest. This positive trend also extends to the delayed posttest for most the error patterns, indicating improved accuracy in student writing.

Figure 4. 8 below provides a clearer visual representation of the developmental pattern for each of the seven primary error types based on their raw counts. For detailed statistics, readers can be referred to Table 4. 11. Compared to the Indirect CF group and FC group, the seven most frequent error types produced by Direct CF group students only demonstrated two shapes for the developmental trend. In contrary to the Indirect CF group and FC group, no errors in the Direct CF group showed an initial increase. In other words, the number of all the error types declined from the pretest to the posttest, which is an indicator of initial and immediate improvement of accuracy in L2 writing once students received the direct corrective feedback. For instance, errors on tense and verb displayed a very slight linear decrease from the pretest to the delayed posttest. Article errors, prepositional errors and parts of speech errors constantly decreased from the pretest to the posttest, followed by a stable and parallel development in the delayed posttest. Regarding plural and subject-verb agreement, a clear drop of the number of errors occurred from the pretest to the posttest while followed by a slight increase from the posttest to the delayed posttest, though it was still less than the number of errors in the pretest. Although the developmental patterns produced by the Direct CF group were not a perfect or the best developmental pattern, they were still desirable in L2 learning. The overall developmental patterns in the Direct CF group clearly showed a consistent decline in the number of errors from the pretest to the delayed posttest.

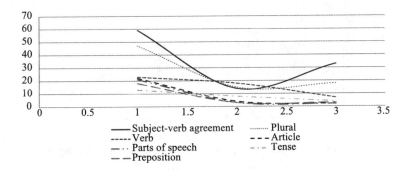

Figure 4. 8 **Raw count of the top seven error types for Direct CF group in the three tests**

Table 4. 12

Means and Standard Deviations of Seven Most Frequent Error Types by Direct CF group in the Three Tests (n = 35)

Test	Sva[a]		Plural		Verb		Article		Tense		Prep. [b]		Pos[c]	
	M	SD	M	SD	M	SD	M	SD	M	SD	M	SD	M	SD
1	1.69	2.25	1.34	1.21	.66	1.28	.63	.77	.37	.69	.51	.74	.51	1.12
2	.40	.60	.43	.70	.51	.89	.11	.40	.23	.55	.09	.37	.09	.28
3	.94	1.03	.51	1.04	.20	.58	.06	.24	.11	.32	.09	.37	.06	.24

Note. a. Sva is the acronym of subject-verb agreement. b. Prep. is the acronym of preposition.
c. Pos is the acronym of parts of speech.

Table 4. 12 presents the means and standard deviations of the seven most frequent error patterns made by the Direct CF group students in the three tests. Information in the table confirmed the previous analysis, which is the overall trend of all seven error types decreasing from the pretest to the delayed posttest. Although the subject-verb agreement and plural errors rose again in the delayed posttest after a fall in the posttest, they confirmed to the trend for the overall occurrence of errors.

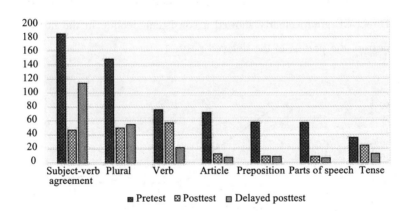

Figure 4. 9 **Normed frequencies of the top seven error types for Direct CF group in the three tests**

In order to better control the effect of writing length on students' writing accuracy, normed frequencies were calculated (i. e. , number of errors / total number of words * 1,000) for the Direct CF group as well. Figure 4. 9 shows the developmental tendency in terms of the total number of each of the seven primary error types in the three tests based on their normed frequencies. Excepting subject-verb agreement and plurals, the other five error patterns (i. e. , verb article, preposition, part of speech and tense) demonstrated a continuous decrease across the three tests. In particular, plural, article, prepositional and part of speech errors in the posttest and delayed posttest declined more than the other error types, which indicated a large degree of error reduction. In addition, although the number of errors on subject-verb agreement and plural increased from the posttest to the delayed posttest. It still can be said that there was a trend toward decreasing errors overall.

Therefore, normed frequency counts also showed the overall decline across the three tests for the Direct CF group. The developmental pattern for each of the seven primary errors indicated an eventual reduction of errors from the pretest to the delayed posttest for the Direct CF group.

Table 4.13

Direct CF Group Students' Aggregate Performance in Accuracy in the Pretest

($n = 35$)

Number of Errors	Sva (%)[a]	Plural (%)	Verb (%)	Article (%)	Tense (%)	Prep. (%)	Pos. (%)
0	11(31.4)	10 (28.6)	23 (65.7)	19 (54.3)	25 (71.4)	22 (62.9)	24 (68.6)
1	12 (34.3)	12 (34.3)	8 (22.9)	10 (28.6)	8 (22.9)	8 (22.9)	8 (22.9)
2	5 (14.3)	6(17.1)	0 (2.9)	6 (17.2)	1 (2.9)	5 (14.3)	2 (5.7)
3	2 (5.7)	5 (14.3)	3 (8.6)	0	1 (2.9)	0	0
4	2 (5.7)	2 (5.7)	0 (2.9)	0	0	0	0
5	1 (2.9)	0	0	0	0	0	0
6	0	0	1 (2.9)	0	0	0	1 (2.9)
8	1 (2.9)	0	0	0	0	0	
10	1 (2.9)	0	0	0	0	0	
Total	35	35	35	35	35	35	35

Note. [a]: (%) = number of students/ 35

Table 4.14

Direct CF Group Students' Aggregate Performance in Accuracy in the Posttest ($n = 35$)

Number of Errors	Sva (%)[a]	Plural (%)	Verb (%)	Article (%)	Tense (%)	Prep. (%)	Pos. (%)
0	23 (65.7)	24 (68.6)	24 (68.6)	32 (91.4)	29 (82.9)	33 (94.3)	32 (91.4)
1	10 (28.6)	7 (20.0)	6 (17.1)	2 (5.7)	4 (11.4)	1 (2.9)	3 (8.6)
2	2 (5.7)	4 (11.4)	3 (8.6)	1 (2.9)	2	1 (2.9)	0
3	0	0	2 (5.7)	0	0	0	0
Total	35	35	35	35	35	35	35

Note. [a] : (%) = number of students/ 35

Table 4.15

Direct CF Group Students' Aggregate Performance in Accuracy in the Delayed-posttest ($n = 35$)

Number of Errors	Sva (%)[a]	Plural (%)	Verb (%)	Article (%)	Tense (%)	Prep. (%)	Pos. (%)
0	15 (42.9)	26 (74.3)	30 (85.7)	33 (94.3)	31 (88.6)	33 (94.3)	33 (94.3)
1	11 (31.4)	4 (11.4)	4 (11.4)	2 (5.97)	4 (11.4)	1 (2.9)	2 (5.7)
2	5 (14.3)	2 (5.7)	0	0	0	1 (2.9)	0
3	4 (11.4)	2 (5.7)	1 (2.9)	0	0	0	0
4	0	1 (2.9)	0	0	0	0	0
Total	35	35	35	35	35	35	35

Note. [a] : (%) = number of students/ 35

Table 4.13, 4.14 and 4.15 present the Direct CF students' aggregate performance with regard to frequency of different error types that occurred in the three tests. The majority of students in the Direct CF group tended to make fewer errors after the treatment from the pretest to the delayed posttest. For example, 71.4% of students made errors in plurals in the pretest, and it dropped to 31.4% in the posttest and 25.7% in the delayed posttest, which was a considerable 40% decrease from the pretest to the delayed posttest. 34.3% of students made verb errors in the pretest, then it dropped to 31.4% in the posttest and 14.3% in the delayed posttest. Almost a 40% dramatic decrease was shown from the pretest (45.7%) and the posttest (8.6%) to the delayed posttest (5.7%) in the frequency of article errors. 28.6% of students made errors on tense and this dropped to 17.1% in the posttest and 11.4% in the delayed posttest. In addition, 31.4% of students made errors in parts of speech and this dropped noticeably to 8.6% in the posttest and 5.7% in the delayed posttest. There was also a noticeable drop for prepositional errors—from 37.1% in the pretest to 5.7% in the posttest and the delayed posttest. An exception to this trend was subject-verb agreement errors, which 68.6% of students made in the pretest. This dropped to 34.3% in the posttest but unexpectedly raised to 57.1% in the delayed posttest. The increased percentage indicated more students paid attention to or attempted to correct their errors but may not truly consciously processed or successfully uptook the direct corrective feedback.

4.1.4 Descriptive Statistics for Across Group Comparison.

Table 4.16 presents the means and standard deviations of the total number of errors for the three groups during the three treatments. Table 4.17 displays the means and standard deviations of the normed frequencies in the pretest, posttest, and delayed posttest for the three groups, which helped control for the effect of text length in the tests. Figure 4.10 is the visual representation of the normed frequencies of error rates across the three treatments in the three groups.

Table 4. 16

Mean and Standard Deviationof the Raw Count for Corrective Feedback by Group in the Pretest ,Posttest ,and Delayed-posttest

Group[a]	Pretest		Posttest		Delayed posttest		N
	M	S	M	S	M	S	
ICF	5. 26	3. 29	2. 23	1. 83	1. 83	1. 77	35
FC	1. 89	1. 95	1. 66	1. 83	0. 97	1. 82	35
DCF	5. 71	4. 19	1. 86	1. 93	1. 97	2. 38	35
Total	4. 29	3. 67	1. 91	1. 86	1. 59	2. 04	105

Note. [a]: ICF = Indirect Corrective Feedback Group; FC = Feedback on Content Group; DCF = Direct Corrective Feedback Group

Table 4. 17

Mean and Standard Deviation of Normed Frequencies for Corrective Feedback by Group in the Pretest ,Posttest ,and Delayed-posttest

Group[a]	Pretest		Posttest		Delayed posttest		N
	M	S	M	S	M	S	
ICF	16. 5	10. 98	7. 3	7. 35	6. 1	5. 91	35
FC	11. 0	13. 45	8. 8	10. 30	5. 6	10. 76	35
DCF	18. 2	14. 08	6. 0	6. 44	6. 5	7. 84	35
Total	15. 2	13. 15	7. 4	8. 20	6. 0	8. 34	105

Note. [a]: ICF = Indirect Corrective Feedback Group; FC = Feedback on Content Group; DCF = Direct Corrective Feedback Group

As shown in Figure 4. 10 , there was a considerable initial decrease of error rates from the pretest to the posttest for both Indirect CF and Direct CF group students. The difference was that after the initial decrease , the Direct CF group was followed by a very slight increase in the error rates in the delayed posttest while the Indirect CF group was followed by a continued decrease in the error rates in the delayed posttest. For students who received feedback on content , there was a slight initial decrease in the error rate from the pretest to the posttest , followed by another slight

Error Rates

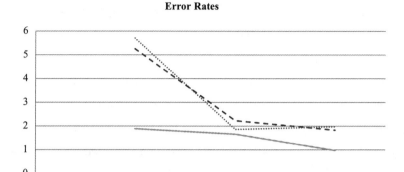

Figure 4. 10 **Mean of error rates of the three groups in the three tests**

decrease in the delayed posttest. Therefore, according to the raw number of errors, it can be concluded that both the Indirect CF and Direct CF had a great degree of error reduction in general. On the other hand, the Indirect CF group and FC group showed a constant decrease of errors in general. In other words, the Indirect CF is the group who showed not only continuous error reduction but also a more consistent decrease. Furthermore, Figure 4. 11 shows student errors per word in their writing, and displays an overall developmental trend for the three groups, which does not differ from the trend in Figure 4. 10.

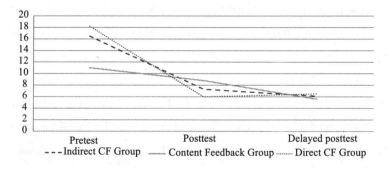

Figure 4. 11 **Mean of normed frequencies of error rates of the three groups in the three tests**

Figure 4. 12 below (on p. 110-111) shows a comparison based on the normed frequencies among the three groups for each of the seven most frequent error types. The majority of errors emerged in relation to subject-verb agreement and plurals for all three groups, indicating students either attempted to use those feature most often or had more difficulties in processing these two grammatical forms. Prepositional and part of speech errors appeared to be least frequently error types for all three groups, indicating students were either less favorable toward the use of the two grammatical features in writing or had less difficulties with the two features. By looking at each error type for their developmental trend within the three groups, it appears interestingly in the figure that seven error types exhibited seven distinguished developmental patterns. For the pattern of subject-verb agreement, the two experimental (CF) groups started with more errors than the control (FC) group on subject-verb agreement in the pretest, which then dropped below the number of the errors the FC group committed in the posttest. Finally, errors in all the three groups slightly picked up in the delayed posttest, in which the Direct CF group had more errors, the FC group in the middle, and the Indirect CF group made the smallest number of errors. Errors in all three groups in the delayed posttest were less frequent than the errors in the pretest.

Regarding errors on plural, the FC group started with the most errors in the pretest. However, it showed an unexpected and near-perfect linear decrease across the three tests. The two CF groups exhibited a considerable drop from the pretest to posttest as well, followed by a slight increase in the delayed posttest, which were still far below the number of errors in the pretest. For errors on tense, the Indirect CF group showed a noticeable drop from the pretest to the posttest, followed by a parallel development with little change, and the Direct CF group had a straight decrease across the tests. Although the FC group had a slight decrease from the pretest to the posttest, no great changes were identified impressionistically as the

difference of normed frequencies between the pretest and posttest was only
0.4 for the mean. With regard to article errors, both the Indirect CF and
Direct CF group displayed a continued error reduction across the three tests
while the FC group did not give an impression of great change from the
pretest to the delayed posttest. With respect to the verb errors and
prepositional errors, the Indirect CF group and the FC group showed the
same developmental curves(i. e. , an upside-down V shape), which were an
initial increase followed by a decrease across the three tests. The Direct CF
group showed a nearly linear decrease on verb errors and a considerable
decrease followed by a stable development on preposition errors across the
three tests. Additionally, it is interesting to note that errors on part of
speech for all three groups showed a noticeable drop over time.

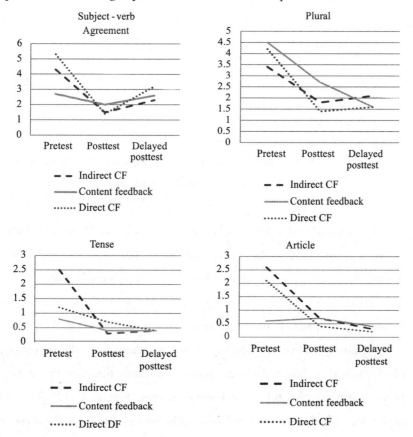

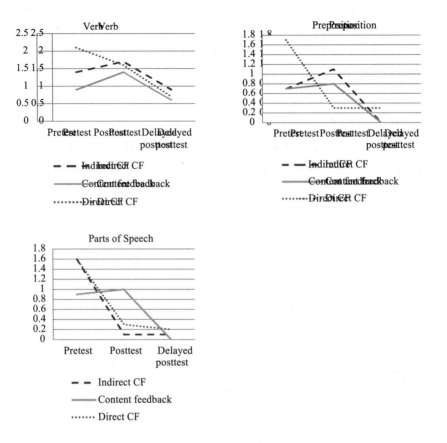

Figure 4. 12 **Comparison across the three groups for each seven primary errors by means of normed frequencies**

To sum up, the developmental patterns shown in the FC group for most the error types (i. e. , subject-verb agreement, tense, article, and verb) showed either a V- shape or an upside-down V-shape without great increase or decrease over time; while the upside-down V-shape pattern for preposition and parts of speech showed a greater decrease from the posttest to the delayed posttest. In addition, errors on plural were the exception, which showed a linear decrease across the three tests for the control group. Regarding the two experimental groups, Figure 4. 12 gives an impression of both a constant and noticeable decrease for six of the seven of the primary error types in the two groups, including subject-verb agreement, plural, tense, article, preposition, and part of speech. The developmental pattern for verb errors was the exception for the Indirect CF group, which as previously mentioned had an initial increase and final decrease as the FC group did. Hence, the data suggest that all three types of feedback—indirect corrective feedback, content feedback and direct corrective feedback could be successful to a certain extent in improving students' writing accuracy over time. As displayed in the figures, it seems that subject-verb agreement, tense, article, preposition, and parts of speech were more likely to be positively affected by indirect CF. Direct CF worked more effectively for subject-verb agreement, plural, article, verb, preposition and parts of speech. FC also affected students' production on plural, preposition and parts of speech.

4.1.5 Inferential Statistics for Within Group Comparisons on Overall Errors.

Paired Samples T-Tests were conducted to see if each group had statistically significant changes regarding both the normed frequencies of errors rates students produced from the pretest to posttest, from the posttest to delayed posttest as well as from the pretest to delayed posttest. Table 4. 18, 4. 19, and 4. 20 below present statistics for the Indirect CF group, the FC group; and the Direct CF group.

As shown in Table 4. 18, a significant decrease was found in the Indirect CF group from the pretest to posttest ($t = 4.08, 34\ df, p = .00, p < .05$) with a medium effect size (Cohen's $d = .44$) and from the pretest to delayed posttest ($t = 4.35, 34\ df, p = .00, p < .05$) with a medium to large effect size (Cohen's $d = .51$), indicating a significant effect of time on indirect CF in students' performance on writing.

Table 4. 18

Paired Samples T-Test for Corrective Feedback in Indirect CF Group in the Pretest, Posttest, and Delayed-posttest (n = 35)[a]

Treatment[b]	M	SD	95% Confidence Interval of the Difference		t	df	Sig. (2-tailed)	Cohen's d
			Lower	Upper				
1-2	9. 18	13. 29	4. 61	13. 74	4. 08 *	34	. 00 *	. 44
2-3	1. 2	8. 78	-1. 81	4. 22	. 81	34	. 42	. 09
1-3	10. 38	14. 13	5. 53	15. 23	4. 35 *	34	. 00 *	. 51

Note. [a]: statistics are calculated based on normed frequencies (number of errors/ total number of words * 1000) of errors. * $p <$. 05 ; [b]: Treatment 1 = pretest, Treatment 2 = posttest, Treatment 3 = delayed posttest.

Concerning the changesof the error rates in the FC group in terms of the three treatments, Table 4. 19 shows that there was no statistical significance found in FC group from the pretest to posttest (t = . 95, 34 df, p = . 35, p > . 05) and from the posttest to delayed posttest (t = 1. 54, 34 df, p = . 13, p > . 05). However, a significant decrease did occur in the FC group from the pretest to delayed posttest (t = 2. 15, 34 df, p = . 04, p < . 05). Although the effect size was small (Cohen's d = . 22), this implies as well that a significant effect of time existed on content feedback in FC group students' performance on writing.

Table 4. 19

Paired Samples T-Test for Feedback in FC Group in the Pretest, Posttest, and Delayed-posttest (n = 35)[a]

Treatment[b]	M	SD	95% Confidence Interval of the Difference		t	df	Sig. (2-tailed)	Cohen's d
			Lower	Upper				
1-2	2. 24	13. 93	-2. 54	7. 03	. 95	34	. 35	. 09
2-3	3. 27	12. 59	-1. 05	7. 60	1. 54	34	. 13	. 15
1-3	5. 51	15. 19	. 30	10. 673	2. 15 *	34	. 04 *	. 22

Note. [a]: statistics are calculated based on normed frequencies (number of errors/ total number of words * 1000) of errors. * $p <$. 05 ; [b]: Treatment 1 = pretest, Treatment 2 = posttest, Treatment 3 = delayed posttest.

Table 4. 20

Paired Samples T-Test for Corrective Feedback in Direct CF Group in the Pretest, Posttest, and Delayed-posttest (n = 35) [a]

Treatment[b]	M	SD	95% Confidence Interval of the Difference		t	df	Sig. (2-tailed)	Cohen's d
			Lower	Upper				
1-2	12. 22	11. 93	8. 12	16. 31	6. 06 *	34	. 00 *	. 49
2-3	-. 48	8. 78	-3. 50	2. 53	-. 33	34	. 75	-. 03
1-3	11. 73	13. 95	6. 94	16. 52	4. 98 *	34	. 00 *	. 46

Note. [a]: statistics are calculated based on normed frequencies (number of errors/ total number of words * 1000) of errors. * $p < . 05$; [b]: Treatment 1 = pretest, Treatment 2 = posttest, Treatment 3 = delayed posttest.

In addition, as shown in Table 4. 20, as the same to the Indirect CF group, a decrease in the Direct CF group turned out to be significant from the pretest to posttest ($t = 6. 06, 34$ $df, p = . 00, p < . 05$) with a medium effect size (*Cohen's d* $= . 49$) and from the posttest to delayed posttest ($t = 4. 98, 34$ $df, p = . 00, p < . 05$) with a medium effect size (*Cohen's d* $= . 46$), indicating that there was a significant effect of time on direct CF for students' performance on writing.

4. 1. 6　Inferential statistics for within group comparisons on individual errors.

Table 4. 21 below summarizes the changes for each of the seven error types in Indirect CF group. As displayed, a significant time effect with a small to medium effect size was clearly shown on subject-verb agreement, plural, article, tense, preposition, and part of speech. In other words, verb error was the only error type that was not affected by indirect CF. To be specific, the decrease of errors on subject-verb agreement ($t = 3. 19, 34$ df, $p = . 00, p < . 05$) and plural ($t = 2. 29, 34$ $df, p = . 03, p < . 05$) was statistically significant from the pretest to posttest. The decrease for article ($t = 2. 73, 34$ $df, p = . 01, p < . 05$; $t = 3. 59, 34$ $df, p = . 00, p < . 05$), tense

$(t = 3.47, 34 \ df, p = .00, p < .05; \ t = 3.17, 34df, p = .00, p < .05)$, and parts of speech errors $(t = 2.88, 34 \ df, p = .0, p < .05; \ t = 2.82, 34 \ df, p = .01, p < .05;)$ was also significant from both the pretest to posttest and from the pretest to delayed posttest. In addition, the decrease for prepositional errors from the posttest to delayed posttest $(t = 2.94, 34 \ df, p = .01, p < .05)$ and from the pretest to delayed posttest $(t = 3.05, 34 \ df, p = .00, p < .05)$ was significant as well. At this point, it could suggests that the significant level of improvement achieved regarding specific grammatical errors in Indirect CF group student writing accuracy can be possibly contributed to the indirect corrective feedback they received over time.

Table 4.21

Paired Samples T-Test for Individual Error Types in the Indirect CF Group across the Three Tests ($n = 35$) [a]

Error type	Treatment [b]	M	SD	95% Confidence Interval of the Difference		t	df	Sig. (2-tailed)	Cohen's d
				Lower	Upper				
Subject-	1 - 2	2.84	5.27	1.03	4.65	3.19 *	34	.00 *	.33
verb agr-	2 - 3	-.84	4.33	-2.33	.65	-1.15	34	.26	.12
eement	1 - 3	1.20	6.41	-.21	4.20	1.84	34	.07	.23
Plural	1 - 2	1.60	4.14	.18	3.02	2.29 *	34	.03 *	.25
	2 - 3	-.23	5.07	-1.97	1.51	-.26	34	.79	.05
	1 - 3	1.38	5.30	-.45	3.20	1.54	34	.13	.17
Verb	1 - 2	-.35	3.20	-1.45	.75	-.65	34	.52	.06
	2 - 3	.30	2.83	-.17	1.78	1.68	34	.10	.18
	1 - 3	.45	3.28	-.68	.1.58	.81	34	.42	.10
Article	1 - 2	1.83	3.98	.47	3.20	2.73 *	34	.01 *	.32
	2 - 3	.48	1.91	-.18	1.13	1.47	34	.15	.16
	1 - 3	2.31	3.81	1.00	3.62	3.59 *	34	.00 *	.39
Tense	1 - 2	2.17	3.70	.90	3.44	3.47 *	34	.00 *	.40
	2 - 3 -	-.13	1.85	-.77	.50	-.42	34	.68	.04
	1 - 3	2.04	3.81	.73	3.35	3.17 *	34	.00 *	.37
Preposition	1 - 2	-.42	2.37	-1.24	.39	-1.05	34	.30	.17
	2 - 3	1.14	2.3	.35	1.93	2.94 *	34	.01 *	.33
	1 - 3	.72	1.4	.24	1.20	3.05 *	34	.00 *	.32

								(Contd.)
Error type	Treatment[b]	M	SD	95% Confidence Interval of the Difference		t	df	Sig. (2 - tailed)	Cohen's d
				Lower	Upper				

Error type	Treatment[b]	M	SD	Lower	Upper	t	df	Sig. (2-tailed)	Cohen's d
Parts of speech	1 – 2	1. 50	3. 09	. 44	2. 57	2. 88 *	34	. 01 *	. 41
	2 – 3	-. 02	. 82	-. 30	. 26	-. 14	34	. 89	. 00
	1 – 3	1. 49	3. 12	. 41	2. 56	2. 82 *	34	. 01 *	. 41

Note. [a]: statistics are calculated based on normed frequencies (number of errors / total number of words * 1000) of errors. * p < .05; [b]: Treatment 1 = pretest, Treatment 2 = posttest, Treatment 3 = delayed posttest.

Table 4. 22 below shows the statistics of the change for each of the seven error types by the FC group. As can be seen, no significant time effect of FC on the error rates ever appeared except for in plural errors (t = 2. 17, 34 df, p = .04, p < .05) with a small effect size ($Cohen's d$ = .25) from the pretest to delayed posttest. In other words, plural was the only error pattern for FC group that could be affected by FC in their writing.

Table 4. 22

Paired Samples T-Test for Individual Error Types in FC Group across the Three Tests (n =35)[a]

Error type	Treatment[b]	M	SD	95% Confidence Interval of the Difference		t	df	Sig. (2-tailed)
				Lower	Upper			
Subject-verb agreement	1-2	. 67	4. 79	. 97	2. 32	. 83	34	. 41
	2-3	-. 57	5. 77	-2. 55	1. 41	-. 59	34	. 56
	1-3	-. 10	5. 89	-1. 92	2. 13	. 10	34	. 92
Plural	1-2	1. 80	7. 36	-. 73	2. 13	1. 45	34	. 16
	2-3	1. 08	4. 51	-. 47	4. 33	1. 42	34	. 17
	1-3	2. 88	7. 88	. 18	2. 63	2. 17 *	34	. 04 *c
Verb	1-2	-. 52	2. 60	-1. 41	. 37	-1. 19	34	. 24
	2-3	. 83	3. 76	-. 46	2. 12	1. 30	34	. 20
	1-3	. 31	3. 58	-. 92	1. 54	. 51	34	. 62

(Contd.)

Error type	Treatment[b]	M	SD	95% Confidence Interval of the Difference		t	df	Sig. (2-tailed)
				Lower	Upper			
Article	1-2	-.17	2.77	-1.12	.79	-.35	34	.73
	2-3	.39	3.68	-.88	1.65	.62	34	.54
	1-3	.22	2.34	-.58	1.03	.56	34	.58
Tense	1-2	.39	2.58	-.50	1.27	.89	34	.38
	2-3	-.00	2.22	-.76	.76	-.00	34	1.00
	1-3	.39	2.17	-.36	1.13	1.06	34	.30
Prep.	1-2	-.04	3.60	-1.27	1.20	-.06	34	.95
	2-3	.75	2.22	-.01	1.52	2.01	34	.05
	1-3	.72	2.62	-.18	1.62	1.62	34	.12
Parts of speech	1-2	-.11	5.39	-1.19	1.74	-.13	34	.90
	2-3	1.01	3.98	-.36	2.38	1.50	34	.14
	1-3	.90	3.36	-.26	2.05	1.58	34	.12

Note. [a]: statistics are calculated based on normed frequencies (number of errors / total number of words $*$ 1000) of errors. $* p < .05.$ [b]: Treatment 1 = pretest, Treatment 2 = posttest, Treatment 3 = delayed posttest. [c]: Cohen's d = .25.

Table 4.23 below presents the statistics of the change for each of the seven error types in Direct CF group. As shown, a significant time effect of direct CF with a small to medium effect size on errors rates was observed on five error patterns, including subject-verb agreement($t = 3.59, 34$ $df, p = .00, p < .05$; $t = -2.57, 34$ $df, p = .02, p < .05$), plural($t = 3.49,$ 34 $df, p = .00, p < .05$; $t = 2.84, 34$ $df, p = .01, p < .05$), article ($t = 3.75, 34$ $df, p = .00, p < .05$; $t = 4.17, 34$ $df, p = .00, p < .05$), preposition($t = 2.90, 34$ $df, p = .01, p < .05$; $t = 2.97, 34$ $df,$ $p = .01, p < .05$) and parts of speech($t = 2.12, 34$ $df, p = .04, p < .05$; $t = 2.24, 34$ $df, p = .03, p < .05$). However, errors on verb and tense did not reach statistical significance, indicating that the two grammatical forms were not likely to be affected by direct CF on student writing accuracy.

Table 4. 23

Paired Samples T-Test for Individual Error Types in Direct CF Group across the Three Tests (*n* = 35)^a

Error type	Treatment[b]	M	SD	95% Confidence Interval of the Difference		t	df	Sig. (2-tailed)	Cohen's d
				Lower	Upper				
Subject-	1-2	3. 92	6. 47	1. 70	6. 14	3. 59 *	34	. 00 *	. 35
verb agr-	2-3	-1. 80	4. 14	-3. 22	-. 38	-2. 57 *	34	. 02 *	. 29
eement	1-3	2. 12	6. 63	-. 16	4. 40	1. 89	34	. 07	. 19
	1-2	2. 80	4. 73	1. 17	4. 4	3. 49 *	34	. 00 *	. 38
Plural	2-3	-. 13	3. 83	-1. 44	1. 19	-. 20	34	. 85	. 04
	1-3	2. 67	5. 57	. 76	4. 58	2. 84 *	34	. 01 *	. 33
Verb	1-2	. 53	5. 16	-1. 24	2. 31	. 61	34	. 54	. 06
	2-3	. 94	3. 72	-. 33	2. 22	1. 50	34	. 14	. 18
	1-3	1. 48	4. 58	-. 10	3. 05	1. 91 *	34	. 07	. 19
Article	1-2	1. 71	2. 7	. 78	2. 64	3. 75 *	34	. 00 *	. 38
	2-3	. 14	1. 7	-. 44	. 73	. 50	34	. 62	. 09
	1-3	1. 85	2. 63	. 95	2. 76	4. 17 *	34	. 00 *	. 44
Tense	1-2	. 46	2. 57	-. 43	1. 34	1. 05	34	. 30	. 13
	2-3	. 30	1. 84	-. 29	. 97	1. 09	34	. 28	. 23
	1-3	. 80	2. 47	-. 05	1. 65	1. 91	34	. 07	. 10
Prep.	1-2	1. 42	2. 89	. 42	2. 41	2. 90 *	34	. 01 *	. 34
	2-3	-. 03	1. 73	-. 63	. 56	-. 12	34	. 91	. 00
	1-3	1. 38	2. 76	. 44	2. 33	2. 97 *	34	. 01 *	. 34
Parts of speech	1-2	1. 38	4. 00	. 01	2. 78	2. 12 *	34	. 04 *	. 23
	2-3	. 05	1. 26	-. 38	. 48	. 24	34	. 81	. 06
	1-3	1. 43	3. 81	-. 13	2. 74	2. 24 *	34	. 03 *	. 25

Note. ^a: statistics are calculated based on normed frequencies (number of errors/ total number of words * 1000) of errors. * $p < $. 05; ^b: Treatment 1 = pretest, Treatment 2 = posttest, Treatment 3 = delayed posttest.

In summary, all the three groups showed an effect of time on the treatment for students' writing accuracy from the pretest to the delayed posttest. The Indirect CF and Direct CF group also obtained significant changes from the pretest to the posttest. In addition, no significant changes were achieved from the posttest to delayed-posttest by all the three groups.

According to the effect size, the two types of corrective feedback worked more effectively in improving students' writing accuracy compared to the feedback on content. Comparing the two types of corrective feedback, indirect corrective feedback functioned somewhat more successfully than direct corrective feedback. Moreover, by examining the effectiveness of feedback on accuracy concerning each of the seven primary error types, both the Indirect and Direct Corrective Feedback group committed fewer errors in subject-verb agreement, plural, article, preposition and parts of speech, indicating the two types of CF worked effectively for certain error types. Tense was the only grammatical pattern that can be positively affected by indirect corrective feedback, and verb was the only grammatical form that was not disposed to be influenced by any of three types of feedback. It was also interesting to note that all types of feedback seemed to have an effect on plural error rates (i. e. , not only the indirect and direct corrective feedback but also the content feedback produced a significance).

4. 1. 7   Inferential Statistics for Across Group Comparisons on Overall Errors.

One-way ANOVA was calculated to see if the three groups were significantly different in the pretest, posttest and delayed-posttest. Table 4. 24 below demonstrates the results of the ANOVA for different types of feedback by treatment group. As can be seen, there was no statistical significance for group effect obtained across the three tests. Thus, the null hypothesis of no group differences was not rejected at this point. This also indicates that the Indirect CF and Direct CF group which received different types of corrective feedback did not outperform the FC group which received content feedback in their performance on writing accuracy.

Table 4. 24

ANOVA Summary Table of the Overall Errors by Group in the Pretest, Posttest, and Delayed-posttest (n = 35)[a]

Treatment	Source	SS	df	MS	F	Sig.
Pretest	Between groups	984. 63	2	492. 31	2. 96	. 05
	Within Groups	16992. 67	102	166. 60		
	Total	17977. 29	104			
Posttest	Between groups	135. 442	2	67. 72	1. 01	. 37
	Within Groups	6854. 52	102	67. 20		
	Total	6989. 96	104			
Delayed posttest	Between groups	16. 84	2	8. 42	. 12	. 89
	Within Groups	7215. 57	102	70. 74		
	Total	7232. 41	104			

Note. [a]: statistics are conducted based on normed frequencies (number of errors/ total number of words ∗ 1000) of errors. ∗ $p <$. 05.

4. 1. 8   Inferential Statistics for Across Group Comparison on Individual Errors.

In order to examine if the changes across the three essays regarding each of the seven most frequent errors are statistically significant, a series of one-way ANOVAs were conducted to evaluate the seven individual error types. Table 4. 25, 4. 26 and 4. 27 summarize the results of ANOVA for the three groups in the pretest, posttest, and delayed posttest.

Table 4. 25

Summary Table of One-Way ANOVA for Seven Individual Error Patterns by Group in the Pretest

Error type	Source	SS	df	MS	F	Sig.
Sva	Between groups	119. 14	2	59. 57	2. 01	. 14
	Within Groups	3019. 38	102	29. 60		
	Total	3138. 51	104			
Plural	Between groups	19. 86	2	9. 93	. 37	. 69
	Within Groups	2726. 69	102	26. 73		
	Total	2746. 55	104			

(Contd.)

Error type	Source	SS	df	MS	F	Sig.
Verb	Between groups	28.46	2	14.23	1.22	.30
	Within Groups	1187.21	102	11.64		
	Total	1215.67	104			
Article	Between groups	75.58	2	37.79	4.87*	
	Within Groups	790.83	102	7.75		.01*
	Total	866.40	104			
Tense	Between groups	53.75	2	26.87	3.91*	.02*
	Within Groups	701.71	102	6.88		
	Total	755.46	104			
Prep.	Between groups	20.97	2	10.49	2.09	.13
	Within Groups	511.06	102	5.01		
	Total	532.03	104			
Pos.	Between groups	12.05	2	6.03	.52	.60
	Within Groups	1179.80	102	11.57		
	Total	1191.85	104			

Note. [a] : statistics are conducted based on normed frequencies (number of errors/ total number of words ∗ 1000) of errors. ∗ $p <$ .05.

Table 4.26

Summary Table of One-Way ANOVA for Seven Individual Error Patterns by Group in the Posttest

Error type	Source	SS	df	MS	F	Sig.
Sva.	Between groups	8.97	2	13.44	1.53	.22
	Within Groups	917.09	102	8.80		
	Total	926.06	104			
Plural	Between groups	26.88	2	.18	.33	.72
	Within Groups	897.65	102	.55		
	Total	924.53	104			
Verb	Between groups	1.86	2	.93	.14	.87
	Within Groups	680.84	102	6.68		
	Total	682.70	104			
Article	Between groups	3.46	2	1.73	.35	.71
	Within Groups	511.83	102	5.02		
	Total	515.30	104			
Tense	Between groups	3.43	2	1.71	.86	.43
	Within Groups	202.65	102	1.99		
	Total	206.08	104			

(Contd.)

Error type	Source	SS	df	MS	F	Sig.
Prep.	Between groups	14. 00	2	7. 00	1. 83	. 17
	Within Groups	391. 33	102	3. 84		
	Total	405. 33	104			
Pos.	Between groups	16. 97	2	8. 48	1. 51	. 23
	Within Groups	573. 31	102	5. 62		
	Total	590. 27	104			

Note. ᵃ : statistics are conducted based on normed frequencies (number of errors/ total number of words * 1000) of errors. *p < . 05.

Table 4. 27

Summary Table of One-Way ANOVA for Seven Individual Error Patterns by Group in the Delayed-posttest

Error type	Source	SS	df	MS	F	Sig.
Sva.	Between groups	13. 72	2	6. 86	. 40	. 67
	Within Groups	1745. 19	102	17. 11		
	Total	1758. 91	104			
Plural	Between groups	5. 82	2	2. 91	. 21	. 81
	Within Groups	1411. 80	102	13. 84		
	Total	1417. 63	104			
Verb	Between groups	2. 24	2	1. 12	. 24	. 79
	Within Groups	475. 41	102	4. 66		
	Total	477. 65	104			
Article	Between groups	. 36	2	. 18	. 14	. 87
	Within Groups	132. 31	102	1. 30		
	Total	132. 67	104			
Tense	Between groups	. 04	2	. 02	. 01	. 99
	Within Groups	208. 51	102	2. 04		
	Total	206. 08	104			
Prep.	Between groups	1. 88	2	. 94	1. 82	. 17
	Within Groups	52. 63	102	. 52		
	Total	54. 51	104			
Pos.	Between groups	. 75	2	. 37	1. 00	. 37
	Within Groups	38. 24	102	. 338		
	Total	38. 97	104			

Note. ᵃ : statistics are conducted based on normed frequencies (number of errors/ total number of words * 1000) of errors. *p < . 05.

As shown, the statistical significance of group effect was only obtained in article errors and tense errors on the pretest. A Post Hoc test was further conducted and detected significant differences for errors with article and tense between the Indirect CF and the FC group and between the Indirect CF and the Direct CF group, which is shown in Table 4.28. Significant differences were also identified on tense errors between the Indirect CF group and the Direct CF group, as well as between the FC group and the Direct CF group.

Table 4.28
Summary Table of Post Hoc Test for Subject-verb Agreement, Article, Tense and Preposition in the Pretest

Error type	Pairs ofGroup	Sig.
Article	Indirect CF- FC	.00 *
	Indirect CF- Direct CF	.04 *
Tense	Indirect CF- FC	.01 *
	FC - Direct CF	.03 *

$*p < .05$

Chapter 5: Mixed Methods Results

This chapter examined RQ2, including questions "which component among grammar, content, and organization do students value the most in their understanding of effective feedback? How do students evaluate their own potential for improving their writing ability? What expectations do students have of grammar corrections in their writing? And how do students' perceptions and preferences vary between different groups?" All 105 students from the three groups participated and responded to the questions in the two questionnaires. Analysis of the 105 students' responses from the three groups to each of the questions in the two questionnaires are presented and discussed in detail. Table 5.1 and Table 5.2 review the questions in Questionnaire 1 and Questionnaire 2.

Table 5.1

Review of Q1-Q5 in Questionnaire 1

---

1. In English classes you have taken before, have you ever learned any English grammar rules?

   Yes, a lot   Yes, but few   No

   If yes, what? _____

   If no, why? _____

2. Have you ever received feedback from teachers?

   Yes, a lot   Yes, but few   No

   If yes, what? _____

   If no, why? _____

3. Do you think teacher feedback is helpful?

   Yes, very helpful   Yes, but not much   No

(Contd.)

4. Do you worry about making mistakes in writing or your language class?

Yes, a lot   Yes, but few   No

5. How do you feel about your English language use, especially grammar, in writing?

Very good   Good   bad

Table 5. 2

Review of Q1-Q10 in Questionnaire 2

1. What is the best way for your English teacher to give feedback on your writing?

Feedback on grammar   feedback on content   feedback on organization   none of these

If others, what is it? _____

2. What is the best way for your English teacher to give feedback about your grammatical errors in your writing?

Direct correction   underline or circle   description and explanation   none of these

If others, what is it? _____

3. What is the easiest way for you to correct your errors?

Direct correction   underline or circle   description and explanation   none of these

If others, what is it? _____

4. Which type of corrective feedback do you think you can learn the most from?

Direct correction   underline or circle   description and explanation   none of these

If others, what is it? _____

5. Whytype of corrective feedback do you like most?

Direct correction   underline or circle   description and explanation   none of these

If others, what is it? _____

6. Do you like the current type of corrective feedback you received from the researcher?

Very much   mostly   a little   not at all

7. Do you understand the type of corrective feedback you received from the researcher?

Very much   mostly   a little   not at all

8. Do you feel discouraged about the correction?

Very much   mostly   a little   not at all

9. Do you think you will apply the correction to your future writing?

Very much   mostly   a little   not at all

(Contd.)

---

10. What did you think or what did you do after you received your writing with feedback from the researcher?

I was eagerly to see the errors I made and wanted to correct the errors immediately because I really wanted to improve my English writing.

I was thinking about the reasons why I made the errors, but I did not know how to correct them and revise my writing.

I just left it on my desk and did not want to look at or revise it.

I believed that I wish I had not written anything.

5.1   Results for Questionnaire 1

5.1.1   Responses from Indirect CF Group.

Table 5.3 presents descriptive statistics of the Indirect CF group students' responses to Questionnaire 1. The table reports the average score for each item in Questionnaire 1 and gives us an idea of how much variability is in the data. All the questions in Questionnaire 1 have three levels of choices, which could respectively reflect students' positive, neutral, or negative points of view toward their English learning background and experiences. Three points were marked for students who chose the positive side, 77two points were given to students who chose the neutral one, and one point was offered to students who chose the negative answer.

Table 5.3

Descriptive Statistics of the Results for Questionnaire 1 in Indirect CF Group ($n = 35$)

Item	M	SD	Min	Max	Skewness	Kurtosis
Q1	2.63	.49	2	3	-.56	-1.80
Q2	2.40	.55	1	3	-.13	-.93

(Contd.)

Item	M	SD	Min	Max	Skewness	Kurtosis
Q3	2. 71	. 52	1	3	-1. 64	2. 00
Q4	2. 03	. 75	1	3	. 05	-1. 15
Q5	1. 46	. 56	1	3	. 71	-. 53
Total	2. 25	. 74	1	3	-. 43	-1. 06

As shown in Table 5. 3, students' overall responses to the five questions were towards the positive spectrum (M = 2. 25). If looking at the questions individually, students' responses to Q1, Q2, Q3, and Q4, as indicated by the mean (M = 2. 63, 2. 40, 2. 71, 2. 03), showed their positive attitudes towards their English learning experiences. In contrast, students' responses to Q5 (M = 1. 46) indicated that most students hold a negative view towards their English language learning ability and use.

Table 5. 4

Frequencies of the Five Items in Questionnaire 1 *for Indirect CF Group* (n = 35)

Item/%	Q1	Q2	Q3	Q4	Q5
Positive	62. 9	42. 9	74. 3	28. 6	2. 9
Neutral	37. 1	54. 3	22. 9	45. 7	40. 0
Negative	0	2. 9	2. 9	25. 7	57. 1
Total	100	100	100	100	100

Table 5. 4 displays the percentage of student responses for each of the five items. As seen, for Q1, all the students had previous English grammar learning experiences. 37. 1% of students learned very few English grammar rules and most of the students (62. 9%) learned more in their previous L2 learning experiences. For Q2, only 2. 9% of students indicated that they did not receive any feedback from teachers in their previous English learning experiences; more than half of the students (54. 3%) received

more feedback from teachers before; and 42.9% students received less from teachers. For Q3, only 1 student thought feedback was not helpful; 22.9% of students thought feedback had a positive effect on their learning, but limited; the majority of the students (74.3%) regarded feedback as very beneficial. For Q4, 71.4% of the students worried about making mistakes when using English. Only a small portion of students (28.6%) did not think using English was a problem for them. For Q5, less than half of the students (42.95%) had confidence in their use of grammar in writing. Among the 42.95%, only one student thought his/her English grammar was very good. The rest of the students, which was more than half (57.1%), thought their English grammar was even bad in writing.

Table 5.5

Correlation between Error Rates across the Three Tests and Students' Attitudes in Questionnaire 1 for Indirect CF Group

Sig.	Q1	Q2	Q3	Q4	Q5
Pretest	.88	.72	.31	.91	.15
Posttest	.01 *a	.15	1.00	.91	49
Delayed-posttest	.44	.37	.24	.44	.85

Note. a: Pearson correlation = -.42.

Table 5.6

Correlation between Error Reduction across the Three Tests and Students' Attitudes in Questionnaire 1 for Indirect CF Group

Sig.	Q1	Q2	Q3	Q4	Q5
Pre _ Post	.23	.62	.40	.88	.43
Pos _ Delayed	.14	.55	.44	.54	.65
Pre _ Delayed	84	.92	.20	.81	.31

Table 5.5 shows the results of correlation between students' attitudes

and their performance in writing accuracy overtime. Table 5.6 displays the correlation between students' responses and error reduction across the three tests. As clearly shown, correlation was not found to be significant at $p < .05$. In other words, there was no significant evidence to conclude that there exists a relationship between students' attitudes and their error rates as well as between students' attitudes and their error reduction in writing. However, an exception happened to the correlation between students' responses to Q1 and the error rates in the posttest, although it did not reveal a strength of the tendency as indicated by the value r (-.42). The r squared of the relationship indicated that 17.6% of the variability in students' accuracy performance can be accounted for by students' prior English grammar learning experiences. It seems like the more students learned English grammar, the fewer errors they tended to make.

Table 5.7

Correlation between the Five Items in Questionnaire 1 for Indirect CF Group

	Pearson Correlation	*Sig.*
Q1 & Q2	.46	.01 *
Q3 & Q4	.40	.02 *
Q4 & Q5	-.39	.02 *

If looking at the correlations among each items in Questionnaire 1, as shown in Table 5.7, correlation coefficients were significant between Q1 and Q2, Q3 and Q4, and Q4 and Q5. All the pairs was moderately correlated as indicated by the value of r (i.e., .46, -.40, -.39). This could reasonably mean: first, the more students learned English grammar, the more feedback they possibly received from teachers; second, the more helpful students thought teacher feedback was, the less students were afraid of making mistakes in their use of English; third, the more students had a lack of confidence in making use of English grammar in writing, the more likely they were to worry about making mistakes in their writing.

5.1.2 Responses from Content Feedback (FC) Group.

Table 5.8 below presents descriptive statistics of each of the five items in Questionnaire 1 for the FC group students. As shown, students' overall responses to the five questions seemed neutral ($M = 2.06$). By checking on each of the questions, students' responses to Q1, Q2 and Q3 ($M = 2.26, 2.54, 2.74, 2.40$) showed their positive attitudes towards their prior English learning experiences. As a clear contrast, students' response to Q4 ($M = 1.60$) and Q5 ($M = 1.17$) indicated students' negative view towards their own English language learning ability.

Table 5.8

Descriptive Statistics of the Results for Questionnaire 1 in FC Group ($n = 35$)

Item	M	SD	Min	Max	Skewness	Kurtosis
Q1	2.26	.56	1	3	.03	-.29
Q2	2.54	.56	1	3	-.71	-.53
Q3	2.74	.44	2	3	-1.16	-.69
Q4	1.60	.70	1	3	.74	-.56
Q5	1.17	.38	1	2	1.82	1.40
Total	2.06	.80	1	3	-.11	-1.41

Table 5.9

Frequencies of the Five Items in Questionnaire 1 for FC Group ($n = 35$)

Item/%	Q1	Q2	Q3	Q4	Q5
Positive	31.4	57.1	74.3	11.4	0
Neutral	62.9	40.0	25.7	37.1	17.1
Negative	5.7	2.9	0	51.5	82.9
Total	100	100	100	100	100

Table 5.9 demonstrates the percentage of students for each of the five

items. As seen, for Q1, more than half of the students (62. 9%) learned very few English grammar rules and 31. 4% of students learned a lot in their previous L2 learning experiences. Differently from the Indirect CF group, there were two students who indicated that they had never learned English grammar before. For Q2, only one student did not receive any feedback, which is the same with the Indirect CF group. More than half of the students(57. 1%) had received a lot of feedback from teachers before, and 40% of students received only little feedback from teachers. For Q3, all the students thought feedback was helpful, among which 25. 7% of students thought feedback had at least, to a certain extent, a positive effect on their learning, and the majority of the students (74. 3%) regarded feedback as very useful. For Q4, a majority of the students (88. 6%) worried about making mistakes when using English. Only a small portion of students(11. 4%) felt comfortable making mistakes while using English. For Q5, 17. 1% of students thought their use of English was good; interestingly, of those 17. 1% of students, zero students thought their English grammar was very good. Far more than half of students(82. 9%) thought their English grammar was bad in writing.

Table 5. 10

Correlation between the Total Number of Errors in the Three Tests and Students' Attitudes in Questionnaire 1 *for FC Group*

Sig.	Q1	Q2	Q3	Q4	Q5
Pretest	. 88	. 86	. 56	. 67	. 94
Posttest	. 40	. 46	. 05	. 13	. 99
Delayed posttest	. 78	. 28	. 64	. 20	. 15

Table 5.11

Correlation between Error Reduction across the Three Tests and Students'
Attitudes in Questionnaire 1 for FC Group

Sig.	Q1	Q2	Q3	Q4	Q5
Pre _ Post	.66	.98	.56	.22	.97
Post _ Delayed	.27	.20	.18	.82	.44
Pre _ Delayed	.62	.30	.58	.35	.54

With respect to the correlation coefficient between the FC group students' attitudes and their accuracy performance as well as between students' attitudes and error reduction across the three tests, there were no significant correlations found. By taking a further look at relationships among the five items, significant correlation was still not identified.

5.1.3 **Responses from Direct CF Group.**

Table 5.12 shows descriptive statistics of each of the five items in Questionnaire 1 for the Direct CF group students. As with the Indirect CF group, students' overall responses to the five questions were also positive (M = 2.32). As displayed, students' responses to Q1, Q2, and Q3, as indicated by the mean (M = 2.69, 2.54, 2.91), showed their positive attitudes towards their English learning experiences. However, students' responses to Q4(M = 1.94) and Q5(M = 1.51) indicated that most students hold a negative view towards their own English language learning and use.

Table 5.13 demonstrates the percentage of student responses for each of the five items. As shown in the table, all the students indicated that they had learned English grammar rules and received feedback before. All the students thought feedback worked, among which 91.4% students thought feedback was very helpful. A majority of the students (77.2%) worried about making mistakes when using English; yet in contrast, 22.9% of students did not think using English was a problem for them. In addition, 48.6% of students had confidence in their use of grammar in their writing, among which only one student (2. 9%) thought his/her English grammar was very good. Over half of the students (51. 4%) thought their English grammar was poor in writing.

Table 5. 12

Descriptive Statistics of the Results for Questionnaire 1 in Direct CF Group
(*n* = 35)

Item	M	SD	Min	Max	Skewness	Kurtosis
Q1	2. 69	.47	2	3	-. 84	-1. 38
Q2	2. 54	.51	2	3	-. 18	-2. 09
Q3	2. 91	.28	2	3	-3. 09	8. 03
Q4	1. 94	.73	1	3	.09	-1. 02
Q5	1. 51	.56	1	3	.47	-. 82
Total	2. 32	.74	1	3	-. 59	-. 94

Table 5. 13

Frequencies of the Five Items in Questionnaire 1 for Direct CF Group (*n* = 35)

Item/%	Q1	Q2	Q3	Q4	Q5
Positive	68. 6	54. 3	91. 4	22. 8	2. 9
Neutral	31. 4	45. 7	8. 6	48. 6	45. 7
Negative	0	0	0	28. 6	51. 4
Total	100	100	100	100	100

Table 5. 14

Correlation between the Total Number of Errors in the Three Tests and Students'
Attitudes in Questionnaire 1 for Direct CF Group

Sig.	Q1	Q2	Q3	Q4	Q5
Pretest	.75	.86	.38	.31	.21
Posttest	.87	.88	.78	.02 * [a]	.34
Delayed posttest	.99	.20	.48	.87	.21

Note. [a] : Pearson correlation = -. 38.

Table 5.15

Correlation between Error Reduction across the Three Tests and Students'
Attitudes in Questionnaire 1 *for Direct CF Group*

Sig.	Q1	Q2	Q3	Q4	Q5
Pre _ Post	.65	.76	.23	1.00	.35
Post _ Delayed	.92	.20	.67	.07	.07
Pre_ Delayed	.75	.59	.19	.27	.04 * [a]

Note. [a]: Pearson correlation = -.36.

Table 5.14 and Table 5.15 demonstrate the correlation coefficient between Direct CF group students' attitudes and their accuracy performance as well as between students' attitudes and error reduction across the three tests. A significant correlation was found between students' responses to Q4 and their error rates in the posttest. The relationship between students' responses to Q5 and error reduction from the pretest to the delayed posttest was found to be significant as well. The strength of the tendency for both correlations is indicated by value of r (-.38 and -.36), which means the two correlations were moderate. The r squared for -.38 indicated that 14.4% of the variability in accuracy performance in the posttest can be explained by students' responses to Q4; and the r squared for -.36 inferred that 13.0% of the variability in error reduction from the pretest to delayed posttest can be accounted for by students' responses to Q5. In other words, the more students worried about making mistakes in writing, the more errors students were likely to make; and accordingly the less confident students felt about their English ability, the more errors students made. When taking a further look at relationships among the five items, significant correlation was not found.

5.1.4 Comparison of Results Across the Three Groups.

One-way ANOVA was conducted to determine if there was any

significant group difference in students' responses to the five questions in Questionnaire 1 (see Table 5. 16). The statistics shows that a significant difference existed across groups in Q1, Q4, and Q5. To further examine where the significant differences occurred across the three groups for the three items, a post hoc test was conducted; the results showed that there was a significant difference between the Indirect CF and FC group as well as the Direct CF and FC group in Q1 and Q5. For Q4, the significant group difference occurred in the Indirect CF and the FC group.

Table 5. 16

Results of One-Way ANOVA for the Five Items in Questionnaire 1 across Groups ($n = 105$)

Item	Source	SS	df	MS	F	Sig.
Q1	Between groups	3. 79	2	1. 90	7. 32*	.00*
	Within Groups	26. 40	102	. 26		
	Total	30. 19	104			
Q2	Between groups	. 48	2	. 24	. 82	. 45
	Within Groups	29. 77	102	. 29		
	Total	30. 25	104			
Q3	Between groups	. 82	2	. 41	2. 25	. 11
	Within Groups	18. 57	102	. 18		
	Total	19. 39	104			
Q4	Between groups	3. 33	2	1. 67	3. 21*	.04*
	Within Groups	52. 91	102	. 52		
	Total	56. 25	104			
Q5	Between groups	2. 36	2	1. 18	4. 56*	.01*
	Within Groups	26. 40	102	. 26		
	Total	28. 76	104			

Table 5.17

Results of Post Hoc Test for Q1, Q4 and Q5 in Questionnaire 1 across Groups
(*n* = 105)

Item	Pairs ofGroup	*Sig.*
Q1	Indirect CF - FC	.00 *
	Direct CF - FC	.00 *
Q4	Indirect CF - FC	.01 *
Q5	Indirect CF – FC	.02 *
	Direct CF - FC	.01 *

* *p* < .05

5.2   Results for Questionnaire 2

5.2.1   Responses from Indirect CF Group.

Table 5.18 presents the descriptive statistics for the Indirect CF group students' responses to each of the ten items in Questionnaire 2. Q1 to Q5 were questions in relation to different types of corrective feedback; and Q6 to Q10 concerned students' overall attitudes and perceptions to corrective feedback. As seen in Table 5.18, students showed very positive attitudes towards corrective feedback as indicated in the means from Q6 to Q10. Table 5.19, Table 5.20 and Table

Table 5.18

Descriptive Statistics of the Results for Questionnaire 2 in Indirect CF Group (*n* = 35)

Item	M	SD	Min	Max	Skewness	Kurtosis
Q6	3.03	.75	1	4	-.50	.29
Q7	3.03	.57	2	4	.01	.40
Q8	3.26	.95	1	4	-1.21	.63
Q9	3.14	.73	2	4	-.23	-1.05
Q10	3.51	.56	2	4	-.59	-.70

5.21 display the percentage of students who responded to each of the ten items. Students' responses to each of the questions are analyzed in detail as follows.

Table 5.19

Frequencies of Q1 in Questionnaire 2 for Indirect CF Group (n = 35)

Item /%	Feedback on grammar	Feedback on content	Feedback on organization	None of these	Two of thee	All of these	Total
Q1	65.7	8.6	11.4	0	5.7	8.6	100

Table 5.20

Frequencies of Q2-Q5 in Questionnaire 2 for Indirect CF Group (n = 35)

Item/%	Q2	Q3	Q4	Q5
Direct correction	14.3	37.1	17.1	22.9
Underline or circle	17.1	11.4	11.4	2.9
Description and explanation	60.0	45.7	68.6	71.4
None of these	0	0	0	0
Two of these	2.9	2.9	2.9	2.9
All of these	5.7	2.9	0	0
Total	100	100	100	100

Table 5.21

Frequencies of Q6-Q10 in Questionnaire 2 for Indirect CF Group (n = 35)

Item/%	Q6	Q7	Q8	Q9	Q10
Very much	25.7	17.1	8.6	34.3	54.3
Mostly	54.3	68.6	8.6	45.7	42.9
A little	17.1	14.3	31.4	20.0	2.9
Not at all	2.9	0	51.4	0	0
Total	10	100	100	100	100

In regards to Q1, 65.7% of students thought feedback on grammar was the best way for teachers to provide feedback for their writing, indicating that students are concerned about their grammar as a way of improving their writing quality. For Q2, the majority of students (60.0%) preferred teacher corrective feedback with description and explanation instead of only correcting or underlining their errors. Regarding Q3, corrective feedback with description and explanation (45.7%) was considered the easiest way for students to correct their errors, and direct correction (37.1%) was considered the second easiest way for error correction. Concerning Q4 and Q5, 68.6% students of thought they learned most from feedback with description and explanation. Direct correction and underlined feedback seemed less favorable by students as they accounted for a small portion of students' responses. Also, 71.4% of students regarded feedback with description and explanation as their favorite type of feedback in writing. When asked about their perceptions of the indirect CF they received from the researcher, 80% of students liked the indirect correction and 85.7% of students expressed that they understood the indirect CF provided by the researcher. Most of the students (82.8%) did not feel discouraged while being corrected, and 80% of students would like to apply the correction to their future writing. Interestingly, 97.1% students believed that they were likely to attend to the errors after receiving the feedback, but one student in particular expressed that she/he just left their writing on their desk and did not want to look at it.

Table 5.22

Correlation between the Total Number of Errors in the Three Tests and Students' Attitudes in Questionnaire 2 for the Indirect CF Group (n = 35)

Sig.	Q6	Q7	Q8	Q9	Q10
Pretest	.93	.21	.47	.32	.57
Posttest	.32	.73	.06	.75	.85
Delayed posttest	.06	.39	.85	.46	.02 * [a]

Note. a. Pearson correlation = -.38

Table 5. 23

Correlation between Error Reduction across the Three Tests and Students'
Attitudes in Questionnaire 2 for Indirect CF Group (*n* = 35)

Sig.	Q6	Q7	Q8	Q9	Q10
Pre _ Post	. 64	. 41	1. 00	. 52	. 71
Pos _ Delayed	. 03 *ᵃ	. 77	. 09	. 44	. 10
Pre _ Delayed	. 39	. 55	. 63	. 28	. 17

Note. a. Pearson correlation = -. 37

Table 5. 22 shows the coefficient correlation between students'
attitudes to corrective feedback and the errors they committed in the three
tests; Table 5. 23 demonstrates the correlation between errors reduction
across the three tests and student attitudes towards indirect CF. The data
indicate that excepting for a correlation between Q10 and error rates in the
delayed posttest, there was not significant evidence to conclude that a
relationship existed between students' responses to the questionnaire and to
their error rates across the three tests. For Q10, there was significant
negative correlation between students' responses and errors rates, indicating
that students who showed a positive attitude towards the application of error
correction were more likely to make fewer errors in the delayed posttest. In
addition, as shown in Table 5. 23, a significant positive correlation occurred
between student responses to Q6 and error reduction from the posttest to the
delayed posttest, indicating that students with a positive attitude toward
indirect CF tended to produce fewer errors from the posttest to the delayed
posttest.

5. 2. 2 **Responses from the Content Feedback (FC) Group.**

Table 5. 24 presents the descriptive statistics of FC group students'
responses to Questionnaire 2. As seen, students showed more positive
attitudes towards corrective feedback in response to Q8, Q9, and Q10 than
their responses to Q6 and Q7. Table 5. 25, Table 5. 26, Table 5. 27 display

the percentage of students who responded to each of the ten items.

Table 5.24

Descriptive Statistics of the Results for Questionnaire 2 in FC Group ($n = 35$)

Item	M	SD	Min	Max	Skewness	Kurtosis
Q6	2.94	.64	2	4	.05	-.38
Q7	2.91	.56	2	4	-.04	.39
Q8	3.03	1.04	1	4	-.72	-.68
Q9	3.17	.57	2	4	.03	.06
Q10	3.54	66	1	4	-1.82	4.97

Table 5.25

Frequencies of Q1 in Questionnaire 2 for FC Group ($n = 35$)

Item/%	Feedback on grammar	Feedback on content	Feedback on organization	None of these	Two of thee	All of these	Total
Q1	60.0	11.4	25.7	0	2.9	0	100

Table 5.26

Frequencies of Q2-Q5 in Questionnaire 2 for FC Group ($n = 35$)

Item/ %	Q2	Q3	Q4	Q5
Direct correction	11.4	25.8	2.9	17.1
Underline or circle	17.1	17.1	11.4	20.0
Description and explanation	68.6	57.1	85.7	62.9
None of these	2.9	0	0	0
Two of these	0	0	0	0
All of these	0	0	0	0
Total	100	100	100	100

Table 5. 27

Frequencies of Q6-Q10 in Questionnaire 2 for FC Group (*n* = 35)

Item/ %	Q6	Q7	Q8	Q9	Q10
Very much	17.1	11.4	11.4	25.7	60.0
Mostly	60.0	68.6	17.1	65.7	37.1
A little	22.9	20.0	28.6	8.6	0
Not at all	0	0	42.9	0	2.9
Total	10	100	100	100	100

As shown in Table 5. 25, 60. 0% of students thought feedback on grammar was the best way for teachers to provide feedback for their writing. 68.6% of students preferred teacher corrective feedback with description and explanation instead of being provided either the direct or indirect correction on their errors. Corrective feedback with description and explanation (57. 1%) was considered by respondents the easiest way to correct their errors, and the same can be said for the Indirect CF group, with direct correction(37. 1%) considered the second easiest way to correct errors. 85.7% of students thought they learned most from feedback with description and explanation. Also, 62. 9% of students regarded feedback with description and explanation as their favorite type of feedback on their writing. In addition, 77. 1% of students liked the content feedback they received from the researcher, and 80% of students expressed that they understood the types of feedback provided by the researcher. Most of the students(71. 5%) did not feel discouraged while being corrected, and 80% of students would like to apply the correction to their future writing. 97. 1% students showed their willingness to attend to the errors after receiving the feedback, but one student expressed that she/he wish they had not written anything.

Table 5. 28

Correlation between the Total Number of Errors in the Three Tests and Students'
Attitudes in Questionnaire 2 for FC Group (n = 35)

Sig.	Q6	Q7	Q8	Q9	Q10
Pretest	.93	.95	.09	.79	.40
Posttest	.35	.73	.79	.35	.06
Delayed posttest	.53	.33	.95	.29	.33

Table 5. 29
Correlation between Error Reduction across the Three Tests and Students'
Attitudes in Questionnaire 2 for FC Group (n = 35)

Sig.	Q6	Q7	Q8	Q9	Q10
Pre _ Post	.55	.75	.07	.67	.57
Pos _ Delayed	.83	.27	.79	.09	.48
Pre _ Delayed	.71	.53	.15	.32	.96

Table 5. 28 and Table 5. 29 show the coefficient correlation between FC group students' attitudes to corrective feedback and their error rates in the three tests, as well as between students' attitudes to CF and error reduction across the three tests. As seen in the data, none of the relationships was significantly correlated.

5. 2. 3 **Responses from Direct CF Group.**

Table 5. 30 presents the descriptive statistics of students' response to the ten questions in Questionnaire 2 for the Direct CF group. As indicated by the means, students showed very positive attitudes towards corrective feedback from Q6 to Q10. Table 5. 31, Table 5. 32, Table 5. 33 display the percentage of students who responded to each of the ten items.

Table 5.30

Descriptive Statistics of the Results for Questionnaire 2 in Direct CF Group $(n = 35)$

	M	SD	Min	Max	Skewness	Kurtosis
Q6	3.09	.56	2	4	.04	.39
Q7	3.14	.69	2	4	-.20	-.81
Q8	3.11	.98	1	4	-.81	-.14
Q9	3.37	.60	2	4	-.34	-.61
Q10	3.89	.40	2	4	-3.81	15.05

Table 5.31
Frequencies of Q1 in Questionnaire 2 for Direct CF Group $(n = 35)$

Item/%	Feedback on grammar	Feedback on content	Feedback on organization	None of these	Two of thee	All of these	Total
Q1	54.3	8.6	20.0	0	2.9	14.3	100

Table 5.32
Frequencies of Q2-Q5 in Questionnaire 2 for Direct CF Group $(n = 35)$

Item/ %	Q2	Q3	Q4	Q5
Direct correction	28.6	40.0	28.6	17.1
Underline or circle	20.0	11.4	14.3	11.4
Description and explanation	42.9	40.0	48.6	65.7
None of these	0	0	0	0
Two of these	0	0	0	0
All of these	8.6	8.6	8.6	5.7
Total	100	100	100	100

Table 5.31 shows that 54.3% of students thought feedback on grammar was the best way for teachers to provide feedback for their writing. 42.9% of students preferred teacher corrective feedback with description and explanation, and more students in the Direct CF group compared to the other two groups considered direct(28.6%) or underlined(20%) correction on errors as the best way for corrective feedback. In addition, both direct

correction(40%) and corrective feedback with description and explanation (40%) were considered the two easiest ways for students to correct their errors. Almost half of the students(48.6%) thought they learned most from feedback with description and explanation. 65.7% of students regarded feedback with description and explanation as their favorite type of feedback to receive in their writing. In regards to their attitudes to the direct corrective feedback received from the researcher, 88.6% of students liked the direct corrective feedback and 82.8% of students expressed that they understood it. Most of the students(94.3%) did not feel discouraged while being corrected, and 80% of students would like to apply the correction to their future writing. As with the other two groups, 97.1% of students were likely to attend to the errors after receiving the feedback, while one student expressed that she/he did not want to look at the feedback and just ignored it.

Table 5.33

Frequencies of Q6-Q10 in Questionnaire 2 for Direct CF Group(n = 35)

Item/ %	Q6	Q7	Q8	Q9	Q10
Very much	20.0	31.4	14.3	42.9	91.4
Mostly	68.6	51.4	8.6	51.4	5.7
A little	11.4	17.1	48.6	5.7	2.9
Not at all	0	0	28.6	0	0
Total	100	100	100	100	100

Table 5.34

Correlation between the Total Number of Errors in the Three Tests and Students'
Attitudes in Questionnaire 2 for Direct CF Group(n = 35)

Sig.	Q6	Q7	Q8	Q9	Q10
Pretest	.67	.39	.82	.23	.74
Posttest	.67	.70	.70	.77	.64
Delayed posttest	.79	.07	.90	.92	.70

Table 5.35

Correlation between Error Reduction across the Three Tests and Students'
Attitudes in Questionnaire 2 for Direct CF Group ($n = 35$)

Sig.	Q6	Q7	Q8	Q9	Q10
Pre _ Post	.47	.22	.63	.11	.89
Post _ Delayed	.94	.06	.86	.76	1.00
Pre _ Delayed	.57	.90	.76	.25	.91

Table 5.34 and Table 5.35 show the coefficient correlation between students' attitudes to corrective feedback and the errors they committed in the three tests, and between student attitudes towards direct CF and errors reduction across the three tests. As seen, there is no significant evidence to conclude that there exists a relationship between students' attitudes and their change in accuracy across the three tests.

5.2.4 Comparison of Results Across the Three Groups.

A one-way ANOVA was conducted to discover if there was any significant group difference in students' responses to the ten questions in Questionnaire 2. The statistics shows that a significant difference existed in Q10 across groups. Then, a post hoc test was conducted, showing that a significant difference was found in Q10 between the Indirect CF and Direct CF group as well as the FC group and Direct CF group.

Table 5.36

Summary Table of One-Way ANOVA for Ten Items in Questionnaire 2 across
Groups ($n = 105$)

Item	Source	SS	df	MS	F	Sig.
Q1	Between groups	5.79	2	2.90	1.22	.30
	Within Groups	241.20	102	2.37		
	Total	246.99	104			

(Contd.)

Item	Source	SS	df	MS	F	Sig.
Q2	Between groups	1.43	2	.71	.56	.57
	Within Groups	129.09	102	1.27		
	Total	130.51	104			
Q3	Between groups	.06	2	.03	.02	.98
	Within Groups	148.57	102	1.46		
	Total	148.63	104		.83	
Q4	Between groups	1.60	2	.80		.44
	Within Groups	98.06	102	.96		
	Total	99.66	104			
	Between groups	1.16	2	.58		
Q5	Within Groups	94.40	102	.93	.63	.54
	Total	95.56	104			
	Between groups	.36	2	.18		
Q6	Within Groups	43.60	102	.43	.42	.66
	Total	43.96	104			
	Between groups	.91	2	.46	1.23	.30
Q7	Within Groups	38.00	102	.37		
	Total	38.91	104			
	Between groups	2.13	2	1.07		.34
Q8	Within Groups	100.40	102	.98	1.08	
	Total	102.53	104			
Q9	Between groups	1.09	2	.54		.27
	Within Groups	41.43	102	.41	1.34	
	Total	42.51	104			
Q10	Between groups	2.99	2	1.50		.01 *
	Within Groups	30.97	102	.30	4.92 *	
	Total	33.96	104			

Table 5.37

Summary Table of Post Hoc Test for Question 10 in Questionnaire 2 across Groups

Item	Pairs of Group	Sig.
Q10	Indirect CF- FC	.83
	Direct CF- FC	.01 *
	Indirect CF- Direct CF	.01 *

*p < .05

5.3   Student Responses to the Open-ended Questions in Questionnaire 1

5.3.1   Indirect CF Group.

Three open-ended questions were designed in Questionnaire 1. The first open question is Q6, which asked "how do you feel when the teacher immediately corrects your error in your writing or in a language classroom?" Student responses were classified into seven categories (refer to Appendix G for the specific examples), including embarrassed (34%), happy (29%), satisfied (23%), sorry (17%), nervous (17%), indifference (6%), and others (34%) (i. e., appreciated, helpful, meaningful, etc.). This clearly reflected that the majority of students (86%) held a positive attitude towards error correction. Overlap existed in students' responses. For example, some students responded as embarrassed but fine; embarrassed but happy; embarrassed but appreciated; embarrassed but satisfied; embarrassed, sorry, nervous but also grateful; happy and satisfied; happy, satisfied, embarrassed, and nervous; indifferent and helpful; sorry but happy; as well as sorry but meaningful. Many students who belonged to the category of "embarrassed" said they only felt a little embarrassed and later on they felt fine because it was helpful. Everyone cannot avoiding making mistakes and individuals should be happy to know their shortcomings, face the errors, and then correct them. Some other students reflected that although they felt embarrassed at the beginning, they realized teachers' correction could help them improve their English skills. Then they felt satisfied and grateful for error correction. Figure 5.1 is the visual representation of students' responses, with percentage adjusted to reach 100%. It is glad to see that no students considered teacher' correction bothersome or overwhelming in the Indirect CF group.

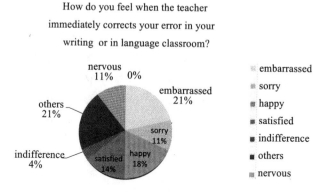

How do you feel when the teacher
immediately corrects your error in your
writing or in language classroom?

Figure 5. 1 **Indirect CF students' responses to Q6 in**
Questionnaire 1

The second open-ended question is Q7. This question inquires "what
feedback do you expect teachers to provide for your writing?" Students'
responses varied in five categories, which are grammar (43%) , writing
skills (29%) , comprehensive requirements of writing (14%) , grades
(3%) , and others(11%). Most students thought teachers should mark the
grammar errors and help them write better, tell them the correct sentence
patterns, and how to use appropriate grammar in writing. In terms of writing
skills, some students expected teachers to tell them how to write effectively
regarding consistency, organization, ideas, etc. In addition, many students
had a comprehensive expectation from teacher feedback. They hoped
teachers could provide feedback on all the elements of writing including
grammar, structure of composition, and content. They also hoped teachers
would provide feedback that is practical and specific. One student asked
how to write well in order to get higher grades(refer to Appendix G for
detailed responses from students).

The last open-ended question asks if students have anything they want
to share with the researcher. 19 students responded to this question and
68% of students believed that English speaking is more important than

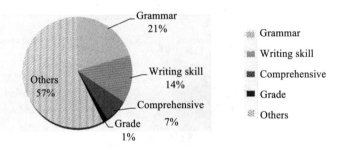

What feedback do you expect teachers
to provide for your writing?

Figure 5. 2 **Indirect CF students' responses to Q7 in**
Questionnaire 1

writing, and asked about the ways to improve their spoken English. Among
those students, one student asked, "Is English grammar important?"
Another student even wrote, "I just think as an English speaker, when your
English is good enough to talk with native speakers that means you
succeed. Not more grammars. That's stupid." One student had concern
about his/her listening, as she/he asked "I don't know why my listening
grade is good but I actually cannot understand what foreigners say." Two
students were concerned about their use of words, as they asked, "How to
remember word accurately?" and "I can memorize a lot of words and
phrases but still my English is bad. I cannot use them in daily
communication." One student wrote "I think feedback vary from person to
person. Each student has different attitudes to feedback." Examples of
other comments students wrote are listed below:

> *e. g. , I want to learn English well, but I just speak or write in easy*
> *ways, not thoroughly. How to improve this?*
> *Easier said than done.*
> *How to concentrate on what teachers say instead of having a bit of*
> *sleeping.*

Is hand writing important in composition?

It is difficult to write something. Really.

5.3.2   Content Feedback(FC)Group.

In terms of Q6 "how do you feel when the teacher immediately corrects your error in your writing or in language classroom?" FC group students' responses are categorized into eight types, including embarrassed (40%), happy (34%), satisfied (34%), sorry (23%), nervous (34%), indifference(11%), bothered(6%), overwhelmed(6%). On the contrary to the Indirect CF group students, the majority of students in FC group held a negative attitude towards teachers' immediate error correction. Overlap also appeared in students' responses. For example, some students who responded as embarrassed also wrote embarrassed but fine; embarrassed but happy; embarrassed but satisfied; embarrassed, nervous and satisfied; embarrassed, sorry, nervous but also happy; and embarrassed, sorry and bothered. Students responded as happy along with emotions like satisfied, nervous and indifference. Students who belonged to the category of "embarrassed" said they feel a little embarrassed but they can benefit from error correction. One student wrote, "a little embarrassed, but the more the happier." Figure 5.3 visually represents students' responses. A small portion of students considered teachers' corrections as bothersome and overwhelming.

Regarding Q7 "what feedback do you expect teachers to provide for your writing?" 22 students responded to this question and there were four types of responses from FC group students: grammar(41%), writing skills (23%), authenticity (3%), and others (32%). Students who expected teachers to provide feedback on grammar wanted teachers to focus on syntactic structures. For example, one student asked "how can use the sentence well or which is the best phrase I can use?" Students who expected feedback on writing skills expressed their concern about how to write logically. For instance, one student was concerned about how to make

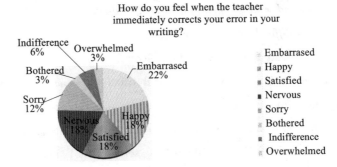

Figure 5. 3 **FC group students' responses to Q**6 **in**
Questionnaire 1

writing that could sound like native speakers. Many students also expressed their willingness to receive encouragements from teachers, such as good job, excellent, etc. (refer to Appendix E for detailed responses from students).

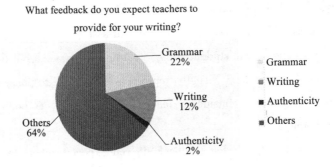

Figure 5. 4 **FC group students' responses to Q**7 **in**
Questionnaire 1

The last open-ended question asked if students have anything they want to share with the researcher. 10 students responded to this question in the FC group and 40% students asked questions about spoken English. For example, one student asked, "I want to speak English well so I can understand what native speakers say." Another student wrote "I think we should enhance our oral English because we don't have a good English environment. " Only one student had concern about his/her writing, as she/ he asked "to be honest, I am eager to improve my writing skills. But when I am writing, I don't know how to organize and how to express my opinions. " The general questions students asked are as follows:

e. g. , *I like English.*

In fact, I am not interested in studying English. What should I do?

I want to know how do you improved your oral English and when you meet obstacles, especially in learning English, how do you overcome it? I want to ask you how hard you study in your undergrad?

I feel that my motivation is not enough ad I am not satisfied with myself. I don't know why.

5.3.3 **Direct CF Group.**

For the question "how do you feel when the teacher immediately corrects your error in your writing or in language classroom?" Direct CF group students' responses are categorized into six types (refer to Appendix E for the specific examples), including embarrassed (31%), happy (34%), satisfied (40%), sorry (26%), nervous (31%), and overwhelmed (6%). Same to the FC group, the majority of students in Direct CF group held a negative attitude towards teachers' immediate error correction.

Regarding the question "what feedback do you expect teachers to provide for your writing?" 24 out of 35 (69%) students expected teachers' feedback on grammar, such as grammar rules, how to make sentences, and how to use grammar correctly. Four students (11%) wanted their teacher to provide feedback on writing skills, such as how to make a summary and how to make the writing vivid. Six students (17%) hoped teachers would provide feedback on not only grammar but also use of vocabulary, content, and also writing skills. One student expected teachers to tell her/him what is good and what is bad in general in the writing.

Only six students responded to the question "anything else you want to share with the researcher?" No surprising results were found as the Indirect CF group students made similar comments with the Indirect CF and FC group. Most students were concerned about their spoken English. As one student said, "Spoken English is the most difficult in learning. I think we should practice more during the spare time." (Refer to Appendix G for more student examples)

How do you feel when the teacher

immediately corrects your error?

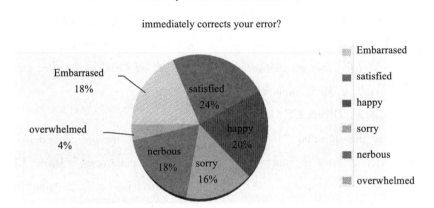

Figure 5. 5 **Direct CF students´ responses to Q6 in Questionnaire** 1

Chapter 6: Qualitative results: Interviews and Classroom Observation

This chapter examines RQ3: how do contextual (e. g. , prior learning experience, educational experiences/context, EFL VS. ESL) and affective (e. g. , motivation and attitudes) factors affect corrective feedback in L2 development?

6.1 Responses to Student Interview

In order to appropriately answer the RQ, 10 out of 35 students from each group were randomly selected to participate in the interview. Figure 6.1, 6.2, and 6.3 below demonstrate the developmental patterns based on the selected students' normed number of errors in the three tests for each of the three groups. The X – axis represents the three tests and the Y-axis represents the normed frequencies of errors in the pretest, posttest, and delayed posttest; each line represents one student in their corresponding group who showed either a linear or V-shape pattern. In general, students from the Indirect CF and the Direct CF group showed more similarities compared to the FC group in their developmental patterns. The selected ten students in the Indirect CF group showed four patterns: linear decrease, V-shape decrease, upside-down-V-shape decrease and linear increase. Students in the FC group showed five patterns: linear decrease, V-shape decrease, upside-down-V-shape decrease, linear increase and upside-down-V-shape decrease. Patterns that occurred in the Direct CF group included: linear decrease and V-shape decrease. These visual representations help explain each student's developmental pattern by matching and contextualizing their responses to the seven interview questions to the trends shown in the Figures. Table 6.1 briefly summarizes each interviewee's response to the seven interview questions. Analysis of the thirty students' responses from the three groups to each of the seven interview questions is described and discussed thoroughly below.

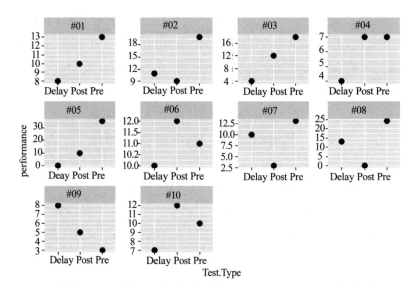

Figure 6. 1 **Developmental patterns demonstrated by ten students' performance in Indirect CF group**

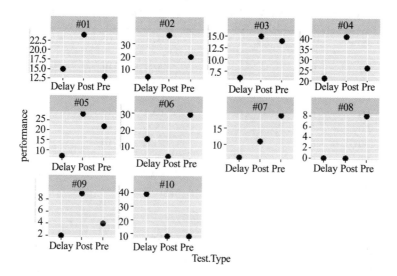

Figure 6. 2 **Developmental patterns demonstrated by ten students'**
performance in FC group

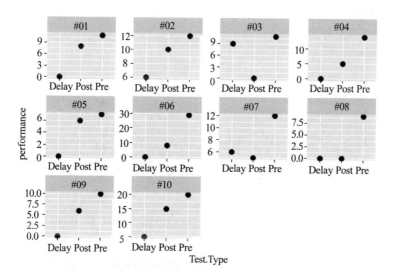

Figure 6. 3 **Developmental patterns demonstrated by ten students'**
performance in Direct CF group

Table 6. 1

Summary of Individual Students' Responses to Questions 1-6 in the Interview

	Pattern	Q1	Q2	Q3	Q4	Q5	Q6
1[a]	LD	G	✓	×	CA/S	DF	A
2	VD	G	✓	×	CA	DF	C
3	LD	G	✓	×	CA	DF	I
4	LD	G	✓	×	CA	PF	M/I
5	LD	G	✓	×	S	DF	C
6	UVD	G	✓	✓	CA/S	DF	A/M
7	VD	G	✓	×	S	DF	C
8	VD	G	✓	×	CA	DF	M
9	LI	G	✓	×	CA/S	PF	A
10	UVD	G	✓		S	DF	C
1[b]	UVI	O	✓	×	CA	LA	C
2	UVD	O	✓	✓	S	PF	M
3	UVD	G	✓	✓	No	PF	C
4	UVD	G	✓	✓	S	LA	C
5	UVD	G	✓	×	S	DF	A
6	VD	O	✓	×	CA	DF	A
7	LD	G	✓	✓	S	DF	M
8	LD	O	✓	×	S	LA	C
9	UVD	O	✓	×	CA	DF	C
10	LI	O	✓	×	S	LA	C
1[c]	LD	G	✓	×	CA	DF	I
2	LD	G	✓	×	CA	DF	A
3	VD	G	✓	×	CA	PF	C
4	LD	G	✓	×	S	DF	C
5	LD	G	✓	×	CA	PF	M
6	LD	G	✓	×	CA	DF	B
7	VD	G	✓	×	other	DF	I
8	LD	G	✓	×	CA	DF	C
9	LD	O	✓	×	CA	DF	A
10	LD	G	✓	×	S	DF	A

Note. [a]: Indirect CF group; [b]: Content Feedback group; [c]: Direct CF group; LD = linear decrease, VD = V-shape decrease, UVD = upside-down-V-shape decrease and LI = linear increase; G = grammar, C = content, O = organization; ✓ = positive answer, × = negative answer; CA = correct all the errors, S = be specific; DF = difficult to find errors, PF = only can find partial errors, LA = lazy; A = attitude, B = belief, C = contextual factors, I = interest, M = motivation.

6.1.1   Question 1: **Which component of writing do you most expect to receive feedback from teachers, grammar, content, or organizations?**

It was interesting to see that all the students interviewed from the three groups picked either grammar or organization as the component of writing they most expected to receive feedback from teachers. For the students who chose *grammar* (10 *from the Indirect CF group*, 4 *from FC group*, *and* 9 *from Direct CF group*) , they explained that even though they had learned many rules of grammar, they did not know when and how to apply the rules to writing appropriately and accurately. Students said they were not confident in using grammar, thus they needed more guidance on grammar use. Some of them also mentioned that the textbook they were using and the materials their teacher implemented in the classrooms were very tedious and not practical, which to a certain extent demotivated them from learning English grammar.

For the students who chose *organization* (6 *from FC group and* 1 *from Direct CF group*) , their perspectives were very realistic in relation to the test-oriented English learning in college. Students pointed out that in order to meet test requirements, it is important for them to make a good first impression on their evaluators, according to which teachers can easily and quickly make a judgment of students' writing and categorize it to different grade levels. Teachers normally did not have much time to look through the whole text carefully, thus it was impossible for teachers to examine each grammatical structure. If the student had a very neat and straightforward organization for the overall writing task, the individual earned a satisfactory grade. Students did not deny the importance of grammar, but they said it was not the most important thing compared to the overall organization in writing since it immediately grabs the readers' attention. In addition, students mentioned that having a good organization reflects whether they had sufficient ability in logical thinking, which was perceived as an advanced skill in writing. One student said that, "grammar can be learned quickly for test requirements, but organization needs to be developed and practiced over a long time. Thus, organization at this point is more important for us. "

6. 1. 2   Question 2: Do you like the type of feedback you received from the teachers and the researcher?

All 30 students from the three groups favored the type of feedback they received from the researcher, and they all said that they were eager to receive any teacher feedback regardless of whether it is in reading, speaking, or writing. Students from the Indirect CF group mentioned that since they had spent so much time learning grammar in high schools for tests, after they entered college, they were sick of learning grammar on a daily basis because they knew they would never have a chance to use it practically. However, because they had to pass TEM-4 (Test for English Majors-Band 4) in their second year of college and TEM-8 (Test for English Majors-Band 8) in their senior year for their degree, they had to learn grammar for these test requirements. In these cases, teachers' feedback on grammar was one way to draw their attention back to grammar, and they liked it. As one student in particular mentioned, she liked the indirect CF the researcher provided, which not only located the errors without discouraging students, but also stimulated their desire for grammar knowledge as well as aroused their curiosity to figure out what the errors were and why the errors occurred. Some students also said that sometimes they could suddenly realize and understand what the errors were, and they felt like the grammar knowledge they ignored had suddenly been retrieved at the moment when they saw the underlined or circled errors. However, one student pointed out that "I like the feedback you provided for me. However, the problem is because the errors were only underlined, even though I corrected them by myself, I did not know whether it was wrong or right. This led me to ignore some errors, and I just did not care about the errors and left them alone. "

One student from the FC group expressed her opinion that because of being pressed by test-oriented learning, she had become too lazy to use her brain to think and even to deal with writing. She said: " I am very sorry that I did not take a look at of the feedback you provided for me. I am lazy and tired. " Another student mentioned that he liked the feedback the researcher provided—the feedback on content. He said, " Even though it was nothing about grammar, the feedback facilitated me to read my own writing once more. I was happy that I corrected some errors by myself!" Another student said, "Sometimes, I like teacher feedback but sometimes I don't. It really depends on which situation I was. I very much welcome teachers' feedback on writing but I do not like to be interrupted in speaking. It is frustrating. "

Students from the Direct CF group in general pointed out that the direct correction was very helpful for them to digest knowledge because it was easy for them to figure out what the problem was with less effort and then they could memorize it for future use. However, one student pointed out that "Sometimes, since it was the teacher who corrected the errors and the answer was provided already, it was hard for me to deeply think about why the error happened. I could easily forget about the errors and not think about them anymore. "

6.1.3 Question 3: Are you confident in your own writing and self-editing ability?

Only one student from the Indirect CF group had confidence in her own writing and her self-editing ability. She said that " Writing is not difficult and it just needs practice. Self-editing is not hard for me, either, and it is like a habit. Whenever I finish writing, I re-read my writing to make sure it is okay to be turned in. Otherwise, I do not feel comfortable. I think I am able to correct some of the errors, though not 100% , by myself and I feel happy about that. " Most of the students mentioned that they were not familiar with or just did not know how to self-edit. In most cases, they knew there was something wrong with their writing, but they did not know how or where to get started with revision and editing.

Four participants from the FC group were confident in either their own writing or their self-editing ability. As one student said, "I am very proud of my writing, and I always have some unique perspectives that are different from my classmates. But I do not really care about self-editing because it is not allowed due to either time limits in tests or lack of opportunities for practice. " Another student mentioned that he did have confidence in writing, but was not sure if he had sufficient self-editing skills. Another student said "it is okay for me to check grammar errors for my peers; but if you ask me to correct my own writing, I am not sure if I am able to do it. It is hard to find errors that I make. Sometimes, people just don't like to read their own writing for no reason. " Still, one student said that "I think my writing is fine but my self-editing ability is just so-so. I have not had many opportunities to edit my own writing because we do not write much. " In addition, many students mentioned that their English writing ability was either positively or negatively affected by their Chinese writing ability, either in the use of language or in their writing style. They didn't think their writing was excellent but that it was good enough for use.

None ofthe students from the Direct CF group showed confidence in their own writing or self-editing ability, and a large portion of students expressed that they lacked confidence in dealing with writing in any circumstances. One student from this group said that, "It is amazing that I have memorized a lot of writing patterns in high school and I can just easily use them when writing for tests. But I have problems in vocabulary not in grammar. I have memorized enough words but still don't know how to use them authentically. I need to improve my writing in this case. " Another student responded that "I don't like writing, so I don't write much unless

I have to practice it for passing tests. " Still, another student reported that "many people can expand their ideas through writing, but for me, I feel like I don't have much to say on whatever topics. I am sad about this but don't know how to deal with this problem. " Another student replied that "I practiced a lot of writings in high school because we had so many English tests, in which writing accounted for a great portion of the overall evaluation. I memorized a number of formulaic expressions in English that I thought I would be able to use in tests. However, in college, we have not had much chance to practice these anymore. Unfortunately, the only formulaic expressions I remember cannot be used in college writing. "

6.1.4 Question 4: What expectations do you have of grammar corrections in your writing from teachers?

All except one student from the three groups indicated that they expected teachers to either correct all their errors or to provide specific examples of grammar use. Interestingly, one student from the Indirect CF group expressed a willingness to receive grammar feedback but it pretty much depends upon her mood. Another student from the Indirect CF group pointed out that "I hope teachers correct all the errors I have in grammar. I am not confident in my use of grammar. Since we entered college, teachers did not give systematic instruction on grammar anymore. Teachers only picked up the knowledge or focused on the things that they thought were important for us, but sometimes what we were taught was not what we expected to learn. Thus, the problems with grammatical structures I encountered in writing can only be fixed through grammar feedback. " Students also suggested that teachers should provide more examples in relation to the errors so they would be able to comprehend and fix the errors more easily.

Students from the Direct CF group also mentioned the same problem that their grammar teacher tended to give lectures on certain grammatical structures and for the rest of the class, students were asked to read the textbook page by page, which was a boring learning process and demotivated students from learning. Sometimes, the grammar class was a lot of fun, but students did not feel they truly learned anything from it. Most of the time, they took notes from the teacher's lecture and read the textbook to digest the knowledge after class. Because students were reluctant to ask questions either in class or after class, the grammatical points were left out. Thus, students expected teachers to provide grammatical feedback not only for their improvement of accuracy in writing, but also as a good way to communicate with teachers as this did not often happen in or after class.

Only one studentfrom the FC group mentioned he did not like to receive grammar correction, pointing out that "the use of English sometimes, no matter in speaking or writing, is a sense of flowing. I speak what I want to speak and write what I want to write. I have a flow of ideas to express in writing and I don't think there are fixed rules for grammar. I believe I have learned English grammar very well. Therefore, I don't have any expectations of grammar correction from the teacher. Another reason is I cannot understand teacher's explanations on grammar. "

6.1.5   Question 5: **What difficulties did you encounter during your revision process**?

All students from the three groups responded that they had difficulties in the editing process because it was hard to find out errors that they had made. Many students mentioned that they understood that their use of language was awkward, especially for the Chinese use of English; however, they did not know how to change it and to make it sound native-like. The only errors that could be easily found were spelling and punctuation, which do not necessarily belong within grammatical errors. One student from the Indirect CF group said that, "when I read my writing first time, I felt like it was such a good writing. After I had read it for the second time, I found some errors on tense, which I think was probably due to my carelessness. Other errors I noticed were the use of clauses and redundant use of main verbs in the sentences. Then, I corrected the errors but still felt like the sentence structures were in disorder, which unfortunately I did not know how to deal with. " Many students expressed that for the errors they were not able to correct, they hoped teachers could take care of it. As these students mentioned, article usage was an example of kind of the errors that students were struggling with and hoped teachers could point out and provide feedback on. One student in the FC group said, "It is a terrible feeling when I have to use articles in my writing. We don't have articles in Chinese but English has so many articles. They are so bothersome. "

6.1.6 Question 6: What other contextual and individual factors (e. g. , attitude, belief, and motivation) do you think may influence your writing ability to benefit from corrective feedback?

Four students from the Indirect CF, six from the FC group, and three from the Direct CF group considered their context of learning as a major factor that influenced their writing ability and benefited from teacher feedback. These students complained about their lack of an authentic English learning environment and they said they needed more opportunities to practice English writing in order to make errors and then to correct those errors. One student from the Indirect CF group said, "The reality is that we do not have many opportunities of practicing English in class. Teachers teach English in Chinese, and do not create an environment that could facilitate our English use in classrooms. " One student from the FC group also stressed that " teachers normally use half of the class time giving lectures and ask us to read the textbook for the rest of class time. I don't like this way of learning because I feel like I was feeding up all the time but still did not gain any weight. I like the speaking class, and it was taught by a foreign teacher. She likes to build up our language sense, and I think this is necessary in writing. However, all the classes followed that class format we had in high school. Teachers spent too much time teaching vocabulary but did not tell us how to appropriately use it in writing. "

Another student from the Direct CF group said, "The contextual factor, I would say, was the teaching and learning style that derived from high school. It was very influential at least for my entire English learning experience. It was the kind of environment that got me stuck. I am a person that like to use my mind and don't like things that are forced into my brain. I need to know its practical value if I want to learn it well. Otherwise, it won't work for me. Thus, compared to the grammar class, I like the listening and speaking class. They are much more fun, from which I learned something I could use in practical life. "

For the other students (6 from the Indirect CF group, 4 from the FC group, and 7 from the Direct CF group), motivation, attitude, belief, and interest were the major factors that affected their writing proficiency and performance. For example, one student from the Indirect CF group said that, "I think I am a perfectionist and I always to want to write perfectly without any errors. Therefore, I tend to use simple sentence structures to avoid making complex errors. I am always highly motivated and hold a positive attitude while learning English. I am interested in English writing and believe my efforts will pay off. " One student from the FC group said, "For me, attitude plays an important role to a larger extent in my life. I am a lazy person in daily English learning and do not really care about if I could write good or bad essays. However, whenever I need to take a test, I could devote much time to preparing for the test because I know I need to get a good grade. When I write English in the test, I can finish writing very quickly and always like to read my writing and revise it over and over again. I enjoy taking tests but do not like to learn anything besides that. " Another student from the Direct CF group said, "I am interested in writing no matter in English or Chinese. Chinese writing is for leisure while English writing, to me, is more professional, which is worthy of more efforts to put in. " In addition, many students stressed that they were not interested in writing because they did not like it. As one student in the Indirect CF group emphasized, "Writing is like a burden to me, and I feel stressed whenever I write. Spoken English is more fun.

6.1.7　Question 7: Do you have anything else that you want to share with the researcher?

When being asked this question, many students complained about their grammar class and asked me questions about my life in the U. S. and how to apply for graduate school, which will not be discussed in detail in this chapter since it is not related to the research questions.

6.2　Responses to Teacher Interview

Three teachers who taught extensive reading, intensive reading, and grammar and writing classes for the three groups also participated in the interview, and their opinions were not divergent in response to the interview questions. To summarize teachers' responses, all three teachers agreed that students valued grammar and organization the most in their understanding of the effectiveness of feedback in writing, and students sometimes asked to be corrected on all the errors in their writing. However, teachers said that they did not have much chance to regularly help students practice their writing and self-correction ability because of the existing syllabus that they could not control. Teachers all stressed that based on their daily observation of student performances, motivation and attitude are the most important factors that may have an impact on student writing ability.

In addition, the grammarteacher brought up the main problem these EFL students encountered about writing, he said, ' It is all about grammar and organization. I think students have particular problems of using correct sentence structures, word order, and verbs, and they don't know how to use the transition words. The extensive reading teacher reported that "I think that students have already mastered the fundamental elements to write well, but they are just not interested in writing. I once gave them a writing assignment, but they kind of rejected it and were not willing to do it. The teacher who taught intensive reading also stated that, "As I see, students would rather read the textbook and do drills practice than writing a composition. It is very hard to ask them to write anything." The grammar teacher also said, "I think we as teachers are always prepared to provide feedback for students whenever they need, and actually I did but only in spoken English. We don't normally ask students to submit the second draft of their writing, and we also believe students don't do what they are expected to do when revising any of their assignments after they receive feedback."

Overall, student and teacher responses to the interview reveal similarities and differences in terms of their beliefs and attitudes towards CF in their English teaching and learning. Both student and teacher interviews not only strengthen findings from the questionnaires and classroom observation but also add value to the whole research as they more explicitly expressed student and teacher perceptions and thoughts on the current issue of CF in writing and grammar learning in an EFL context.

6.3　Report from Classroom Observation

This section details the findings from classroom observation in the grammar and writing course at the target university, including descriptions of lessons presented, teacher feedback, as well as teaching practice. Findings from the classroom observation were not surprising, but interesting. Students from all three groups in general did not show much difference in their performances in the classroom.

Here are major things I did while observing the grammar and writing class. I focused on how students' grammar and writing was taught, and how the teacher approached the lessons and activities, along with evaluating whether the teaching practice and approach were effective by identifying both the strengths and problems of teaching. I attempted to identify the type of feedback the teacher provided for students in the classroom, along with assessing whether the feedback was effective. I also evaluated student interaction.

Basically, the teacher spent the first half class (approximately 45 minutes) presenting the grammar points from the textbook, through which a great deal of grammar knowledge was lectured and explained by the instructor, even though students seemed not to be interested in these lectures. Then the teacher asked students to read the textbook for the rest of the class (approximately 45 minutes). Students were assigned to the specific pages of textbook reading, but they did not have to finish all the reading.

A number of issues regarding teaching lecture and feedback practice were noticed during the observation:

1. The lesson tended to be teacher-centered. The teacher did most of the talking, and students mainly passively received information from the teacher.

2. The teacher followed the textbook very closely. Flexibility of learning was lacking. There were no authentic materials incorporated into grammar instruction.

3. The teacher spent a lot of time explaining grammar, following prescribed textbooks without any contextualization of the grammar use in real discourse contexts. In other words, the teacher did not make any connections between the grammatical items and how they could be applied in writing.

4. Activities were based on the textbook and none was derived from other materials beyond the textbook, which was less motivating for student learning.

5. Since no writing or spoken tasks were provided in the course, the effect of written CF was not observed.

6. Pair or group work was rarely conducted. Students were not encouraged to ask questions in class for any grammatical explanations.

Limitation of classroom observation should also be noted: First, lessons were not audio recorded because the teacher did not like the class recorded. Second, teachers and students' behaviors in the classroom may have been influenced by my presence, which may bias their behaviors. Third, due to the restriction of time (only one observation and 90 minutes for each group), it is difficult to have a reliable picture covering all the teaching issues in one observation. Students did not have a chance write anything or express themselves in class because the teacher spent the whole class time on textbook-oriented grammar explanations and reading. This made it challenging to observe any practice on feedback by the teacher or interactions between teachers and students.

Chapter 7: Discussion

This chapter discusses the quantitative, mixed-methods, and qualitative results presented in Chapters 4, 5, and 6, and follows them with a further discussion and interpretation of the three research questions.

*RQ*1: Does accuracy in the use of certain grammatical structures improve as a result of the provision of CF in student L2 writing? Which type of corrective feedback (i. e. , indirect CF and direct CF) better helps facilitate students' L2 writing accuracy?

*RQ*2: What are students' and teachers' expectations and preferences for feedback on students' writing? (E. g. , which component among grammar, content and organizations, do students value the most in their understanding of effective feedback? How do students evaluate their own potential for improvement of their writing ability? What expectations do students have for grammar corrections in their writing?)

*RQ*3: What are the contextual(e. g. ,EFL vs. ESL) , affective(e. g. , attitudes and beliefs) and other individual factors(e. g. ,proficiency level) associated with EFL learners' understanding the effectiveness of CF in L2 writing?

7.1 Quantitative Results

7.1.1 Time Effect of Feedback on Overall Errors for Each Group.

With regard to the effectiveness of corrective feedback (CF) in improving advanced EFL learners' general accuracy of L2 writing, a few conclusions are drawn as follows. First, the developmental trend of student performance in the Indirect CF group showed a continued decrease in error rates across the three tests. The change of error rates was also statistically significant from the pretest to the posttest and from the post- to the delayed posttest with a medium effect size. This indicates a successful application of indirect CF and eventual improved accuracy in the Indirect CF student writing over the research period.

For the FC group, an overall decrease occurred in the number of errors across the three tests as well. However, the significant decrease was only observed from the pretest to the delayed-posttest and the effect size was small. This not only implies a significant time effect of content feedback on student writing accuracy but also indicates that content feedback to a certain extent may play a role in raising students' awareness of the value of self-editing their writing, which accordingly facilitates students' noticing on grammatical features and leads to improvement in grammatical accuracy.

The initial production of grammatical errors by the Direct CF group was higher than the Indirect CF and the FC group. However, students showed a consistent improvement in accuracy on all the errors from the pretest to the posttest and from the pretest to the delayed posttest. Despite the lack of significant change of the error rates from the posttest to the delayed posttest, the increase of accuracy exhibited from the pretest to the posttest and from the pretest to the delayed posttest was substantial, reaching statistical significance with a medium effect size. This indicates Direct CF had a time effect on improving student writing accuracy as well.

Therefore, the overall trend of student performances in writing is apparent as indicated in statistical analysis. The two experimental groups (i. e. , the Indirect CF and Direct CF) showed improved accuracy throughout the whole treatment process while the significant trend was not consistent for the control group (i. e. , the FC group). To explain this phenomenon, we should take into account the fact that FC group did not make as many errors as the two CF groups did from the beginning in the pretest, which led them to be less likely to have remarkable error reduction rates in the posttest and the delayed posttest. The results also indicate that teacher feedback on writing in general could play a positive role in reducing grammatical errors no matter the type of feedback.

7.1.2   Time Effect of Feedback on Individual Error Types for Each Group.

Concerning the change of individual error types in the Indirect CF group, the tendency reveals a clear drop for all seven primary error types: subject-verb agreement, plural, verb, article, tense, preposition and parts of speech from the pretest to the delayed posttest. Of these, article errors was the only error type that constantly decreased across the three tests. However, the statistical significance of time effect with a small to medium effect size only appeared on subject-verb agreement, plural, article, tense, preposition, and part of speech; verb error was not significantly affected by the indirect CF. The results suggest a potential over-time effect of the Indirect CF for specific grammatical error types on helping L2 learners to write accurately.

With regard to the development of accuracy for the FC group, with the exception of subject-verb agreement and plural errors, students demonstrated a slight improvement on verb, article, tense, prepositional, and parts of speech errors from the pretest to the posttest while no significant time effect was found on the change of error rates. Plural was the only error type that continuously declined and obtained a statistical significance of improvement across the three tests with a small effect size. Subject-verb agreement errors were an exception; they did not show any positive trend of error reduction from the pretest to the delayed posttest. The results from the FC group indicate content feedback could positively affect the use of certain grammatical features(e. g. , plural)in improving L2 writing accuracy.

In contrary to the Indirect CF and the FC group, all the seven error types in the Direct CF group showed an initial decrease from the pretest to the posttest, indicating a noticeable and immediate improvement of accuracy in student writing once they received the direct CF. All the errors in the direct CF group also showed an eventual reduction from the pretest to the delayed posttest. In particular, subject-verb agreement, plural, article, prepositional and part of speech errors in the posttest or the delayed posttest declined more than verb and tense errors, on which a significant time effect was identified with a small to medium effect size. Students' performance on these errors indicated their frequent attempts to correct them and probably it turned out to be either successful corrections or ignorance of certain errors. The trend also suggested a positive role for direct CF on specific error types for students' improvement on writing accuracy. However, errors on verb and tense did not reach statistical significance, indicating that the two grammatical forms may be unlikely to be affected by direct CF on student writing accuracy in a treatment of short duration.

In addition, by looking at students' aggregate performance on the percentage of different error types, the majority of students from all the three groups tended to commit fewer errors after the treatment from the pretest to the delayed posttest. This indicated that students more often attempted to and successfully corrected their errors through the provision of teacher feedback in their writing.

7.1.3 Group Difference of Feedback on Overall Errors.

Taken as a whole, the data reveal a unified tendency across the three groups. The overall developmental trend for all three groups exhibits a decline of error rates across the three tests, with more variance in the pretest which became less in the post- and the delayed posttest as the Indirect CF and Direct CF group started with much more errors produced than the FC group.

All three groups showed an effect of time on error frequency from the pretest to the delayed posttest, but no significant changes were achieved from the posttest to delayed-posttest by the three groups. The Indirect CF and Direct CF group also obtained significant changes from the pretest to the posttest.

Moreover, no group effect was found to be statistically significant on the total number of errors that the three groups committed. This indicates that the two experimental groups – Indirect CF and Direct CF —did not work more effectively and efficiently than the control group that only received content feedback. In particular, it can be concluded that the two types of CF (i. e. , Indirect vs. Direct CF) in fact are not statistically distinct from each other regarding their impact on EFL learners' improved writing accuracy.

7. 1. 4 **Group Difference of Feedback on Individual Error Types.**

The findings are in particular encouraging and surprising in regard to the effectiveness of feedback on specific accuracy concerning each individual error type. It is interesting to note that subject-verb agreement and plural errors turned out to be the majority of errors committed by all three groups, indicating all three groups of students preferred and more often attempted to use these features but had more difficulties in correctly processing or producing them. Prepositional and part of speech errors appeared to be least frequent among the seven primary error types in the three groups, which indicates students were either less favorable in using or had fewer difficulties with the two features in their writing. Another possibility is that students did not have access to many opportunities to use these two features in their writing. Within this tendency, the difference in the production of errors among the three groups is that the Indirect CF students tended to produce more tense and article errors in their writing; while the Direct CF group were likely to produce more verb and article errors.

Moreover, both the Indirect and Direct CF group committed fewer errors in subject-verb agreement, plural, article, preposition and part of speech after the treatment. The only grammatical pattern that was positively affected by the indirect CF was tense. Verb was the only error type that was not disposed to be influenced by any of the three types of feedback. This finding contradicts Ferris et al. (2000) and Ferris and Roberts (2001) study, which found a substantial progress over a semester in reducing verb errors but no reduction in article errors. This finding is also congruent with Ferris (2006) and Rahimi (2009), who found that verb errors were not as amendable to CF as other error types, such as articles. Rahimi (2009) even argued that verb errors can be considered as untreatable for Persian EFL learners. It was also interesting to note that all types of feedback seemed to have an effect on plural error rates. Not only the indirect and direct CF but also the content feedback reached a statistical significance on plural errors. Thus, it can be concluded that subject-verb agreement, tense, article, preposition, and part of speech were more amendable to the indirect CF. The direct CF worked more effectively for subject-verb agreement, plural, article, preposition and part of speech. Feedback on content could also affect students' production of grammatical features, such as plural.

7.1.5　Conclusion.

Based on the above-mentioned results, a few observations can be made: First, there was no group effect as students who received CF did not produce more accurate texts than those who received no error correction but only feedback on content. This may suggest that students receiving any feedback, no matter whether the feedback is on content or grammar, does not attribute their improved writing accuracy to the CF.

The findings are not only consistent with some previous research (e. g. , Ashwell, 2000 ; Truscott and Hsu, 2008 ; Bruton, 2009), which shows written CF did not significantly affect student ability to write accurately, but also correspond to the studies that found no group difference between different types of feedback (e. g. , Lalande, 1982; Semke, 1984; Robb et al. ,1986; Kepner, 1991). Kepner's (1991) study showed that within a 12-week timeframe no significant difference in errors showed for intermediate EFLs between the group with an explicit correction and a message group with no correction. Robb et al. (1986) targeted EFL undergraduate students in Japan and assigned them into four groups, respectively receiving explicit correction, coded correction, highlighting and a marginal count of errors in each line. All the groups showed substantial gains, but group performances did not differ significantly. Thus, they argued that the different effect on accuracy was not found to be statistically significant between the indirect and direct CF.

In addition, the findings don't show strong evidence in favor a significant positive effect for CF on student writing in line with previous research(e. g. ,Bitchener and Knoch, 2008 ,2009 ,2010; Ferris & Roberts, 2011; Chandler,2013; Ferris, et al. ,2013, Liu, et al. ,2013; Shintani & Ellis,2013). For example, Chandler(2013) and Ferris, et al. (2013) found a strong relationship between teacher's error correction and successful error reduction in students' subsequent writing. However, the effectiveness of CF may be attributed to differences in research design. For example, Bitchener and Knoch's(2008) study only had experimental groups and only examined English articles while the current study also included a control group and had a broader scope of focus on different types of errors. Therefore, Bitchner and Knoch's (2008) research was unable to attribute gains in overall accuracy to corrective feedback.

Second, while looking at the time effect, it can be assumed that teacher feedback may play a role in helping EFL learners develop their ability to write accurately. It does not matter which type of feedback is involved in teaching and learning practice because all the treatments in the current research seemed to be virtually identical in their effect on changing the error rates. Both corrective (i. e. , indirect and direct CF) and content feedback could possibly facilitate students' noticing of grammatical forms and thereby foster their self-editing ability in their writing. The findings conform to some previously conducted research. For example, Ferris and Roberts (2001) found the two types of corrections—indirect and direct CF—were nearly identical in their value for improved accuracy. They claimed that error correction and feedback help L2 learners reduce their errors in the writing. They also found some of the changes extended to new pieces of writing and the time effect was substantial. Thus, no specific types of feedback should be considered superior to any other in writing practice.

Another point is worth discussing in terms of the three groups' writing accuracy across the three tests. As can be seen, in the pretest, the Indirect CF group and Direct CF group made many more errors than the FC group; while in the posttest, errors in the Indirect CF group and Direct CF group became fewer than the FC group. Then, in the delayed posttest, although the FC group student errors were slightly lower than the Indirect CF group and the Direct CF group, there was very slight variance in their writing accuracy among the three groups. In this case, it can be inferred from the phenomenon that students in the Indirect CF and the Direct CF group attempted to work hard on the type of corrective feedback they received and finally caught up with the FC group. Considering the FC group, as they started with a remarkably lower number of errors compared to the Indirect and Direct CF groups, it was reasonable that no considerable change occurred in the FC group across the three tests. Also, because the FC group had the shortest writing length (see Appendix F for the information of writing length) , they were more likely to commit fewer errors at the beginning and kept a stable developmental trend overtime. Therefore, it could be stated from a practical (though impressionistic) viewpoint that the two experimental groups—Indirect CF and Direct CF— revealed more improvements on their writing accuracy due to the treatment of CF from the researcher.

Moreover, it can be concluded that different error types were not equally amenable to the treatment as different types of errors decreased at different rates. This finding is consistent with some previous studies that explored the effect of CF on different error types and showed different levels of improvement on writing accuracy (e. g. , Beunnigen et al. , 2012; Bitchener, et al. , 2005; Ferris, 2006; Ferris & Roberts, 2001; Lalande, 1992; Sheppard, 1992). It seems that all the primary seven error types except for verb are likely to be affected by the indirect CF, including subject-verb agreement, plural, article, tense, preposition, and parts of speech. Subject-verb agreement, plural, article, preposition and parts of speech are prone to be affected by the direct CF as well. It is also interesting to see that plural is the only error type that is more amendable to treatment of all three types of feedback while verb is the only error type that is not affected by any type of feedback (see Table 7. 1 below).

Table 7. 1

Amenability of Error Types to Different Types of Feedback

	Sva	Plural	Article	Tense	Verb	Prep.	Pos.
Indirect CF	+ [a]	+	+	+	--	+	+
FC	-- [b]	+	--	--	--	--	--
Direct CF	+	+	+	--	--	+	+

Note. a. + means amenable; b. – means non-amenable

By looking at the trend in individual students' performance over time, some students improved slightly while others greatly improved and then consolidated mastery of these grammatical forms. This indicates that within each group, individual students' achievements varied from low to high achievers. Some students may have benefited significantly from CF, but that was not revealed in ANOVA since their performance did not affect the overall results.

7.1.5.1 **Potential Factors and Reasons.** There are some possible explanations for the absence of significant differences among the three groups. First, EFL learners' advanced English proficiency can be accounted for as a factor that potentially affects their production of accurate writing. Even though students from the three groups were identical in their overall English proficiency based on their scores in the college entrance exam, students were not actually equal in their initial writing proficiency as they performed differently in accuracy in the pretest. The control (FC) group exhibited more accurate performance in the pretest. However, in general all three groups wrote fairly accurate essays across the treatments. In this case, it can be assumed that because of their advanced English proficiency whether or not students received feedback and correction on their first writing did not seem to influence their performance on the subsequent writing assignments.

The second possible explanation to why CF did not show any effect on student writing accuracy might be because of the insufficient duration of the treatment. The research lasted for only ten weeks, which was a short period of time. A two-month experiment with only two treatments may not be enough to reveal the influence of CF on student writing accuracy.

It is also possible that students may not benefit from CF because of their attitudes in dealing with CF in their self-correction process. As revealed in students' responses to the questionnaire and interview, some students were not willing to deal with or not interested in understanding how the CF could work and help them improve their writing. Some students also expressed that they could not understand the feedback, which may raise a certain level of anxiety and discouragement, consequently leading to their incapability of fixing the errors.

Moreover, cross-linguistic differences between Chinese and English could be a source of certain types oferrors that are not amenable to corrections. Such differences seem to be especially significant in the context of China since the majority of English classes are still taught in Chinese with much emphasis on the explicit teaching of grammatical rules by the teachers and the conscious application of the rules by the students. Hence, it is important to deal with this issue in this EFL context and to examine the extent to which the teacher's CF effect is influenced by such cross-linguistic errors. For instance, mastering the use of articles correlates with high proficiency in English skills. However, Chinese students often have difficulties deciding whether a definite, indefinite, or zero article is needed for a noun because Chinese does not have articles in its language system. Instead, individuals tend to use demonstratives or quantifiers to express the meaning of articles in English.

Another factor to consider is the negative nature of CF(i. e. , negative evidence) and the positive nature of CF(i. e. , positive evidence). Taking into consideration the ethical issue, although the control group did not receive any corrective feedback, they received feedback on the content of their compositions. It is likely that the control group benefited from the feedback as most of the comments were positive(e. g. , praise) , which to a certain extent indirectly encouraged students to attend to feedback for errors during their writing process. This indicates a potential effect of positive feedback in aiding teacher's effort to provide constructive corrections.

Another factor may be related to the EFL learning context. As indicated in Kang and Han (2015) , learners in EFL tend to benefit less from corrective feedback than learners in an ESL environment. An alternative explanation according to Ferris(2010) could be that EFL classes are more concerned about writing as a product instead of as a process, in which EFL learners have fewer opportunities to revise and edit their writing.

With regard to students' improved writing performance over time within each group, since no group effect was found, it is not appropriate to claim that students' improvement is attributed to the CF because the control group which received only content feedback also showed improvement in general accuracy. Therefore, other factors that might have influenced student performances should be noted, from which some possible explanations can also be suggested for the improved accuracy within each group. The first factor considers EFL learners' English proficiency. For advanced EFL learners in college, they may already have had a certain level of self-editing ability even though they did not accept the fact, as indicated in student responses to the interview. Thus, different types of feedback may not make distinctions in their effectiveness in improving student writing accuracy. Probably for advanced level EFL learners, any type of feedback could have an effect in improving their writing accuracy, and the effect could be significant as shown in the Indirect CF and Direct CF group. Regarding the FC group's performance, the results are also reasonable. Because of a fairly low number of errors committed at the beginning of the treatment, it is unlikely that any significant changes occurred for this group over time.

Another possible reason for within-group significance can be detected from student responses to the questionnaires and interview, in which most of the students held a positive belief of CF. As the majority of students mentioned, they were not discouraged by error corrections but felt grateful for the feedback from the researcher; they liked the type of feedback provided by the researcher and were also willing to apply it to their future writing. Therefore, a possibility exists for a relationship between the treatment from the researcher and students' attitudes during the two-month research period. The provision of feedback not only brought students' attention to their writing, but also inspired them to work hard in the process of correcting errors and learning grammar. Students with a more positive attitude towards CF would be more likely to attend to the errors and self-edit their writing, leading to a substantial change from the beginning of the treatment to the end over the two months period of time, and to a successful uptake of feedback for their development of linguistics competence. In contrast, some students from the two CF groups may not like to see the red ink for their errors from the researcher. This could lead students to ignore the feedback intentionally.

In particular, in respect to student improvement on specific grammatical forms, many studies have examined hypotheses to account for the acquisition order and processing difficulties of different grammatical structures. Thus, problems can be caused as a result of syntactic complexity of certain error forms. Ferris (2001) defined and distinguished between treatable(e. g. , subject-verb agreement, plural and article) and untreatable errors(e. g. , word order, word choice and idiomatic usage). Some error types are more correctible than others because they are relatively simple and can be treated as discrete items; while other error types may be an integral part of a complex sentence structure or a more complex system which are not amenable to CF (Truscott, 2001). Another possibility to explain why certain grammatical errors are more likely to benefit from CF than others is because of the fact that their acquisition not only depends on understanding their forms but also the meaning and use in relation to the language system. According to Larsen Freeman (2015), grammatical structures not only consist of forms(morpho-syntactic) but also are meaning-related (semantics) for communicative purposes in varied contexts (practical). Some errors are only form-based and occur in a rule-governed way, and learners can refer to grammar books to deal with these errors(e. g. , subject-verb agreement, plural, and tense) ; while others are meaning and use-related that are more likely to pose difficulties (e. g. , articles, prepositions and word choice).

It can be concluded that these EFL learners preferred to attend to, use, or were more accessible to the structurally easier grammatical patterns, which were less linguistically and cognitively demanding, instead of the more difficult ones after they received CF. It is also possible that the less problematic grammatical forms that individuals produce may be the ones they use more frequently in their writing. For example, the most frequent error types— subject-verb agreement and plural— accounted for the most errors committed by students in all three groups. These errors were also comprehended and produced considerably better than the other types of errors in the subsequent writing tasks. To correct an error in subject-verb agreement, one only needs to check its form in terms of whether the subject of a clause is third person singular(i. e. , she, he, it) without considering its meaning or use. If the answer is affirmative, one needs to add a $-s, -es$, or-*ies* as a suffix to the verb to maintain the agreement between the subject and the verb. To fix an error in plural, one only needs to either add a $-s, -es$, or-*ies* to the noun to make it plural or remove a $-s, -es$, or-*ies* from the noun to make it singular. Meaning and use are not involved, either. Therefore, it seemed that if students were only exposed to a limited number of options to choose from to correct an error or the error form did not contain any meaning or use, they were more likely to successfully correct these errors.

In addition, grammar instruction from the students' teacher can be regarded as a factor in ultimate reduction of errors; teaching materials and activities in classrooms may also have a certain effect on student learning outcomes(i. e. , application of CF and uptake of CF) , although I did not notice any specific writing tasks or any other opportunities in writing practice offered for students during classroom observation. Errors could also be amendable to self-correction based on exposure alone. According to Francis(2011) , it cannot be denied that by means of rich comprehensible input alone even without any explicit grammar instruction, learners can still make progress in their grammatical competence in terms of both fluency and accuracy. Thus, it is likely that students' writing accuracy improved because of the many types of grammatical input they received from other sources during the treatment, the intensive or extensive exposure to other

English courses they had during the two months, and any other grammar or writing practice they had in or out of class.

Moreover, some other confounding factors are worthy of being considered. First, the difficulty of the essay topics may affect student performance in writing accuracy. Some students may have sufficient knowledge of the topic the researcher offered, whereas others may regard the topic as too challenging or demanding for them. Besides, peer pressure could limit their performance in writing, and some unexpected practical issues may also produce negative influence in students' application of CF. Last but not least, some personal characteristics, such as insufficient English knowledge and limited or passive personal devotion in writing, could negatively affect students' writing accuracy. Some students did not take CF seriously, and therefore did not write much and improve much because of their being less motivated.

7.2　Mixed-methods Results

Questionnaire 1 was conducted on the first day of the experiment, eliciting student responses regarding their prior English learning experiences with CF and grammar. Questionnaire 2 was administrated at the end of the experimental study, focusing on students' experience and perceptions of CF from the treatment. Expectations based on findings from the questionnaires match and explain the findings and provide additional evidence regarding whether or not corrections have value for grammatical accuracy.

7.2.1　Questionnaire 1.

About students' responses in Questionnaire 1, significant group effect was obtained for students' grammar learning background, anxiety of making mistakes, as well as confidence of using English among the three groups. Students in general from all three groups held a positive belief of their prior

English learning experiences but had a negative view of their own English ability. 100% of students from the Indirect CF and Direct CF groups, and 94. 3% from the FC group had previous grammar learning experiences. 97. 2% of students from the Indirect CF and the FC group, and 100% from the Direct CF group had received teacher feedback before. 97. 2% of students from the Indirect CF group, 100% from the FC and Direct CF group thought feedback was beneficial. However, only 28. 6% of students from the Indirect CF group, 11. 4% from the FC group, and 22. 8% from the Direct CF group were not afraid of making mistakes while using English; the majority of students— 97. 1% from the Indirect CF, 100% from the FC group, and 97. 1% from the Direct CF group— lacked confidence of dealing with grammar use in writing.

A significant negative correlation was found between the Indirect CF students' prior language learning experience and their performances in the posttest, indicating that the more experiences students had with English grammar, the fewer errors they made. Results also revealed significant correlations between the Indirect CF student responses to different items in the questionnaire, which basically shows that students who had more experiences with English grammar also had more experience with teacher feedback, and thus thought feedback was beneficial; accordingly, students felt less stressed about making mistakes and more confident of using English in writing.

Moreover, significant negative correlations appeared in the Direct CF students' responses to Q4 and their error rates in the posttest, as well as their responses to Q5 and error reduction from the pretest to the delayed posttest. The results interestingly indicate that the more students were afraid of making mistakes in writing, the more errors they tended to commit; and the less confident students felt about their English ability, the more errors students were inclined to make.

7.2.2 **Questionnaire** 2.

Over half of the students—65.7% from the Indirect CF group,60% in FC group, and 54.3% in Direct CF—regarded error correction as the best type of teacher feedback on their writing. 60% of Indirect CF students, 68.6% of FC, and 42.9% of Direct CF students preferred error correction with explanation and description. 45.7% of Indirect CF students, 57.1% of FC students, and 40% Direct CF students considered grammar feedback with explanation and description the easiest way for them to figure out the errors and correct them. There were also 40% of Direct CF students who considered direct correction the easiest way for corrective feedback. In addition, the majority of students from all three groups expressed their favor for and understood the type of feedback they received, did not feel discouraged by corrections, and would like to attend to and apply the corrections to their future writing.

When asking students to rate their English language skills and confidence in writing, with the purpose to see if their self-evaluation matched their language and writing skills reflected in their performances in the three tests, most of the students rated their skills as weak or bad and only a small number of students regarded their English as good. However, as I observed, most students under-evaluated their English proficiency as they wrote more accurate essays than expected and performed very well in the three tests.

In terms of correlations between student perception and attitudes to different types of feedback and their performances in accuracy, a significant negative correlation appeared in Indirect CF students' responses to Q10 and error rates in the delayed posttest, and a significant positive correlation showed between student responses to Q6 and error reduction from the posttest to the delayed posttest. This indicates that students with more positive attitudes towards the application of indirect CF committed fewer errors; in particular students with positive attitudes towards indirect CF had a greater decline in error rates. In addition, a significant group difference was achieved in Q10 between the Indirect CF and FC group, and between the Indirect CF group and Direct CF group, indicating students responded differently after they received written feedback from the researcher.

Regarding the open-ended questions in the questionnaire, the majority of students from the Indirect CF and Direct CF group felt happy about, satisfied with or grateful for immediate teacher correction. As a clear contrast, the FC group students generally had a negative perception (e. g. , embarrassed, nervous, bothered, overwhelmed) of immediate teacher corrections. Most students from all three groups expected teachers to focus on grammatical issues while providing written feedback.

7.2.3 Conclusion.

Similar to previous findings (Diab, 2005; Ferris, 2011, 2013; Mustafa, 2012; McMartin-Miller, 2014), students in the current study revealed a great concern about accurate writing and cared about having their written errors corrected. Students from all groups highly appreciated the type of feedback received from the researcher and were very positive about the benefits of corrective feedback. They expressed their desire for more CF from teachers but had different preferences. The majority of students from the Indirect CF and FC group preferred teachers to provide corrections with descriptions and explanations; the Direct CF students were favorable toward not only corrections with descriptions and explanations but also direct correction. Contrary to expectations, only a very small portion of students showed favorable attitudes towards indirect CF in their questionnaire responses. Also, it can be assumed that lack of feedback may lead to students' anxiety in writing, which consequently decreases their motivation and lowers their confidence. This collaborates the medium to large correlation found between learners' attitudes toward feedback and error reduction in the mixed-methods analysis.

However, it is also crucial to discuss another phenomenon, which may not be easily identified from the statistics: Regarding certain non-significant correlations between students' responses to the questionnaires and their error rates, it is possible that students who had positive attitudes did not demonstrate improvement in their accuracy of writing over time; in contrast, students who did not like being corrected may show a certain level of improvement during the research time. Hence, no clear conclusion can be drawn because of no existed relationships between students' attitudes towards CF and their improvement of writing accuracy.

7.3 Qualitative Results

Interviews were conducted in the study to gain some in-depth understanding of students' production and perceptions of CF, and to explain student improvement or lack of improvement in their writing accuracy over time. A detailed examination of students' perceptions of effectiveness of CF through interviews showed interesting differences and similarities between the groups and among individual students. This led the researcher investigate the reasons for their responses and achieve a better understanding of their writing.

Responses from students and teachers showed similarities and differences regarding their perceptions of CF. The findings from interviews also corresponded to those from the questionnaires regarding student and teacher attitudes towards error correction. On one side, students in general valued teacher feedback and took it seriously in writing. They felt they had gained more grammar knowledge from the CF, because it was more interesting than the textbook-based materials, even though some CF had revealed challenges. Some students showed their expectations for teachers to correct all the errors; and others hoped teachers could provide feedback on various writing aspects rather than only concentrating on grammar. On the other hand, teachers agreed on the importance of corrective feedback for improving student English proficiency and writing accuracy, but they complained that many students would not take it seriously after they received feedback. Thus, teachers usually do not follow up with students after providing feedback and students in return do little after they receive feedback as the teacher never asks them to revise and resubmit for the second time.

A clear contrast occurred between the two experimental (Indirect CF and Direct CF) groups and the control (FC) group in student responses to the interview. First of all, almost all the interviewees from the two CF groups desired to receive teacher feedback on grammar for their writing, while most of the students in the FC group emphasized more the importance the organization possessed over grammar for good writing quality. Second, only one student from the Indirect CF group and none of students from the Direct CF group felt confident in their writing and self-editing ability; while 40% of the interviewees from the FC group showed their confidence in writing proficiency. This corresponds to the fact that the FC group produced more accurate essays in the pretest.

When asked about the possible confounding factors affecting their production of writing based on the current English environment, most students from the two CF groups thought motivation, attitude, belief, and interest were the major factors either facilitating or inhibiting their writing accuracy. Students believed that individuals who have positive attitude and high motivation would have more interest in the process of writing and editing towards their errors, and possibly more chance to improve their writing accuracy over time. While the majority interviewees from the FC group considered the context of learning as a major factor that influenced their writing ability, and even inhibited their progress as capable L2 writers and self-editors. Students pointed out that they had little motivation to learn grammar due to their lacking authenticity and practicality in the current English learning environment at schools.

By looking at individual students' responses and performances as shown in their developmental trends, variations were found between learners who demonstrated different developmental patterns, and their responses to the interview questions varied. Students who demonstrated continued improvements in their writing accuracy tended to value teachers' feedback by being actively involved in the process of writing and editing. They tried to apply teacher feedback to their writing more often than those who did not gain much improvement in accuracy. However, some students were not actively involved in the process of writing and editing, and did not actually attempt to correct their errors or to apply the feedback to their writing. The conclusion drawn here is that students who tended to self-edit their writing were more likely to make improvements in accuracy over time than those who did not. It also seems that students who were good at self-editing or confident of their own writing ability tended to demonstrate a reduction in errors from the posttest to the delayed posttest. In contrast, students who were not successful in reducing errors were those who did not like writing or did not like to devote time to revisions and editing. In this case, attitude can be regarded as a confounding factor which may play an important role in affecting student development of writing accuracy.

In addition, classroom observation only provides limited clarification regarding students' and teachers' expectations, perceptions, and attitudes toward CF. Observations not only confirmed student complaints, but also suggested an essential role of teacher instruction and practice in classrooms, which could lead to several effects on students' cognition, behavior, and affect. For example, students came to favor certain types of CF but were disinterested in others; students tended to ignore the CF; students became demotivated by the CF provided by the teacher.

Chapter 8: Implications, Recommendations and Conclusion

This chapter consists of five sections: (a) summary of the major results for the three research questions; (b) implications and practical recommendations for EFL teachers; (c) strength of the current study; (d) limitations of the current study; and (e) future direction for research on corrective feedback.

8.1 Summary of Results

As can be seen, findings from students' writing, questionnaire, interview and classroom observation shared some common features but contrasted in others. Although not all quantitative results were validated by responses for the questions in the questionnaires and interviews and student improvement in writing accuracy, certain conclusions can still be reached based on the results.

RQ1: "Does accuracy in the use of certain grammatical structures improve as a result of the provision of CF in student L2 writing? Which type of corrective feedback (i. e. , indirect CF and direct CF) better helps facilitate students' L2 writing accuracy?" While this study did not reveal statistically significant group differences between the two CF groups and the FC group in individual error rates, it is doubtful that the improved accuracy is attributed to CF. However, except for verb in indirect CF group and verb and tense in direct CF group, students from the two CF groups showed significant improved accuracy over time in their use of subject – verb agreement, plural, article, preposition and parts of speech. Students in the FC group did not show any significant change except plural. The fact that significant gains were found for the CF group while no gains for the control (i. e. , FC) group indicates that students' improved accuracy in the use of certain grammatical forms could be associated with CF.

Meanwhile, no significant group differences existed for the total number of errors but with a time effect within each group from the pretest to the delayed posttest. In other words, either this study does not provide sufficient evidence to show a superior effect of CF over the content only feedback or the stronger effect of either type of CF(e. g. , indirect or Direct CF) was not significant enough to be observable on student writing accuracy, because the control (FC) group that did not receive CF also improved. Therefore, although impressionistically students from the two CF groups(i. e. , indirect CF and direct CF) appeared to benefit from the treatment in some way above and beyond what would have occurred in a non-CF treatment as revealed in the statically significant time effect, the results did not indicate which type of CF leads to greater gains or a higher level of correction in either short-term revision or long-term written accuracy. This is supported by Kang and Han's (2015) meta-analysis, which did not show any clear-cut differences between the indirect and direct CF on their efficacy in writing.

Finally, I would argue that although the study did not show a statistically significant positive effect of CF on student writing accuracy(CF may not play a large role and the relationship between CF and writing is not clear based on the current study), we cannot conclude that CF is completely ineffective or even harmful; we cannot deny the potential benefit of CF, either. The application of CF could be potentially influenced, either in a positive or negative means, by internal and external factors such as student English proficiency, research design, the length of experiment, instructional context, etc.

RQ2: "What are students' and teachers' preferences and expectations for feedback on students' writing?" In terms of the perceived value of corrective feedback, all participants confirmed the importance and value of CF to improve their writing accuracy and general English ability, and they showed favorable attitudes towards CF in language learning. Students in particular showed positive attitudes to error corrections with descriptions and explanations. Students also expressed that they did not feel discouraged by CF, and they would like to apply the corrections to their future writing. In addition, students expressed their desire for more CF from teachers. Some students expected that teachers should correct all grammatical errors; others hoped teachers could provide feedback on various writing aspects beyond just grammar.

However, there isa contradiction between what the teachers believed and their actual practices in the classroom. Although teachers believed feedback was important and beneficial, they seemed not to use it often in their daily instruction. Teachers did not usually meet with students to discuss their writing problems, either. Student responses to interviews indicated that teachers did not meet student expectations and needs for CF, which was confirmed from the classroom observations.

RQ3: "What are the contextual (e. g. , EFL vs. ESL) and affective (e. g. , attitudes) factors associated with EFL learners' understanding of the effectiveness of CF in L2 writing?" The EFL learning context as suggested in student responses to the interview and classroom observations may suggest a clear and decisive relationship between students' perception of the difficulty in understanding and correcting the errors and their eventual improvement in writing accuracy. Students expressed that they were full of enthusiasm and motivation in learning English. However, most of the classes in Asian countries focus on grammar and vocabulary lecturing and explanations at the expense of students' active participation and interaction with other English skills, such as writing and speaking. Teachers seldom focused on students' writing process as they rarely practiced writing in the classrooms. Most of the time, students were asked to finish their writing tasks back home and then to submit it later on in school. Teacher would only give a grade on students' compositions but with little follow-up afterwards. For example, teachers did not explain the major errors students committed; there were no face-to-face conferences to discuss the errors and students' writing problems. The limited teacher practice of writing and error feedback obviously did not benefit students. Students also mentioned the learning style they cultivated over the years in high school was continuously developed while they were in college, which demotivated their creative learning. Instead, they were accustomed to accept knowledge that was forced into their brain and lacked knowing its practical value.

Moreover, students' attitude is a potential factor that has an impact on students' application of CF and continued error reduction. Students in general were being positive and active during the process of writing and error correction. The majority of students in this study stressed that they were eager to see the errors they made and then to correct the errors immediately because they wanted to improve their English writing. Some students tended to think about the reasons they made the errors. Therefore, students who showed more positive attitudes seemed to have more improvement in their writing accuracy. This corroborates the medium correlation found between students' attitudes towards feedback and error reduction in the quantitative analysis. However, students also expressed a lack of confidence in dealing with their writing and self-editing ability. Statistics shown from the questionnaires revealed that the more students worried about making mistakes in their writing, the less accurate essays they tended to write; meanwhile, the less students felt confident of their own writing ability, the more errors they were likely to commit.

8.2 Pedagogical Implications and Recommendations for EFL Teachers

The current research provides a practical perspective on how language teachers need to be more aware of the challenges and benefits of using corrective feedback during grammar learning. In particular, this study informs teachers of English in international settings (e. g. , China) how to better develop materials, activities, and tasks that are applicable for L2 students in form-focused instruction. The study also shows how language teaching should lessen students' difficulties instead of posing more challenges. EFL teachers need to consider when and how to provide appropriate corrective feedback and to incorporate grammar learning materials that take into account students' individual differences, such as their English proficiency level, motivation, and attitudes. Factors that contribute to influencing L2 learners' writing accuracy cannot be intuitively discerned and must be identified by L2 instructors.

Though some individual students dislike being corrected and think judgment of errors might be too tough on them, the occurrence of errors will not stop happening if students do not give enough consideration to error correction. It is also true that although L2 learners may be able to generatea great idea in writing tasks, readers could still have a difficult time understanding the texts if they are filled with errors. Therefore, it is important for teachers to help students understand how feedback is intended to affect their L2 learning, and why it is given in the way it is. Otherwise, students might not be able to interpret how beneficial feedback can be.

Ellis(2009) proposed the following guidelines for correcting learners' errors, constituting an explicit set of principles teachers can reflect on when determining their own policy for CF and to eliminate the potential negative effects of CF. First, teachers should ascertain their students' attitudes towards CF, appraise them of the value of CF, and negotiate agreed goals for CF with students. The goals are likely to vary according to different contexts. Second, teachers should let students know that CF works for both accuracy and fluency in writing, and that students should not be afraid of CF. Third, focused CF is potentially more effective than unfocused CF, so teachers should identify specific linguistic targets for correction. Fourth, teachers need to be able to implement a variety of written CF strategies and to adapt the specific strategies they use to the particular student they are correcting. For example, teachers can start with an implicit form of correction by simply indicating an error, and then if the student is unable to self-correct, to move to a more explicit and direct form of correction. This requires that teachers be responsive to the feedback they get from students on their own corrective feedback. Fifth, teachers need to provide extra time following the corrective feedback for students to show uptake of the CF; in other words, students need the opportunity to attend to corrections and to revise their writing. Moreover, teachers should be prepared to vary who, when, and how they correct in accordance with the cognitive and affective needs of the individual learner. This means that teachers do not need to follow a consistent set of procedures for all students. Teachers should also be prepared to correct specific errors on several occasions to enable students to achieve full self-regulation. Additionally, teachers should monitor the extent to which CF causes anxiety in learners and should adapt the strategies they use to eliminate students' anxiety. Based on Ellis' principles, a number of implications can be drawn from the study that can also be applied to EFL contexts.

8.2.1 Considering Learner Factors.

Many researchers have proposed suggestions on pedagogical practices in L2 classrooms in order to limit the negative effect of certain kinds of CF for L2 learners, such as students' increased anxiety when being corrected. Based on my research findings, when providing corrective feedback, it is important for EFL teachers to take into consideration a wide range of learner factors so that teachers can obtain a better understanding of the origins of their students' errors and provide efficient and appropriate feedback that help their students progress in their language growth. In particular, language teachers should consider students' perspectives, sensitivities, personalities, expectations, preferences, and affective needs when providing corrective feedback. Teachers should not impose their own assumptions on students and should deal with conflicts between students' beliefs and instructional practices. In addition, since many studies suggested that teacher feedback had a great potential for miscommunication and misunderstanding, it is recommended that teachers build up a connection between students' expectations and teachers' beliefs by having dialogues and interactions with students to negotiate the aims and expectations of feedback. For instance, because learner preferences and expectations for CF could vary from group to group over time, it is recommended that EFL teachers use surveys to discover individual students' preferences and expectations regarding various CF strategies. Survey data should not be the only source of information used for planning classroom instruction, but it can be used as a tool to reduce the discrepancy between what students expect for CF and what techniques the teachers apply to error treatment. This could be beneficial and enhance both the teachers' and students' efforts in their teaching and learning process, and prevent potential conflicts between students' beliefs and teachers' instructional practices.

Sadler (1989) noted that teacher feedback is effective when it identifies the gap between what is understood and the learning target. Before providing feedback, teachers need to first determine whether the student is a good candidate for it. This helps students to take full advantage of CF. Hattie and Timperley (2007) wrote that when students do not have partial understanding of the learning target, feedback techniques are not effective. However, for students who have partial knowledge, providing feedback can help them recognize and correcttheir misconception or confusion in regard to the learning target or extend their current level of understanding.

8.2.2 Developing Self-correction Strategies.

EFL teachers are responsible for helping L2 learners recognize errors, develop self-revision skills, and to make the best use of error feedback for further language tasks. To be more specific, different error types need to receive various treatments from teachers, such as complex sentence structures, word choice, and other idiosyncratic uses of language forms. It is necessary for EFL teachers to carefully identify and respond to different types of errors by providing detailed grammar explanations and to teach students the correct way of responding to errors. In other words, teacher should explicitly train students for self-correction strategies in class. For instance, the teacher can have their students engage in group work to identify and correct errors that commonly occur in their peers' writing. Peer correction can consolidate students' grammar knowledge and make the knowledge explicit in order to benefit each other. This could be a productive way of helping students explain to themselves the errors and then to find the correct answers.

In addition, due to their prior knowledge of English grammar, some students may be capable of self-editing discrete lexical errors while others may be capable of self-correcting sentence level errors. In this case, students tend to focus on the errors that are easily fixed while ignoring those that require more effort to correct. This poses the challenge that teachers need to be prepared to effectively treat students' written errors by carefully planning a course design which considers students' needs, backgrounds, and the instructional context. For example, teachers can have students engage in the process of self-identifying and addressing the most frequent error patterns in their writing. After the teacher points out all the errors, students need to take an active role of keeping records of what type of errors they have committed in their writing assignment. Students then need to identify the most frequent error types, examine the context where the errors occurred, and then review relevant grammar rules. This can be a useful technique for advanced EFL learners to develop an awareness of proofreading errors in their future writing.

8.2.3   Focused CF Instead of Comprehensive Correction.

An over-focus on all error corrections can lead students to use the sentence structures that they are confident in and ignore other complex sentence structures, which may result in the unsuccessful development of their writing skills. Thus, it is better for EFL teachers to be selective in their feedback and to point out the errors that most frequently occur or significantly confuse the audience. Teachers do not have to provide all the corrections, but they should provide specific, targeted, and systematic corrections in a way that facilitates students' own recognition of the existence of problems and leave corrections for the students themselves to deal with. Based on findings from this study, teachers need to offer different treatments to different error types. For example, EFL teachers can provide indirect CF (i. e. , indicating where the errors are by underlining and circling) for students' tense errors. Because verb errors are not likely to be affected by any type of feedback, teachers can try to provide both indirect and direct CF along with descriptions and explanations. Another technique is to have students participate in the design of CF approaches themselves. Students as a group or as individuals decide the approach they would like their teachers to adopt for specific written errors.

8.2.4   Integrating Grammar Instruction.

As explicit instructions on grammar are crucial in language classrooms, effective and efficient grammar instruction needs to be integrated into the correction process. Especially for Asian students, grammar instruction has a significant impact on language learning because of their language proficiency and previous learning experience in countries where English teaching and learning involves strongly stressed explicit grammar instruction. Schulz (2001) provided data that showed students from different cultures shared the view that the interaction between grammar instruction and feedback plays a positive role in language learning. In this case, we do not deny that learners could automatically acquire and learn language as long as they are exposed to a foreign language environment from which they receive rich and comprehensible input, but a formal Form Focused Instruction (FFI) course design could help and foster EFL learners' ultimate mastery of a foreign language.

In addition, considering many countries under the EFL context have limited time available for teaching all the grammatical rules, selective grammar teaching is needed. Similar to the selected CF of written errors, grammar teachers should choose the grammatical structures that cause learner difficulty in understanding and internalizing their grammar knowledge. Carefully planned courses that focus on specific grammar structures could help learners learn English more rapidly and achieve higher level of grammatical competence than non-instructed learners.

8.2.5 Designing Appropriate Learning Materials and Activities in Class.

Since grammar is often perceived as difficult, boring, and irrelevant by students, it might be effective that instead of made-up examples and teaching sequencing, teachers intentionally present teaching materials and activities following the accessibility sequence. In the meantime, teachers should have students play around with grammar in authentic texts and guide students as active rather than as passive learners by making use of contextualized language and exploratory learning. For example, activities should not only locate the errors without discouraging students, but also stimulate students' desire for grammar knowledge as well as arouse students' curiosity to figure out what the errors are and why the errors occur.

For some students, they need to be constantly pushed and encouraged to read teacher CF and use it. Therefore, corrective feedback in EFL classrooms should not only draw students' attention to the problematic grammatical forms they have encountered, but also raise students' awareness to elicit their own self-correction. For example, the EFL teacher could list the most frequent errors on a blackboard. The errors could be collected from students' daily writing tasks or any other sources, such as journal writing. The teacher could say "I noticed these errors occurred very frequently in some of your compositions. I would like to invite some volunteers to come up here and correct the errors. This would be a good opportunity for you to help your peers recognize and correct their errors." It is not guaranteed that every student will fully attend to the teacher's instruction about the errors. This strategy is potentially valuable as it helps reduce students' anxiety of being exposed to correction and encourages students to retrieve the correct grammatical forms from their linguistic repertoire.

Teachers should also engage students in more frequent and timely writing practices so as to provide students with frequent, timely, and manageable feedback. The more compositions students write, the more opportunities there are for students to practice error editing, and the more likely that students will then improve their writing accuracy. For example, students could be asked to write essays thirty minutes per day and three times a week during a four-month semester. Then, students should be required to revise their writing each time following the teacher's CF before final submission. More frequent and timely exposure to CF, practice in writing, and performance in error correction may contribute to a long-term improvement in accuracy.

In order to foster all the above mentioned ideas, either the department or the college need to conduct workshops designed for EFL teachers and train them how to effectively and efficiently provide corrective feedback by using varied means (e. g. , direct and indirect correction). During the workshop, EFL teachers need to have an awareness of how important it is to have students compose different drafts for their writing, and how beneficial it is to discuss the most frequent errors with students. Teachers need to allocate time during their office hours for meeting with students regularly to talk about their students' writing problems.

8.3   Strengths

First, my research provided consistent treatments of feedback schemes and attempted to deal with both the methodological and ethnic dilemmas addressed by Ferris (2004). Ferris (2004) claimed the necessity that researchers need to address the issue of the effectiveness of CF by conducting future research in the following: two intact classes with the same instructor need to be compared over time. In one class, the teacher could simply indicate what the errors are; and in the other class, the teacher provides direct error corrections in student texts. For students in the control group, they should still receive feedback but about something not related to grammar. Second, all the tests were given to students without conflicting with their daily courses. This raises the possibility that all students were more likely to participate during the whole process of researching. In addition, the sample size in the current study was relatively large. Thus, there were more possibilities of sufficiently drawing credible conclusions from student essays. Lastly, the population in the current study is in general homogeneous. All the participants had the same Chinese background with an advanced English proficiency and similar prior learning experiences. Hence, the unique learner variables in the current study can be considered representative and allow for the drawing of conclusions and the making of recommendations for this specific group of EFL learners.

8.4   Limitations

This study has several limitations that must be noted. First, drawbacks may exist in the research design since no plausible reasons could be explained for why the control group wrote short but more accurate essays at the beginning of the treatment. It was statistically difficult to compare the two CF groups with the control group because they were not equal and the control group had a higher level of performance on writing accuracy at the beginning. The unreliability of the control group potentially distorted the results of this study.

Moreover, because of no significant group effect on CF, we cannot decide whether observed gains in writing accuracy were only accounted for by corrective feedback or by other intervening factors that existed but could not be controlled. For example, all students received English instruction on a daily basis. Any English input over time, such as content-based English activities and intensive reading, can lead to a gradual increase in students' accuracy regardless of the type of feedback students received. Thus, even though students showed consistent and significant improvements in writing accuracy over time, the findings did not tell us a superior value of CF in comparison to content-only feedback.

This phenomenon is also related to the time limit of this study, which is another issue that is worth emphasizing. The study only lasted 10 weeks for the treatment. In retrospect, it was impractical to expect a surprising significant group difference in error rates over ten weeks with only two treatments, especially given students' fairly high accuracy at the beginning of the treatment. Accordingly, it is insufficient to claim whether corrective feedback had a statistically significant positive impact on students' accuracy.

8.5   Future Direction

The limitations of the current study discussed earlier lend themselves to several directions for future investigation. First, in terms of research design, it is recommended to carry out a true experimental study with randomly allocated individuals and numbers of groups. This can be more reliable and quantified, and less susceptible to certain confounding effects that cannot be identified in advance. There is also a need for research that utilizes a long-term study design in the future. For example, the researcher could ask students to write the three different essays (i. e. , pretest, posttest and delayed posttest) during a whole semester or one year to examine the lasting effect of CF on written accuracy.

Moreover, because students' preferences to CF could be dynamic over time based on different courses they take or various activities they are involved in, items designed in questionnaires and interviews should be adapted to reflect how students' attitudes change in different courses and activities. This could help the researcher examine whether the nature of exposure to rich input affects student preferences to error correction over time.

Future studies will also be needed to investigate variables that influence pedagogical effectiveness of CF in L2 classrooms. The following questions involved in the ongoing scholarly discussions necessitate additional thoughts and explorations on research: the first question considers how different types of corrective feedback in EFL contexts function with students of varied English proficiencies and how EFL teachers can incorporate CF into these specified groups of L2 learners to help them explore language and solve problems independently and progressively. For example, because students' English proficiency may correspond with their ability to benefit from corrective feedback, it is necessary for the researcher to have two experimental groups: students with lower English proficiency and students with higher English proficiency. Both groups should be treated the same by receiving the same type of corrective feedback, and other intervening factors should be controlled. The researcher then could examine the group difference and may detect some interesting findings.

Another question for research that needs to be explored asks how explicit are the processes students use to apply CF in their revisions? To address this issue, the researcher could ask the experimental group students to redraft their compositions at least twice compared with the control group which would be asked to neglect the redrafting process. This could help the researcher better understand how students apply the feedback to their errors and their understanding of CF.

Another issue in need for further investigation considers the effect of focused(e. g. , targeted) vs. unfocused (e. g. , comprehensive) corrective feedback so as to inform syllabus design in EFL contexts. Individual students' reactions to the effectiveness of CF also needs further clarification due to learner variations(e. g. , CF could work for one student but not for another).

Overall, all the above issues have been involved in heated discussions but are still worthy of future investigations. These issues also foster research that is designed to answer the overarching question of whether or not corrective feedback helps students achieve ultimate improvement in their writing accuracy in their L2.

8.6   Conclusion

Topics on corrective feedback raise many interesting and potentially relevant issues in the area of SLA and L2 grammar pedagogy. The importance of CF for L2 learners has been addressed by many linguistic researchers regarding its effectiveness and efficacy in L2 learning. This study focuses on seven error types: subject-verb agreement, plural, verb, tense, article, preposition and parts of speech based on their frequency distribution, and lends support to the argument that we cannot dismiss error correction's and feedback's potential effect on L2 writing accuracy.

This research is important because it increases EFL teachers and learners' understanding of how feedback practice and form-focused instruction can be implemented more effectively in writing and grammar classes. The findings also provide a practical perspective for EFL teachers to better develop CF strategies and to design materials that are applicable for EFL learners and their English learning. More importantly, the innovative part is that this study addresses the value of CF for specific error types and contributes to our understanding of how different error types react to different types of CF. The study also facilitates the recognition of new insights into specific treatment of errors for EFL students in terms of particular linguistic structures. As the debate on the effectiveness of CF is inconclusive and ongoing, it provides me with future topics for my own research in EFL writing classrooms to address these many unanswered questions.

References

Andringa, S. and Curcic, M. , "How Explicit Knowledge Affects Online L2 Processing: Evidence from Differential Object Marking Acquisition. " *Studies in Second Language Acquisition* , 37, 2015, 237-268.

Ashwell, T. , "Patterns of Teacher Response to Student Writing in a Multi-draft Composition Classroom: Is Content Feedback Followed by Form Feedback the Best Method?" *Journal of Second Language Writing* , 9, 2000, 227-257.

Baleghizadeh, S. , and Gordani, Y. , "Academic Writing and Grammatical Accuracy: The Role Of Corrective Feedback. " *Gist Education and Learning Research Journal* , 6, 2012, 159-176.

Biber, D. , Johansson, S. , Leech, G. , Conrad, S. , Finegan, E. , *The Longman Grammar of Spoken and Written English*. London: Longman. 1999.

Bitchener, J. , and Knoch, U. , "Raising the Linguistic Accuracy Level of Advanced L2 Writers with Written Corrective Feedback. " *Journal of Second Language Writing* , 19, 2010, 207-217.

Bitchener, J. , and Knoch, U. , "The Contribution of Written Corrective Feedback to Language Development: Aten Month Investigation. " *Applied Linguistics* , 31, 2009, 193-214.

Bitchener, J. , and Knoch, U. , "The Relative Effectiveness of Different Types of Direct Written Corrective Feedback. *System* , 37, 2009, 322-329.

Bitchener, J. , and Knoch, U. , "The Value of Written Corrective Feedback for Migrant and International Students. " *Language Teaching Research*, 12, 2008, 409-431.

Bitchener, J. , "Evidence in Support of Written Corrective Feedback. " *Journal of Second Language Writing*, 12, 2008, 102-118.

Bitchener, J. , & Ferris, D. , *Written Corrective Feedback in Second Language Acquisition and Writing*. New York, NY: Routledge. 2011.

Bitchener, J. , "The Effect of Different Types of Corrective Feedback on ESL Student Writing. " *Journal of Second Language Writing*, 14, 2005, 191-205.

Bitchener, J. , Young, S. , & Cameron, D. , "The Effect of Different Types of Corrective Feedback on ESL Student Writing. " *Journal of Second Language Writing*, 14, 2005, 191-205.

Bruton, A. , "Designing Research into the Effect of Grammar Correction in L2 Writing: Not So Straightforward. " *Journal of Second Language Writing*, 18, 2009a, 136-40.

Bruton, A. , "Improving Accuracy Is Not the Only Reason for Writing, and Even If It Were···" *System*, 37, 2009b, 600-613.

Carrol, S. , and Swain, M. , "Explicit and Implicit Negative Feedback: An Empirical Study of the Learning of Linguistic Generalization. " *Studies in Second Language Acquisition*, 15, 1993, 357-386.

Chandler, J. , "The Efficacy of Various Kinds of Error Feedback for Improvement in the Accuracy and Fluency of L2 Student Writing. " *Journals of Second Language Writing*, 12, 2003, 267-296.

Check, J. and Schutt, R. , *Research Methods in Education*. CA: SAGE Publications. 2012.

Diab, R. , "EFL University Students' Preferences for Error Correction and Teacher Feedback on Writing. " *TESL Reporter*, 38, 2015, 27-51.

Ellis, R. , "A Typology of Written Corrective Feedback Types. " *ELT Journal*, 63, 2009, 97-107.

Ellis, R. , "Current Issues in the Teaching of Grammar: An SLA Perspective. " *TESOL QUARTERLY*, 40, 2006, 83-107.

Ellis, R. , "Does Form-focused Instruction Affect the Acquisition of Implicit Knowledge? A Review of the Research. " *Studies on Second Language Acquisition*, 24, 2002, 223-236.

Ellis, R. , "Introduction: Investigating Form-focused Instruction. " *Language Learning*, 51, 2001, 1-46.

Ellis, R. , "Principles of Instructed Language Learning. " *System*, 33, 2005, 209-224.

Ellis, R. , Sheen, Y. , Murakami, M. , & Takashima, H. , "The Effects of Focused and Unfocused Written Corrective Feedback in An English as a Foreign Language Context. " *System*, 36, 2008, 353-371.

Ellis, R. , *The Study of Second Language Acquisition*. Oxford: Oxford University Press. 1994.

Ellis, R. , *Understanding Second Language Acquisition*. Oxford: Oxford University Press. 1985.

Evans, N. , Hartschorn, K. , and D. Krause. , "The Efficacy of Dynamic Written Corrective Feedback for University Matriculated ESL Learners. " *System*, 39, 2011, 229-239.

Evans, N. , Hartschorn, K. , and Tuioti, E. , "Written Corrective Feedback: Practitioners' Perspectives. " *International Journal of English Studies*, 10, 2010, 47-77.

Felix, S. , "The Effect of Formal Instruction on Second Language Acquisition. " *Language Learning*, 31, 1981, 87-112.

Ferris, D. R. , & Roberts. B. , "Error Feedback in L2 Writing Classes: How Explicit Does It Need to Be?" *Journals of Second Language Writing*, 10, 2001, 161-84.

Ferris, D. , "Second Language Writing Research and Written Corrective Feedback in SLA. " *Studies in Second Language Acquisition*, 32, 2010, 181-201.

Ferris, D. , "The Case for Grammar Correction in L2 Writing Classes: A Response to Truscott (1996). " *Journal of Second Language Writing*, 8, 1999, 1-11.

Ferris, D. , "The "Grammar Correction" Debate in L2 Writing: Where Are We, and Where Do We Go from Here?" *Journal of Second Language Writing*, 13, 2004, 49-62.

Ferris, D. , *Treatment of Errors in Second Language Student Writing.* Ann Arbor, MI: University of Michigan Press. 2002.

Ferris, S. , Liu, H, Sinba, A. , and M. Senna. , " Written Corrective Feedback for Individual L2 Writers. " *Journal of Second Language Writing*, 22, 2013, 307-329.

Guenete, D. , and Lyster, R. , " Written Corrective Feedback and Its Challenges for Pre-service ESL Teachers. " *The Canadian Modern Language Review*, 69, 2013, 129-153.

Guenette, D. , "Is Feedback Pedagogically Correct? Research Design Issues in Studies of Feedback on Writing. " *Journal of Second Language Writing*, 16, 2007, 40-53.

Harley, B. & Swain, M. , "The Interlanguage of Immersion Students and Its Implications for Second Language Teaching. " In A. Davies, C. Criper & A. Howatt (eds.), *Interlanguage.* Edinburgh: Edinburgh University Press, 1984, 291-311.

Hendrickson, J. , " The Treatment of Error in Written Work. " *Modern Language Journal*, 64, 1980, 216-221.

Hyland, F. , " Focus on Form: Student Engagement with Teacher Feedback. " *System*, 31, 2003, 217-30.

Hyland, K. , & Hyland, F. , " Feedback on Second Language Students' Writing. " *Language Teaching*, 39, 2006, 83-101.

Jessner, U. , *Linguistic Awareness in Multilinguals: English as a Third Language.* Edinburgh, UK: Edinburgh University Press. 2006.

Jwenigan, J. , and Mihan, F. , " Error Treatment Preferences of Adult

Intensive English Program Students: Does Proficiency Matter?" *The CATESOL Journal*, 20, 2008.

Kang, E., and Han, Z., "The Efficacy of Written Corrective Feedback in Improving L2 Written Accuracy: A Meta-analysis." *The Modern Language Journal*, 99, 2015, 1-18.

Kao, C., "Effects of Focused Feedback on the Acquisition of Two English Articles." *The Electronic Journal for English as a Second Language*, 17, 2013, 1-15.

Kepner, C., "An Experiment in the Relationship of Types of Written Feedback to the Development of Second Language Writing Skills." *Modern Language Journal*, 75, 1991, 305-313.

Kormos, J., "The Role of Individual Differences in L2 Writing." *Journal of Second Language Writing*, 21, 2012, 390-403.

Kranshen, S., *The Input Hypothesis: Issues and Implication*. Oxford: Pergamon Press. 1985.

Krashen, S., *Explorations in Language Acquisition and Use: The Taipei Lectures*. Portsmouth: Heinemann. 2003.

Krashen, S., *Principles and Practice in Second Language Acquisition*. New York: Pergamon Press. 1982.

Krashen, S., *Second Language Acquisition and Second Language Learning*. Oxford: Oxford University Press. 1981.

Lapkin, S., Hart, D., & Swain, M., "Early and Middle French Immersion Programs - French-Language Outcomes." *Canadian Modern Language Review*, 48, 1991, 11-40.

Larsen-Freeman, D., "Research into Practice: Grammar Learning and Teaching." *Language Teaching*, 48, 2015, 263-280.

Lee, I., "Error Correction in L2 Secondary Writing Classroom: The Case of Hong Kong." *Journal of Second Language Writing*, 13, 2005, 285-312.

Lee, I., "L2 Writing Teachers' Perspectives, Practices and Problems Regarding Error Feedback." *Assessing Writing*, 8, 2003, 216-37.

Lee, I. , " Student Reactions to Teacher Feedback in Two Hong Kong Secondary Classrooms. " *Journal of Second Language Writing* ,17 ,2008 , 144-164.

Leki, I. , "The Preferences of ESL Students for Error Correction in College-level Writing Classes. " *Foreign Language Annals* ,24 , 1991 ,203-218.

Lightbown, P. , "Anniversary Article: Classroom SLA Research and Second Language Teaching. " *Applied Linguistics* ,21 ,2000 ,431-462.

Li, S. , " The Effectiveness of Corrective Feedback in SLA: A Meta-analysis. " *Language Learning* ,60 ,2010 ,309-365.

Liu, M. and Braine, G. , " Cohesive Features in Argumentative Writing Produced by Chinese Undergraduates. " *System* ,33 ,2005 ,623-36.

Mackey, A. , " Feedback, Noticing, and Instructed Second Language Learning. " *Applied Linguistics* ,27 ,2006 ,405-430.

McMartin-Miller, C. , " How Much Feedback Is Enough?: Instructor Practices and Student Attitudes toward Error Treatment in Second Language Writing. " *Assessing Writing* ,19 ,2014 ,24-35.

McMillan, J. , *Educational Research: Fundamentals for the Consumer.* Boston: Pearson Education. 2012.

Mustafa, F. , " Feedback on the Feedback: Sociocultural Interpretation of Saudi ESL Learners' Opinions about Writing Feedback. " *English Language Teaching* ,5 ,3 ,2012.

Myles, J. , " Second Language Writing and Research: The Writing Process and Error Analysis in Student Texts. " *TESL-EJ* ,6 ,2002.

Nassaji, H. , " Research Timeline: Form-focused Instruction and Second Language Acquisition. " *Language Teaching* ,49 ,1 ,2016 ,35-62.

Polio, C. , " The Relevance of Second Language Acquisition Theory to the Written Error Correction Debate. " *Journal of Second Language Writing* , 21 ,2012 ,375-389.

Prabhu, N. , *Second Language Pedagogy.* Oxford: Oxford University Press. 1987.

Rahimi, M. , "The Role of Teacher's Corrective Feedback in Improving EFL Learners' Writing Accuracy Over Time: Is Learner's Mother Tongue Relevant?" *Reading and Writing*, 22, 2009, 219-243.

Robb, T. , Ross, S. & Shortreed, I. , "Salience of Feedback on Error and Its Effect on EFL Writing Quality. " *TESOL Quarterly*, 20, 1986, 83-95.

Russell, J. , & Spada, N. , "The Effectiveness of Corrective Feedback for the Aquisition of L2 Grammar: A Meta-analysis of the Research. " In J. Norris & L. Ortega(Eds.) , *Synthesizing Research on Language Learning and Teaching*(pp. 133-164). Amsterdam: Benjamins. 2006.

Scheffler, P. , " Theories Pass, Learners and Teacher Remain. " *Applied Linguistics*, 33, 2012, 603-607.

Schimidt, R. , " Awareness and Second Language Acquisition. " *Annual Review of Applied Linguistics*, 13, 1993, 206-226.

Schimidt, R. , "The Role of Consciousness in Second Language Learning. " *Applied Linguistics*, 11, 1990, 129-158.

Schulz, R. A. , "Cultural Differences in Student and Teacher Perceptions Concerning the Role of Grammar Instruction and Corrective Feedback: USA-Colombia. " *The Modern Language Journal*, 85, 2001, 244-58.

Schwartz, B. , " On Explicit and Negative Data Effecting and Affecting Competence and Linguistic Behavior. " *Studies in Second Language Acquisition*, 15, 1993, 147-163.

Sheen, Y. , Wright, D. and A. Moldawa. , "Differential Effects of Focused an Unfocused Written Correction on the Accurate Use of Grammatical Forms by Adult ESL Leaners. " *System*, 37, 2009, 556-569.

Shintani, N. , Ellis, R. , & Suzuki, W. , "Effects of Written Feedback and Revision on Learners' Accuracy in Using Two English Grammatical Structures. " *Language Learning*, 64, 2014, 103-131.

Shintani, N. , & Ellis, R. , " The Comparative Effect of Direct Written Corrective Feedback and Metalinguistic Explanation on Learners' Explicit and Implicit Knowledge of the English Indefinite Article. "

Journal of Second Language Writing, 22, 2013, 286-306.

Spada, N. , "Beyond Form-focused Instruction: Reflections on Past, Present and Future Research. " *Language Teaching*, 44, 2011, 225-236.

Spada, N. , Jessop, L. , Tomita, Y, Susuki, W. , and A. Valeo. , "Isolated and Integrated Form-focused Instruction: Effects on Different Types of L2 Knowledge. " *Language Teaching Research*, 18, 2014, 453-473.

Storch, N. , "Critical Feedback on Written Corrective Feedback Research. " *International Journal of English Studies*, 10, 2010, 29-46.

Swain, M. , "Communicative Competence: Some Rules of Comprehensible Input and Comprehensible Output in Its Development. " In S. Gass & G. Madden(eds.) , *Input In Second Language Acquisition*. Rowley, MA: Newbury House, 1985, 235-253.

Truscott, J. and Hsu, A. , " Error Correction, Revision, and Learning. " *Journal of Second Language Writing*, 17, 2008, 292-305.

Truscott, J. , " Evidence and Conjecture on the Effects of Correction: A Response to Chandler. " *Journal of Second Language Writing*, 13, 2004, 337-343.

Truscott, J. , "Review Article: The Case against Grammar Correction in L2 Writing Classes. " *Language Learning*, 46, 1996, 327-69.

Truscott, J. , "Selecting Errors for Selective Error Correction. " *Concentric: Studies in English Literature and Linguistics*, 27, 2001, 93-108.

Truscott, J. , "The Case for "The Case against Grammar Correction in L2 Writing Classes": A Response to Ferris. " *Journal of Second Language Writing*, 8, 1999, 111-122.

Truscott, J. , "The Effect of Error Correction on Learners' Ability to Write Accurately. " *Journal of Second Language Writing*, 16, 2007, 255-72.

Van Beunnigen, C. , " Corrective Feedback in L2 Writing: Theoretical Perspectives. Empirical Insights, and Future Directions. " *International Journal of English Studies*, 10, 2010, 1-27.

Van Beunnigen, C. , De Jong, N. , and F. Kuiken. , "Evidence on the

Effectiveness of Comprehensive Error Correction in Second Language Writing. " *Language Learning*, 62, 2012, 1-41.

Van Beunnigen, C. , De Jong, N. , and F. Kuiken. , "The Effect of Direct and Indirect Corrective Feedback on L2 Learners' Written Accuracy. " *International Journal of Applied Linguistics*, 156, 2008, 279-296.

Vyatkina, N. , "Writing Instruction and Policies for Written Corrective Feedback in the Basic Language Sequence. " *L2 Journal*, 3, 2011, 63-92.

Wang, Z. , "Chinese High School Students' L2 Writing Instruction: Implications for EFL Writing in College: A Qualitative Study. " *Chinese English Language Education Association*. 2011. Retrieved from http:// www. celea. org. cn/pastversion/lw/pdf/wangzhaohui. pdf

Yoshida, R. , "How Do Teachers and Learners Perceive Corrective Feedback in the Japanese Language Classroom?" *The Modern Language Journal*, 94, 2010, 293-314.

Zareil, A. and Rahnam, M. , "The Effect of Written Corrective Feedback Modes on EFL Learners' Grammatical and Lexical Writing Accuracy: From Perceptions to Facts. " *International Journal on Studies in English Language and Literature*, 3, 2013, 1-14.

Zobl, H. , " Converging Evidence for the " Acquisition-learning " Distinction. *Applied Linguistics*, 16, 1995, 35-56.

Appendix A Grading Criteria for Linguistic Accuracy

Linguistic feature	Accuracy level	Numbers	Individual score	Examples
Subject-verb Agreement				
Plural	Inappropriate use			
	Redundant use			
	Missing			
		Total	Total	
Verb	Inappropriate use			
	Redundant use			
	Missing			
		Total	Total	
Tense				
Article	Inappropriate use			
	Redundant use			
	Missing			
		Total	Total	
Prepositions	Inappropriate use			
	Redundant use			
	Lack of use			
		Total	Total	
Parts of speech				

Notes:

1. Scores to be assigned to the seven target forms on linguistic accuracy only.

2. Participant's accuracy score is calculated following this procedure: (1) calculate the individual number of the seven types grammatical errors students make; (2) calculate the overall number of the seven types of grammatical errors; (3) generate the score for each grammatical error based on the frequency. The total possible score is 100 points (e. g. , If students have made 10 errors, they receive 90 points) ; (4) calculate the sum score for all the seven types of grammatical errors based on the total number.

Appendix B Test Prompts

Pretest prompt:

Positive effect vs. Negative effect of technology: Does technology affect our lives? How? *Please provide at least three reasons for your argument.*

Posttest prompt:

Competition vs. Cooperation: Which is good for college students? *Please provide at least three reasons for your argument.*

Delayed posttest prompt:

Do colleges put too much stock in standardized test scores? *Please provide at least three reasons for your argument.*

Appendix C Questionnaires

Questionnaire 1   Name _____

1. In English classes you have taken before, have you ever learned any English grammar rules?

   Yes, a lot   Yes, but few   No

   If yes, what? _____

   If no, why? _____

2. Have you ever received feedback from teachers?

   Yes, a lot   Yes, but few   No

   If yes, what? _____

   If no, why? _____

3. Do you think teacher feedback is helpful?

   Yes, very helpful   Yes, but not much   No

4. Do you worry about making mistakes in writing or your language class?

   Yes, a lot   Yes, but few   No

5. How do you feel about your English language use, especially grammar, in writing?

   Very good   Good   bad

6. How do you feel when theteacher immediately correct your error in your writing or in language classroom? (e. g. , angry, embarrassed, sorry, happy, satisfied, bothered, indifference, nervous, and overwhelmed)

   _____

7. What feedback do you expect teachers to provide for your writing?

   _____

8. Anything else you want to share with the researcher?

   _____

Questionnaire 2   *Name* _____

1. What is the best way for your English teacher to give feedback on your writing?

   Feedback on grammar feedback on content feedback on organization none of these

   If others, what is it? _____

2. What is the best way for your English teacher to give feedback about your grammatical errors in your writing?

   Direct correction underline or circle description and explanation none of these

   If others, what is it? _____

3. What is the easiest way for you to correct your errors?

   Direct correction underline or circle description and explanation none of these

   If others, what is it? _____

4. Which type of corrective feedback do you think you can learn the most from?

   Direct correction underline or circle description and explanation none of these

   If others, what is it? _____

5. Why type of corrective feedback do you like most?

   Direct correction underline or circle description and explanation none of these

   If others, what is it? _____

6. Do you like the current type of corrective feedback you received from the researcher?

   Very much   mostly   a little   not at all

7. Do you understand the type of corrective feedback you received from the researcher?

   Very much   mostly   a little   not at all

8. Do you feel discouraged about the correction?

   Very much   mostly   a little   not at all

9. Do you think you will apply the correction to your future writing?

   Very much   mostly   a little   not at all

10. What did you think or what did you do after you received your writing with feedback from the researcher?

    I was eagerly to see the errors I made and wanted to correct the errors immediately because I really wanted to improve my English writing.

    I was thinking about the reasons why I made the errors, but I did not know how to correct them and revise my writing.

    I just left it on my desk and did not want to look at or revise it.

    I believed that I wish I had not written anything.

11. Any other comments?

    _____

Appendix D Interview Questions in Chinese

For students:

学生回答的问题:

Which component of writing do you most expect to receive feedback from teachers, grammar, content, or organizations?

关于写作的哪个方面，你最希望收到来自老师的意见？这几个方面是:语法,内容,组织结构。

Do you like the type of feedback you received from the teachers and the researcher?

你喜欢你的的老师和研究人员提供的反馈信息吗?

Are you confident of your own writing and self-editing ability?

你对自己的写作能力和自我修改作文的能力有信心吗?

What expectations do you have of grammar corrections in your writing from teachers?

你对老师对于你语法上的纠正或反馈有什么期望?

What difficulties did you encounter during your revision process?

你在自我修改作文的时候有什么困难?

What other contextual and individual factors (e. g. , attitude, belief, and motivation) do you think may influence your writing ability to benefit from corrective feedback?

你认为有哪些环境或个人因素会影响你从反馈中受益？或者你认为其他与你相关的背景和个人因素，比如,态度,信仰,动力,会影响你的写作能力的培养吗?

Do you have anything else that you want to share with the researcher?

你还有什么要和研究人员分享的吗?

(Contd.)

For teachers:	Which component do you think among grammar, content and organizations, students value the most in their understanding of effective corrective feedback?
老师回答的问题:	
	你认为关于写作的哪个方面的反馈，学生会最重视？这几个方面是：语法，内容，组织结构。或者你认为学生最希望获得来自老师对于写作哪个方面的反馈？
	Do you regularly help students practice their writing and self-editing ability?
	你经常帮助学生练习写作和自我修正和编辑的能力吗？
	What expectations do you think students would have of grammar corrections in their writing from teachers?
	你认为学生对于你在语法上的反馈和纠正有什么期望？
	What contextual and individual factors do you think may influence your students' writing ability to benefit from corrective feedback? Any factors from teachers?
	你认为有哪些环境或个人因素会影响你的学生从反馈中受益？有没有任何来自老师方面的因素呢？
	Do you have anything else that you want to share with the researcher?
	你还有什么要与研究人员分享？

Appendix E Examples of Student Errors across Pretest, Posttest, and Delayed Posttest in the Three Groups

GROUP #1 Indirect Corrective Feedback

Examples of Error Types in Pretest-Writing #1

Subject-verb agreement

e. g. ，People could find that more and more problemshas shown up.

Ourlives has been greatly changed.

Whentechnology bring to our lives many advantages，we cannot ignore the disadvantages.

（Many verbs used after technology，such as do，help，affect，create，have，bring，promote，broden，cause，and become）

The invention of computers dramatically increases work efficiency and help compete many difficult tasks that were impossible in the past.

Thanks to technology，our life pace continue to speed up，which increase the productivity of the whole society.

The progress of science improves human abilities to explore the world.

Plural

e. g. ，each coin has twoside.

They even don't spend time reading some useful book.

Science and technology at the same time also resulted in a number of disaster.

In recent years, [the] technology has broughtmany positive effect for them.

Education plays an important role in our life.

Now, if you use internet, all becomes a piece of cake.

Tense

e. g. , When I got a fever, I don't have to go down stairs to buy medicine.

Although we use technology to improve our life standard, we became lazier and more dependent.

Decades ago, ⋯ they have no software for calculation.

As the society developed, the technology plays a more and more important role.

Once upon a time, people use letters to contact each other, and it takes a lot of times. But now, ⋯

When the computer come in to our lives, it is praised by most of us. .

Article

Redundant use of article

In recent years, the technology has brought many positive [effects] for them.

In a conclusion, the technology has a large number [of] advant ages⋯.

Lack article

Thanks to development of science and technology, the society has enjoyed continuous prosperity and more convenience.

Wrong use of article

e. g. , Technology playsa important role in working.

Verb

Wrong use of verb form (after modal verbs)

e. g. , we willbecame helpless with the internet.

Technology can···. , may, ···. , will influent the society's economy···

Without technology, the economy will notdeveloped to the point.

But we candoomed that technology indeed affects our lives.

Technology will not only benefit us, but also bringing some adverse
effects.

Some of you mayheard the clean-robot before···

But now, we canshopping on internet.

Lack main verb/copula verb

e. g. , In the past, it was difficult to go somewhere far, ··· but now is
different, ···.

Technology like a sword with two edges.

Last but not the least, technology greatly convenient for information
communication.

···. seeing a film, relaxing in amusement parks, learning in
modernmuseums, ···. These all owing to the development of technology.

Technology also good for people's communication.

Redundant use of main verb

It is help to save time.

Technology isimprove the quality of our lives.

Preposition

Wrong use of prep.

e. g. , Nowadays, with the development with technology, ···

We can send emails with the friends in the distance.

Technology plays an important role to change our lives.

Lack prep.

Besides, it provides us [safer] food.

On one hand, technology makes our lives more convenient. On the other hand, it makes us indulge virtual world.

In [a] conclusion, [the] technology has a large number of advantages.

Pronoun

Lack pronoun(relative pronoun)

e. g. , However, there [are] some people think it is bad for us.

Redundant use of pronoun

e. g. , But each coin has it two sides.

Technology not only brings us in to date information but also it makes our lives a more convenient.

Lack subject

Beforetaking a taxi have to wait a long time.

Wrong use of possessive

e. g. , As far as my concerned, ···

Existential There is/are Existential There

e. g. , However, there is some people [who] think it is bad for us.

e. g. , I cannot even imagine what life will be like if there is not have technology.

Comparatives

e. g. , Transportation and communication become easier, which makes the connection between each othermore close.

With a telescope, it ismore clear to observe stars and galaxy.

Technology is developing more andmore fast.

Parts of speech

Wrong use of adv.

The development of science and technology is quickly.

It is very slowly and inconveniently.

People's thoughts are more openly.

Wrong use of adj.

We can also finish our work more effective.

More obvious, they did not have software for calculations decades ago.

We need to clean our eyes, proper use the technology products, ⋯

In the same time, technology brings us a lot of convenient.

It also brings much potential dangerous.

Wrong use of verb

e. g. , The development of technology has a significant affect on the
society.

In addition, the develop of technology has good influence on mode of
production.

Wrong use of noun

It is convenience and also harmful.

Lack "to" in infinitive clauses

e. g. , In a word, technology has two sides. What you need to do is be
yourself in your life.

Redundant use of 'that'

More andmore people realize that the importance of using a smart
phone.

Examples of Error Types in Posttest-Writing #2

Subject-verb agreement

e. g. , If someone has [problems,] others will help, which make a
great contribution to establishing friendship.

When confronting with cooperation and competition, people seems to
have a difficult time in choosing them.

It not only save my time but also helps me to promote the
communication.

Cooperationmake students have a good mood.

The evolution of Darwin point out that evolution of species cannot do
withcomperation.

Plural

e. g. If one person's idea [is] just a piece of demos of innovation, many people's idea will give supreme advantages over single idea.

If someone has problems, others will help, which make a great contribution to establishing friendship.

Once my biology teacher asked me to do some researches for the next class.

In many case, individual ability alone cannot fully address different problems.

Maybe onestudents find some mistakes in another student's work.

Tense

e. g. , we can ask them for help when we needed.

Article

Redundant use of article

e. g. , The cooperation also helps students work quickly and be happier.

In fact, after realizing the importance of the competition, you can already overcome such feelings.

We can organizea vital events.

The second, cooperation makes a better study condition.

Lack article

Thanks to development of science and technology, the society has enjoyed continuous prosperity and more convenience.

Wrong use of article

e. g. , Technology playsa important role in working.

Verb

Wrong use of verb form(after modal verbs)

e. g. , Cooperation canhelps people overcome the difficulties and calm you down when you have a hard time.

Lack main/copula verb

e. g. , If one person's idea just a piece of demos of innovation, many people's [ideas] will give supreme advantages over single idea.

It very necessary to compete if human society wants to advance.

It all good for students' development.

Redundant use of main verb

e. g. , Competition is benefit to the growth of talents

Wrong use of main verb

e. g. , why does cooperation better than competition?

Passive voice

e. g. , If this kind of cooperation cannot be control, students will choose a wrong way.

The treasure cannot buy but it is the most expensive thing in the world.

Reasons are lists as follows.

Only in this way, the party can hold successfully.

Cooperation is alwaysneed in our daily lives.

Preposition

Wrong use of prep.

e. g. , in the other hand, teamwork can also exercise the ability of individuals to make individuals grow together.

Stay in campus, we should do more cooperative activities to adapt to the society.

We develop a good relationship for our roommate.

Each individual can choose the task for which he is most capable.

Everyone can make their own contribution in a study group.

Lack prep.

e. g. , as we all know, cooperation is the engine that the human society relies.

Redundant use of prep.

e. g. ,In nowadays, it is quite common that we compete with each other for various competitions.

It is hard to imagine what will offer our world with so much energy to move forward.

Pronoun

Lack pronoun(relative pronoun)

e. g. ,However, there [are] some people think it is bad for us.

Redundant use of pronoun

e. g. ,But each coin has it two sides.

Lack subject

Beforetaking a taxi have to wait a long time.

Possessive

Wrong use of possessive

e. g. ,Competition makesstudent's potential to be fully played.

It can stimulate student's interaction and enthusiasm in order to their efficiency of learning.

Lack possessive

Students can find own advantages and help the team to complete it.

Peer interaction in cooperative learning is vital to promote students socialization.

Existential There is/are

e. g. ,However, there is some people [who] think it is bad for us.

Comparatives

e. g. ,in this way, not only the team but also the individual can become more andmore strong.

Parts of speech

Wrong use of noun

We will [be] sure to feel sad and depression.

Lack "to" in infinitive clauses

e. g. , All you have to do is finish the work on time.

Examples of Error Types in Delayed-Posttest-Writing #3

Subject-verb agreement

e. g. , College is different from high school which put grades as standards of everything.

Though the education level is improved, it stillhave many flaws, such as···

Theschool just see students' standardized tests instead of other things like morality···

First of all, this restrict students' proper activities, and students have no time to do exercises.

College put much stock in standardized tests, but itneglect their daily performance.

Some of them alsodoes not put much stock in standardized tests.

Plural

e. g. , You can publish some articles by yourself and take part in some academic forum.

Nowadays, more and more college put much stock in standardized tests.

Students should not live so hard and their life should be a wonderful life.

For example, we can go to some of the speech contest.

There [exists] a variety of community and student organization in college.

Firstly, the time that is spent preparing students for the exams could be used more effectively on teaching students different aspect that will help them in the long run···

Manystudent do not pay attention to the usual class.

Tense

e. g. ,When we were in high school,grade is the only way to evaluate a student.

Standardized test is still the most popular method of assessment. College concerned more about the level of students' learning result.

In the past,students who get great grades in tests are regarded as the excellent students.

Article

Lack article

e. g. ,The result is same as above.

They just need 'pass'.

Wrong use of article

e. g. ,In college test as a important standard to prove students' study is popular among the schools.

It is nota only choice to evaluate students.

Verb

Wrong use of verb form(before or after modal verbs)

e. g. ,students may not consciouslylearning.

They are might good at paying instrument,sports or painting.

Since no one can performs [stably] all the time.

Lack main verb/copula verb

e. g. ,but I do think that bad.

That is why college different from high school.

Standardized tests not the only way to check our achievement.

I thinks the ability of putting learning into practice more important than the mards in standardized tests.

Redundant use of main verb

e. g. ⋯but in fact,college is still put much stock in standardized tests.

Passive voice

e. g. , whether you can get scholarship or not is depended on your grades.

Students are permit to know or do what they are interested in.

Existential There is/are

e. g. , There exist a variety of [communities] and students [organizations] in college.

Parts of speech
Wrong use of adj.

e. g. , Since no one can [perform] stable all the time.

Lack "to" in infinitive clauses

e. g. , All we need to do is remember the knowledge from the textbooks.

Redundant use of 'that'

e. g. , ···but this result does not mean that all of our achievements.

GROUP #2 Content Feedback

Examples for Different Error Types in Prettest-Writing #1

Subject-verb agreement

e. g. , Technologymake people lazy.

Technology promote the development of business and other related products.

Technology exactly affect our lives or even change our lives.

We listen to the news on radio and watching TV.

Technology are applied more widely in our lives.

* does technology affects our lives?

Plural

e. g. , with the development of technology, we have more choice to relax than before.

These tools provide us [with] a better way to learn about different culture.

Technology is connected with our daily life.

A strange social phenomena appeared in our daily lives.

Technology has brought many conveniences to our lives.

There [are] a lot of negative side here.

Tense

e. g. , technology is widely used in our daily lives as the society developed.

A strange social [phenomenon] appeared in our daily lives. When people stay in a room together, it is likely that they are playing mobile phone rather than talking with each other.

I found a lot of primary and secondary school children are wearing glasses.

I think technology occupied an important position in modern society.

Thedevelopment of science and technology in the 20th century create two overall great achievements.

Article

Redundant use of article

e. g. , there is no doubt that we benefit a lot from the technology.

···it reduces the opportunities of the face to face communication.

Wrong use of article

e. g. , e-commerce is playinga important role in the growth of economics.

Verb

Redundant use of main verb/ be verb

e. g. , technology is just suit for young people.

I think technology is benefit to our lives.

Technology makes it is easy to dins and contact with each other.

Electronic waste is not onlyaffect air environment.

Science and technology is benefits a lot to our lives.

Passive voice

e. g. , everything you want to get could get [from] the internet.

Preposition

Wrong use of prep.

e. g. , when we walk in the street, we will find that more and more people wear glasses.

Everything you want to get could [be got] for the internet.

Lack prep.

e. g. , These tool provide us a better way to learn about different [cultures].

It provides us a new way to make friends all over the world.

Existential There is/are

e. g. , there is a lot of negative [sides] here.

Comparatives

e. g. , people oppose to it, because it makes people especially young people more andmore lazy.

The development of technology is more and more fast.

Parts of speech

Wrong use of adv.

e. g. , because of the rapidly development of technology, more and more people become lazy.

Wrong use of adj.

e. g. , more obvious, they did not have the software for calculation.

Wrong use of verb

E. g. , the development of technology has a significant affect on the society.

Wrong use of noun

e. g. , computer makes our lives more convenience.

Examples of Error Types in Posttest-Writing #2

Subject-verb agreement

e. g. , the child study [harder] and honor parents.

Cooperationhelp students to play an important role in society.

We don't like competitions which is full of our studying.

I must study hard to compete with other students whoseages is as big as me.

Although cooperation is significant for us, competition is more useful, because it build our characteristics.

We will work hard together because we havean everyday appointment that encourage us.

Plural

e. g. , we are member of society.

Some people say that cooperation is better for student.

They are careless about some important thing.

We should not put cooperation and competition [in] different position.

Tense

e. g. , we have good cooperation so we won.

Article

Redundant use of article

e. g. , obviously, the competition is better for students.

Although the cooperation is significant for us, the competition is more useful.

Verb

Wrong use of verb form(after modal verbs)

e. g. , in order to make advances, we need cooperates with others.

Redundant use of main verb

e. g. , completion is alwaysexist and it usually makes people creative.

Learning cooperation isbenefit us a lot.

It is not onlyhelp others but also push ourselves forward.

We are usuallythink which is more important.

Passive voice

e. g. , Walking along the street, you listen to the music that made by accomplished musicians and singers.

Preposition

Wrong use of prep.

e. g. , now let me give you anexample about the issue.

Lack prep.

e. g. , we should not put cooperation and competition different [positions].

Redundant prep.

When we face with a difficult task, we need cooperation.

Pronoun

Lack subject

e. g. , Which is better for students? I think is cooperation.

Comparatives

e. g. , the child [studies] more hard and [honors] parents.

Animalswho are more stronger beat the weaker ones.

Parts of speech

Wrong use of adj.

e. g. ‚I should learn patient and conscientious from my friends.

Wrong use of verb

e. g. ‚it makes us create and positive.

Wrong use of noun

e. g. ‚it is more and more important to success by studying the skill of cooperation.

Examples of Error Types in Delayed-Posttest-Writing #3

Subject-verb agreement

e. g. ‚college put much stock in standardized tests.

It nourish our spirit and keep us going.

Newspaper have reported a student who is smarter enough to enter into college earlier than others.

Standardized tests doesn't seem important to many [colleges], especially many famous [colleges].

College provide a stage that every student can show and learn things,
…

Theschool pay more attention to the quality of the students.

I think theuniversity still depend on the standardized tests to evaluate students.

Plural

e. g. ‚we should evaluate students from all aspect.

Standardized tests [don't] seem important to many college, especially many famous college.

Tense

e. g. ‚⋯but he cannot live by himself after he entered into college.

Article

Redundant use of article

e. g. , Students will lack of self development.

Verb

Wrong use of verb form(after modal verbs)

e. g. , standardized tests do can evaluate students but it is only one
sided.

Lack main verb/copula verb

e. g. , modern college students should have some talents that different
from standardized education.

Redundant use of main verb

e. g. , for these people, it isbenefit our innovation.

GROUP #3 Direct Corrective Feedback

Examples of Error Types in Pretest-Writing #1

Subject-verb agreement

e. g. , Itbroden our horizon and penetrate our lives in many respects.

I have to say that technology have [a] good effect on our lives.

Technology not only widens our sights but also let others learn
aboutourselves.

Technology are developing [faster].

Technology affect our lives and make our lives easier.

Technology benefit us so much ⋯ it play an essential role, promote
productivity, make urbanization and modernization, liberate people's mind,
improve our country's comprehensive strength, enhance international
influence, improve people's living standard and make the society
[develop] steadily and harmoniously.

Scientists invents technological productions day by day.

Technology become, bring, produce, affect, make, boost, help ⋯

Plural

e. g. , It [spills] over into many filed.

Shopping online can save our shopping time.

There are more and more scientific products in our daily life.

We just need to type thekeyboardand the result come to us at once.

Although it [has] advantage and disadvantage, I think its advantage is more than its disadvantage.

People will think about the influence of their behavior before they do it.

Technology can make more contribution to us.

Some developed countries, such as the U. S. , Germany and UK, have the core technology and can always make more profit.

Tense

e. g. , The new technology made our lives simpler and more [convenient] thatn before.

Now, it spilled over into many [fileds].

Today, everyhousehold were using high-tech products.

In the past, we just go hiking.

The electric map can show me where I was, and introduce me to the place where I want to visit.

In ancient, tribes are dispersed.

Article

Redundant use of article

e. g. , I believe the technology brings significant impact to our lives⋯

The another example is our computer.

In a word, the technology provides great convenience for our lives and makes our lives more wonderful.

Lack article

e. g. , It also [presses] us to do something beneficial to world and [helps] us set up a correct sense of worth.

Wrong use of article

e. g. ,I have to say that technology [has] an good effect on our lives.

We cannot have an easy life without using technology.

Technology also playsa important role.

Verb

Wrong use of verb form(after modal verbs)

e. g. ,Technologybenefit us so much···it [improves] people's living standard and make the society developing steadily and harmoniously.

We canplaying computer games, watching movies and shopping online.

Along with the progress of medicine technology, more and more difficult miscellaneous diseasesbe cured.

That is helpful to make the culture has a new carrier.

Lack main verb/copula verb

e. g. , With the 4G technology [extensively] used, mobile phone, computer, etc. appeared, this really a disaster.

Technology is really convenience and it really helpful to make our lives more colorful.

In the 20th century, it very important for everyone to use technology.

Science and technology everywhere, and I think it useful in our lives.

The development of things much faster.

Redundant use of main verb

e. g. ,technology is not only widens our sights but also let others learn about ourselves.

Although it is have advantage and disadvantages, I think its advantage is more thanits disadvantage.

It is not only [broaden] the circle of friends but also [makes] people become closer.

Preposition

Wrong use of prep.

e. g. , we can also use them to share our feelings to others.

For the one hand, it can give us convenience.

We can also get more and more messages by computer.

Lack prep.

e. g. , Telephones provide us much convenience to call [who] we want to talk.

Technology provide us a colorful and new life.

I want to travel to a country where I am not familiar at all.

Redundant prep.

People can use the mobile phone to contact with others in anytime.

With the rapid development of science and technology has brought great changes to human life.

With the development of social technology is more and more important in our daily lives.

Pronoun

Lack pronoun(relative pronoun)

e. g. , I'd like to say that I really enjoy technology bring me something.

Redundant use of pronoun

e. g. , Some developed countries, such as the U. S. , Germany and UK, they have the core technology and can always make more profits.

Some developing countries, such as Brazil and some African countries, they can only offer materials.

Wrong relative pronoun

e. g. , Telephones provide us [with] much convenience to call that we want to talk.

Lack subject

e. g. , ···. now , don' t worry about it because the GPS and map in the phone will help you.

We had to go to the library or bookstore to findinformation , sometimes spent the whole day there.

Replying on its rapiddevelopment , also enabled us to become the part of the modern science and technology.

Comparatives

e. g. , Technology [is] developing more and more fast.

Technology has made our livesmore simple.

Our society will become more and more nice and bright.

It provides us [with] more safe food ··· which makes our bodymore healthier.

Parts of speech

Wrong use of adv.

e. g. , I think this way to pay money is rapidly and handily.

Wrong use of adj.

e. g. , with the rapid development of technology , the social also has a world-shaking change.

With the 4G technology extensive used , mobile phone , computer , etc. appeared , this really a disaster.

It is good for our human healthy.

All kinds of transportation make people travel more convenient.

Wrong use of verb

e. g. , The rapid development of technology has brought great affect to our lives.

Wrong use of noun

e. g. , the new technology [makes] our lives simpler and more convenience than before.

Technology is really convenience to use.

I think if we could use technology correctly, our earth would become more and more harmony and beautiful.

Technology development faster and faster.

Lack "to" in infinitive clauses

e. g. , people can use the mobile phone contact with others anytime.

All students can use the phone do some reading.

Redundant "to" in infinitive clauses

Technology not only widens our sights but also let others to learn about ourselves.

Redundant use of 'that'

e. g. , ···but I guess you realize that the importance of the development of technology.

Examples of Error Types in Posttest-Writing #2

Subject-verb agreement

e. g. , Fierce competition make you be passive.

It promote automatic learning.

In history, ourancestors is relying on the power of unity and cooperation.

With the development of economy, more and more aspectsneeds it.

No matter how fast our society develop, I am greatly convincedthat only in this way we can make greater contribution to our society.

Teammates have a chance to help each other solve problems, which make a great contribution to establishing friendship.

Today, weis more inseparable from the cooperation.

Plural

e. g. , I can see my own shortcoming and can better correct my own shortcomings.

We can know a lot of thing that we don't know.

Cooperation is one of the most effectiveway to extend our personal relationship.

It offers a platform for people tocommunciate an share your idea with others.

Underthese circumstance, we can get the things we really want.

It emphasizes the joint contributions of member, ⋯

Tense

e. g. , In today' ssoceity, more and more parents gave their children mroe stress, and hoped they can succeed by themselves.

In history, ourancestors is relying on the power of unity and cooperation.

Cooperation is better for students and itwaltered the successful flowers.

When we cooperated with others, we can also strengthen our relationships or make more friends.

For example, Bill Gatesccoperate with others to develop Microsoft and apply it to computer.

Mars and Engel work together to develop Marxism.

Article

Redundant use of article

e. g. , It [promotes] the automatic learning.

As is known to all, in the student career, competition and cooperation [are] always together.

Wrong use of article

e. g. , everyone has a idea of positive competition, which will better promote the developmentof a group.

Competition isa important motivation in one's life.

Verb

Wrong use of verb form(after modal verbs)

e. g. , we should to learn to cooperate with others.

The best choice for students is to ask help from others and cooperating with others to deal with them.

They maygetting selfish and arrogant because of their feat.

Cooperation means work together andmake it good. Competition means work alone and compare with someone.

Lack main verb/copula verb

e. g. , As is known to all, in student career, competition and cooperation always together.

As it always said , many hands make light work.

You may not sure whetheryoru thoughts are correct or not.

Cooperation and competition sound really opposite in our lives , but there must be one that more better for students.

Two heads better than one.

Redundant use of main verb

e. g. , None is perfect , that's means when we face a problem and need to solve it , we need help.

It's also show us the importance of cooperation.

Cooperation makes the world more peaceful and beautiful , and it is also helps us develop ourselves and gives us more chances to understand other , to love others and to know about ourselves.

Preposition

Wrong use of prep.

e. g. , We share our results to others.

Lack prep.

e. g. , Studying with others [provides] us a change to communicate with them.

Pronoun

Redundant use of pronoun (relative pronoun)

e. g. , cooperation and competition which sound really opposite in our lives.

Wrong use of relative pronoun

e. g. , companies need talented people that must have a sense of competitiveness.

Lack subject

e. g. , often compete with friends to build up your confidence.

It emphasizes the joint contributions of [members] , can get realcolletive achivements.

Parts of speech

Wrong use of verb

e. g. , Upheaval will have a great affect onourselves.

Wrong use of noun

e. g. , we should cooperation with others to solve the difficulties.

I think cooperation is a peace and useful way.

Redundant 'to'

e. g. , Competition is not only to the requirements of the society.

Teammates have a chance to help each other to solve problems, which [makes] a great contribution to establishing friendship.

Examples of Error Types in Delayed-Posttest-Writing #3

Subject-verb agreement

e. g. , It represent your spent more time on this course.

I don't support that college put much stock in standardized tests.

School require students to take standardized tests.

Thetest need adaquate preparation.

The aims of standard tests is to tell the companies that this student have this kind of skill.

Therefore, the college have not occasion to demand that we must take [the] standard test.

Thepolicy have changed.

Thereasons is obvious.

Plural

e. g. , In fact , many college put much stock in standardized tests.

Somecompany prefer to employ people with more skill.

If you havethese certificate , you will have more opportunity to gain the position.

Our country actively reformed the education policy. It introduced some teaching method from some developed country.

Almost everystudents have known about the standard tests.

Everyuniversities should ue different papers according totheir students' level.

It maylimits students' thoughts and developments.

Tense

Ourcountry actively reform the education policy. It introduce some teaching [methods] from some developed [countries].

People always pay attention to the standardized tests that were connected to students' learnign levels.

Now , we entered university. Does the situationchange ?

They were asked to remember lots of knowledge so that they can not think things deeply in a creative way.

Article

Wrong use of article

e. g. , Therefore , the college [has] not occasion to demand that we must take an standard test.

The standard test isa important way.

Verb

Wrong use of verb form(after modal verbs)

e. g. , it maylimits students' thoughts and development.

Lack main verb/copula verb

e. g. , standard test just like TEM4 , CET4 and CET6.

Students' thoughts rigid.

The reasons as follows.

Redundant use of main verb

e. g. , our college is pay attention to it.

Many colleges are also put much attention to it.

Preposition

Wrong use of prep.

e. g. , It represents your spent more time in this course.

Standard test does not have some [true] effect to our English ability.

Many colleges also put much attention on it.

Lack prep.

e. g. , I don't agree it.

Pronoun

Lack subject

e. g. , if put much stock in standard tests, they won't learn knowledge
carefully.

Parts of speech

Wrong use of adv.

e. g. , We can learn things quickly and firm.

It is commonly that college students are not important as before.

Standard test does not have sometruely effect [on] our English
ability.

Redundant use of 'that'

e. g. , The aims of standard tests is that to tell companies that this
student [has] this kind of skill.

Appendix F Mean and Standard Deviation for Writing Length by Group in Pretest, Posttest, and Delayed-posttest

Group	Pretest		Posttest		Delayed posttest		N
	M	S	M	S	M	S	
Indirect CF	333.17	57.36	332.20	50.89	307.11	45.89	35
FC	193.26	49.42	197.83	36.71	190.69	44.04	35
Direct CF	319.97	48.70	323.74	52.30	310.34	53.98	35
Total	282.13	81.65	284.59	77.42	269.38	73.50	105

Note. Writing length was counted by words.

Appendix G Examples of Students' Responses to the Open-ended Questions In Questionnaire 1

Group 1—Indirect CF group

Question 6. How do you feel when the teacher immediately correct your error in your writing or in language classroom?" **Students responded as follows:**

Embarrassed but fine.

E. g. ,I feel a little embarrassed but later I will be fine and think it is helpful to me. Kind of embarrassed , but it is almost peaceful.

Embarrassed but happy.

e. g. , Embarrassed but happy. Everybody will make mistakes and we should face them and correct them.

I feel satisfied and happy because it improves my English skill. Sometimes , I felt a little embarrassed.

A little embarrassed , but it does not matter and I am happy to know my shortcomings.

A little embarrassed but happy.

Embarrassed , but appreciated.

e. g. , Very appreciated but a little embarrassed.

Embarrassed but grateful.

Embarrassed but satisfied.

Embarrassed, sorry, nervous but also grateful.

e. g. , Inner feelings are contradictory. Embarrassed, nervous and happy.

Nervous, embarrassed but appreciated.

Embarrassed.

e. g. , After the teacher corrected the errors, she was waiting for me to complete the sentence in front of class.

Happy and satisfied.

e. g. , Happy and satisfied because it should be a good improvement for me.

I am happy because I can correct my mistakes timely.

Happy, satisfied and thankful.

Happy, nervous and satisfied.

e. g. , A little nervous and embarrassed, but still satisfied.

Nervous but happy. I can improve my writing.

Happy, satisfied, embarrassed, and nervous.

Appreciated.

Indifferent and helpful.

Sorry but happy.

Sorry but meaningful.

Question 7. What feedback do you expect teachers to provide for your writing?

Grammar.

e. g. , I hope teacher could note the grammar errors and helpme to write better.

Some problems of grammar rules or how use theword to make a phrase better.

How to use correct grammar in writing.

Sentence pattern and grammar error.

Articles.

Grammar and sentence pattern.

I expect the teacher can provide the details of my writing mistakes and how to correct them.

Not only correcting errors but also giving examples.

Writing skills.

e. g. , How to express effectively.

Writing skills , consistency , and contextual influence.

Suggestions about how to write well.

Comprehensive.

e. g. , Structure of composition, advanced words and sentences and whether the main idea is correct.

Writing techniques , writing structure and how to get a higher grade. Grammar and how to make my writing vivid.

I hope teacher to provide some feedback helpful , practical and specific.

Grades.

e. g. , How to write well and get more grades.

Others in general.

e. g. , It is difficult to write something.

Question 8. Anything else you want to share with the researcher?

Spoken English.

e. g. , How to improve spoken language and aural comprehension.

English knowledge learned in high school was a bit unpractical. Welearned less in oral English. Is English grammar important? I want to speak good English. How should I do? I am afraid of speaking English in public.

I just think as an English speaker , when your English is good enough to talk with nativespeakers , that means you succeed. Not more grammars. That's stupid.

Listening.

e. g. , I don't why my listening grade is good but I actually cannot understand what foreigners say.

Words.

e. g. , How to remember word accurately.

I can memorize a lot of words and phrases but still my English is bad. I cannot use them in daily communication.

Feedback.

e. g. , I think feedback vary from person to person. Each student has different attitude to feedback.

Others in general.

e. g. , I want to learn English well, but I just speak or write in easy ways, not thoroughly. How to improve this?

Easier said than done.

How to concentrate on what teachers say instead of having a bit of sleeping.

Is hand writing important in composition?

It is difficult to write something.

Group 2— FC group

Question 6. **How do you feel when the teacher immediately correct your error in your writing or in language classroom**?

Embarrassed butfine.

e. g. , A little embarrassed, but I can learn new knowledge.

Embarrassed and happy.

e. g. , A little embarrassed, but the more the happier.

Sometimes, embarrassed, sometimes happy.

I think I alwaysbe happy but sometimes I will be embarrassed.

A little embarrassed but happy.

Embarrassed.

e. g. ,A little embarrassed.

I will feel very embarrassed.

Embarrassed but satisfied.

e. g. ,Satisfied and a little embarrassed.

Embarrassed, nervous and satisfied.

Embarrassed, sorry, nervous but also happy.

Embarrassed, sorry and bothered.

Happy.

Happy and satisfied.

e. g. ,Happy, satisfied, helpful.

Happy and nervous.

e. g. ,Happy, maybe a little nervous. / Nervous but happy.

Happy, nervous and indifference.

Satisfied.

e. g. ,Feel satisfied and I can benefit from it.

Satisfied and nervous.

e. g. ,Satisfied but a little nervous.

Sorry, happy and satisfied.

Sorry and satisfied.

Sorry.

Indifference.

Nervous and overwhelmed.

**Question 7. What feedback do you expect teachers to provide for
your writing?**

Grammar.

e. g. , Grammar and spelling.

Correct my grammar errors.

English grammar and special use.

Grammar and handwriting.

Syntactic structure.

How can use the sentence well or which is the best phrase I can use.

I suppose teachers will provide more information about my English grammar and writing skills.

More about sentence structure and grammar. Give me some suggestions to do better.

Writing skills.

e. g. , It is difficult to write something.

How to write logical writing?

Logic.

Writing skills. I suppose teachers will provide more information about my English grammar and writing skills.

Authenticity.

e. g. , How to make writing sound like native?

Others in general.

e. g. , Whether I made progress or not.

You did a good job.

I expect she can tell me where is wrong and how to write is better.

I hope I can get thefeedback which have criticized words.

Both good and bad remarks.

Encouragement.

Correct my error and encourage me.

Question 8. *Anything else you want to share with the researcher*?

Spoken English.

e. g. , I want to speak English well so I can understand what native speakers say.

How can I speak English fluently?

I think we should enhance our oral English because we don't have a good English environment.

Writing.

e. g. , To be honest, I am eager to improve my writing skills. But when I am writing, I don' t know how to organize and how to express my opinions.

Others in general.

e. g. , I like English.

In fact, I am not interested in studying English. What should I do?

I want to know how do you improved your oral English and when you meet obstacles, especially in learning English, how do you overcome it?

I want to ask you how hard you study in your undergrad?

I feel that my motivation is not enough ad I am not satisfied with myself. I don' t know why.

Group 3— Direct CF group

Question 6. How do you feel when the teacher immediately correct your error in your writing or in language classroom?

Embarrassed, sorry and happy.

Embarrassed, sorry and nervous.

Embarrassed, sorry and satisfied.

Embarrassed and nervous.

Embarrassed and sorry.

Embarrassed.

e. g. , I feel embarrassed sometimes.

Maybea little embarrassed, I think.

Happy.

e. g. , I am so happy because I can revise it soon.

Very happy.

Happy andwant to correct it next time.

I am glad to receive my teachers' advice.

Happy and satisfied.

Happy, nervous and satisfied.

Happy, satisfied, nervous, and sorry.

e. g. , Happy and satisfied. However, sometimes I can be nervous and sorry for my error.

Happy, nervous and sorry.

Happy and embarrassed.

e. g. , I feel happy but also feel embarrassed.

Happy and a little embarrassed.

Little embarrassed but happy.

I feel embarrassed and happy.

Ifeel a little embarrassed but I think it is very useful, then I feel happy.

Happy, nervous, and embarrassed.

Happy and overwhelmed.

Satisfied, nervous and sorry.

Nervous.

Satisfied.

e. g. , I feel satisfied. I like this way and I don't feel embarrassed. / I feel satisfied because I learned.

Question 7. What feedback do you expect teachers to provide for your writing?

Grammar.

e. g. , Grammar rules.

English grammar and how to make sentences.

Tell me other different sentence patterns.

Grammar and how to write good sentences and structures.

How to use the grammar in writing andtell me why I need to use it.

How to use grammar better in sentence?

Errors in grammar.

The use of words and sentences which can make my writing more good.

English grammar rules.

English grammar rules.

Use grammar correctly.

*How to learn and use grammar. I expect teachers could correct my
mistakes in writing.*

*How to use grammar correctly and what ways can make writing improve
better.*

*Mistakes in grammar and howto write like a native person. Some
grammar terms and writing rules.*

Writing skills.

*e. g. ,I hope teachers teach us more writing skills like how to make a
summary and how to start my writing.*

Structure of writing.

How to make my composition vivid?

I want to learn the writing ideas.

Comprehensive.

e. g. ,Writing skills in grammar ,words and content.

Content and grammar.

*I expect the teachers can give me some advice about how to write more
and better.*

Tell me where I am wrong.

Mistakes of my writing and how to make progress.

Correct grammar mistakes in writing and provide the skill of writing.

Others in general.

*e. g. ,I expect teachers to tell me what I write is good or what is not
good.*

Question 8. Anything else you want to share with the researcher?

Spoken English.

e. g. , I am eager to improve my oral English and now I practice

English every day, morning and night. I am looking for a foreigner to talk with me now.

I think we should practice our spoken English.

Spoken English I the most difficult learning. I think we should practice more during the spare time.

Grammar.

e. . g, Grammar, in my opinion, is very important. Especially for me, so I want to improve it by exercising more.

Feedback.

e. g. , Feedback is important for our English writing. Everyone should have a positive attitude to it.

Others in general.

e. g. , I want to know how to communicate better with the teacher.

In my view, English is very flexible, so sometimes I am worried about that I cannot explain clearly to make the reader understand.

Appendix H Abbreviations

ANOVA	Analysis of Variance
CF	Corrective Feedback
EFL	English as Foreign Language
ESL	English as Second Language
FC	Content – only
FFI	Form – focused Instruction
FonFs	Focus on Forms
FonF	Focus on Form
IEP	Intensive English Program
L2	Second Language
SLA	Second Language Acquisition